James Frederick Ferrier

Selected Writings

Edited and Introduced
by Jennifer Keefe

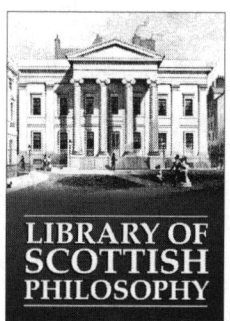

IMPRINT ACADEMIC

Copyright © Jennifer Keefe, 2011

The moral rights of the author have been asserted
No part of any contribution may be reproduced in any form
without permission, except for the quotation of brief passages
in criticism and discussion.

Published in the UK by Imprint Academic
PO Box 200, Exeter EX5 5YX, UK

Published in the USA by Imprint Academic
Philosophy Documentation Center
PO Box 7147, Charlottesville, VA 22906-7147, USA

ISBN 978 1845402433
A CIP catalogue record for this book is available from the
British Library and US Library of Congress

Full series details:

www.imprint-academic.com/losp

Contents

Series Editor's Note iv

I   **Introduction** 1

II   **'An Introduction to the Philosophy of Consciousness'** . . 13
Selection 1. Part II: Chapter I, Chapter II 13
Selection 2. Part III: Chapter III 29
Selection 3. Part IV: Chapter II, Chapter III,
                    Chapter IV, Chapter V 35
Selection 4. Part V: Chapter I 49
Selection 5. Part VI: Chapter I, Chapter II 57

III   **'Berkeley and Idealism'** 75

IV   **'Reid and the Philosophy of Common Sense'** 93

V   *Institutes of Metaphysic* 123
Selection 6. Introduction 123
Selection 7. Epistemology 126
Selection 8. Agnoiology 158
Selection 9. Ontology 171

VI   *Scottish Philosophy: the Old and the New* 195
Selection 10. Abridged 195

Index 201

Series Editor's Note

The principal purpose of volumes in this series is not to provide scholars with accurate editions, but to make the writings of Scottish philosophers accessible to a new generation of modern readers in an attractively produced and competitively priced format. In accordance with this purpose, certain changes have been made to the original texts:

- Spelling and punctuation have been modernized.
- In some cases, the selected passages have been given new titles.
- Some original footnotes and references have not been included.
- Some extracts have been shortened from their original length.
- Quotations from Greek have been transliterated, and passages in foreign languages translated, or omitted altogether.

Care has been taken to ensure that in no instance do these amendments truncate the argument or alter the meaning intended by the original author. For readers who want to consult the original texts, full bibliographical details are provided for each extract.

The Library of Scottish Philosophy was originally an initiative of the Centre for the Study of Scottish Philosophy at the University of Aberdeen and the first six volumes were commissioned with financial support from the Carnegie Trust for the Universities of Scotland. In 2006 the CSSP became one of three research centers within the Special Collections of Princeton Theological Seminary, and with the Seminary's financial support more volumes have been published. *James Frederick Ferrier: Selected Writings* is the twelfth volume in the series and has been prepared for publication by Olivia Lane.

Acknowledgements

The CSSP gratefully acknowledges the financial support of the Carnegie Trust and Princeton Seminary, the enthusiasm and excellent service of the publisher Imprint Academic, and the permission of the University of Aberdeen Special Collections and Libraries to use the engraving of the *Faculty of Advocates* (1829) as the logo for the series.

Gordon Graham,
Princeton, March 2011

I

Introduction

This volume contains selections from the philosophical writings of James Frederick Ferrier. Ferrier was born on the 16th of June in Edinburgh into a well-connected Edinburgh family; his aunt was the novelist Susan Ferrier and family friends included notable figures such as Thomas De Quincey and John Wilson or 'Christopher North' who afterwards became Ferrier's father-in-law. He started his university education in Edinburgh in 1825, which he later completed at Magdalen College in Oxford, graduating in 1832. Yet, Ferrier did not begin to develop a serious interest in philosophy until after university. From 1838 he published a number of philosophy articles in *Blackwood's Magazine* and in 1842 he acquired his first academic chair when he became the Professor of Civil History at the University of Edinburgh. A few years later, in 1845, he moved to St Andrews to become the Professor of Moral Philosophy and he remained there until his death in 1864. His contribution to philosophy was initially well-received yet his failure to acquire two key academic chairs at the University of Edinburgh in the eighteen-fifties[1] coupled with the poor reception of his major work, the *Institutes of Metaphysic*, contributed towards his total obscurity until George Davie's reconsideration of his work in the nineteen-sixties. Nevertheless, Ferrier is an interesting figure in the history of Scottish and British philosophy. Not only is he one of the first post-Hegelian British idealists but he develops his system of absolute idealism via a rejection of the Scottish school of common sense and Enlightenment philosophy in general. Ferrier's intellectual interests include both literature and philosophy. His philosophical writing is quintessentially nineteenth century; poetic descriptions and vivid metaphors as well as a sharp wit, which is rather vicious at times, pervade his discussion of abstract metaphysics. These selections focus on his primary philosophical interests: epistemology and ontology. Ferrier denies the

---

[1] *Moral Philosophy* (1852) and *Logic and Metaphysics* (1856).

possibility of a science of man and suggests that philosophy should focus on self-consciousness, the defining feature of humanity.

I

He was strongly influenced by his friend and mentor, Sir William Hamilton, who tried to reconcile Reid's common sense philosophy with Kant's transcendental idealism. Hamilton was unsuccessful in this task and the increasing influence of German philosophy in Britain coincided with the demise of the common sense school. Ferrier inherits some of his philosophical interests from Hamilton; for instance, both philosophers recognize that the immediate facts of consciousness are the starting-point for philosophy. However, Ferrier completely breaks with the common sense school and provides a system of absolute idealism focusing on epistemology and metaphysics. Indeed, he is the first in a series of Scottish Idealists, including figures such as Edward Caird and D.G. Ritchie.[2] The emergence of British idealism can largely be explained by the influence of Kant and the German idealists. Ferrier does not show much appreciation for the philosophy of Kant; he rarely mentions him and when he does it is to criticize the German philosopher's commitment to the existence of things-in-themselves. Nevertheless, he both read and respected the philosophy of the German idealists, specifically Fichte, Schelling and Hegel. Yet, Ferrier's idealism largely depends upon his reaction to British philosophy. He defends the idealism of Berkeley and attacks the enlightenment goal to develop a 'science of man', directing much of his rancor towards the Scottish school of common sense. In the late nineteenth century and early twentieth century a leading school of philosophy in Britain was idealism. Hence, Ferrier provides a system of absolute idealism that anticipates the type of philosophy that was to dominate British philosophy in the following decades. Yet, unlike the later British Idealists, he was not part of a group of like-minded and influential thinkers. His philosophy was not well-received by his contemporaries and he was intellectually isolated. Nevertheless, his philosophy bridges the transition from one school of Scottish philosophy to another.

---

[2] See Boucher, David, *The Scottish Idealists: Selected Philosophical Writings*, Imprint Academic (Exeter 2004).

II

Ferrier dismisses the Enlightenment project of trying to develop a 'science of man' as a mistaken and impossible undertaking. The basis for this view is rooted in his account of consciousness. According to Ferrier, philosophy should not be modeled on the science of the world because the scientist of humanity, unlike the natural scientist is at once the subject and object of her study. In his view, the characteristic aspect of human beings, the feature that separates humans from all other living things, is consciousness.[3] It follows that if the scientist of humanity wishes to study humanity then she must attend to consciousness, its most peculiar feature. However, consciousness is something that the scientist of humanity employs in all of her endeavours, including her study of humanity. She is therefore presented with a cognitive impasse; she either engages in a substandard study and neglects consciousness, the defining feature of her object, or she invests her object with consciousness and diminishes the subject of the study, rendering the science impossible. Ferrier believes that Enlightenment philosophers tend towards the former option and objectify the self, thereby depriving it of consciousness. He argues that as a direct consequence of this only a vapid picture of a human can be provided by a science of man, merely "a wretched association machine".[4] Given the special status of human beings as conscious creatures Ferrier contends that philosophy should not be a science but rather a systematic form of consciousness.

III

There are similarities between Ferrier's philosophy and the Scottish tradition of common sense. Yet, this is defined purely in terms of a shared agenda because he rejects the methods and the focus of common sense philosophy in favour of an idealist system of metaphysics. Although Ferrier cannot be considered as a common sense philosopher, he works within the parameters of the Scottish philosophical tradition; a tradition in which common sense played a large part. Ferrier accepts, along with Reid, that the theory of ideas is a mistaken project. He acknowledges that there are no intermediate entities—ideas—between the knower and the object of her knowl-

---

[3] Ferrier uses the term consciousness but he means self-consciousness; the awareness of the self that accompanies all experience.
[4] 'An Introduction to a Philosophy of Consciousness', Part IV, Ch.1.

edge. The problem with common sense philosophy, he believes, is that Reid hasn't gone far enough in vanquishing imaginary philosophical entities and displacing representationism. In Ferrier's view, Reid's realism separates an act of cognition into a subject and an object, namely, the perceiver and the perceived. In 'Reid and the Philosophy of Common Sense' he refers to such accounts of perception as the 'psychological doctrine' and asserts that any such analysis of perception is not only false but retains the very basis for the representationism that Reid sought to overcome. The separation of 'the perception of matter' into 'the perception of' and 'matter' provides both an immediate object of knowledge (the perception of x) and a mediate object of knowledge (x-as-it-is-in-itself). In order to avoid representationism the 'perception of matter' cannot be broken down into parts. Indeed, according to Ferrier's idealist metaphysics, any instance of cognition is an inseparable synthesis: subject-*with*-object, or, as Ferrier's says: "[the] perception-of-matter is one mental word, of which the verbal words are mere syllables."[5]

IV

Throughout his philosophical works Ferrier is primarily concerned with the laws of thought. His ultimate goal, which he attempts to realize in the *Institutes of Metaphysic* is a complete system of metaphysics, including an ontology. However, his ontology wholly depends upon his epistemology; this, for Ferrier, is the correct starting-point for the philosopher: what does knowledge entail, what is the minimum unit of cognition and what, as a knowing subject, may the philosopher coherently ask? In fact, Ferrier was the first philosopher to denote this branch of philosophy 'epistemology', and whilst his term for the philosophy of knowledge has had enduring appeal his own epistemology has not. Yet, his epistemology is crucial to an understanding of his philosophy as a whole; it is at the centre of his idealist metaphysics and it features in all of his philosophical works.

In his view, knowledge can only be of the absolute: oneself in synthesis with some object. It is impossible to know selves or things *in themselves*. So, for instance, when considering one's perception of a tree it is impossible to know either oneself or the tree in itself. The things, which are commonly referred to as the subject (the self) and the object (in this case, the tree) are the phenomena of knowledge.

---

[5] 'Reid and the Philosophy of Common Sense'.

The subjective phenomenon is the universal and necessary part of knowledge, whereas, the objective phenomenon constitutes the particular and contingent part of knowledge. In this way, *my*self is the constant concomitant of all of my cognitions, although the subjective phenomenon can change from one moment to the next. Neither the subjective nor the objective phenomenon can be known in itself but only in synthesis with one another. According to this view, the subjective and objective aspects of a subject-*with*-object synthesis cannot be abstracted from one another; when we think of the subjective aspect of the synthesis (oneself) we focus on the subjective aspect but the whole object of thought remains subject-*with*-object (oneself perceiving the tree) rather than the subject *per se*. Neither the ego *per se* nor matter *per se* is knowable; each may only be known in conjunction with the other. He argues that the object and the subject can be distinguished in cognition but they cannot be separated. In this way we can refer to the subject or the object but we can never truly conceive of either of them abstracted from the other; whenever we think of an object (such as the tree) it is as a potentially known object, and whenever we think of a subject (oneself) it is in terms of what she knows.

One of Ferrier's most unique contributions to the History of Philosophy is his account of ignorance or his Agnoiology, which forms the second part of his *Institutes of Metaphysic*. His theory of ignorance both completes and strengthens his idealist epistemology. He defines ignorance as a deficiency; it is the lack of knowledge and involves not knowing something that could be known. Given that knowledge can only be of the absolute it follows that we can only be ignorant of the absolute. Under this definition, not knowing either component of the absolute, a self-in-itself or a thing-in-itself, cannot be ignorance. Indeed, not knowing a thing-in-itself is tantamount to not knowing a contradiction such as a square circle and so is in accordance with the laws of thought rather than a deficiency of some kind. Hence, Ferrier calls not knowing the unknowable nescience. Ignorance, by contrast, reveals a deficiency, a *lack* of knowledge, which is in principle remediable. That is not to say that any individual could overcome ignorance on all matters. Ferrier is concerned with the laws of thought that apply to all knowers (supposing other knowers besides humans exist) and not humans *per se*. It may well be the case that some things are permanent objects of ignorance for human beings, although they may be known or knowable to other forms of intelligence. Objects of nescience, by contrast, could never be known by any intelligence, including a supreme intelligence, because they violate the laws of thought and knowledge. By defining ignorance in this way Ferrier again shows that it is impossible to conceive of a thing-in-itself, a feat which would even escape an omniscient being; thing-in-themselves are the contradictory and are therefore neither objects of knowledge nor ignorance for any intelligence.

V

This collection of Ferrier's writings begins with several selections from his early series of articles 'An Introduction to The Philosophy of Consciousness' published by *Blackwood's Magazine* between 1838 and 1839. These articles represent the best and clearest statement of Ferrier's philosophy and here we see the central themes that all of his subsequent philosophical writings are devoted to.

In Part II he argues against the philosophical notion of a mind as identical to the self, dismissing it as a fictional entity which violates Ockham's razor. He does not specify the target of his criticisms, instead arguing against those he calls 'metaphysicians'.[6] Nonetheless, this discussion contributes to Ferrier's rejection of a 'science of man' in general and his particular focus is the philosophical notion of a mind. He objects to a 'science of man' modeled on the sciences of the world in which the 'mind' rather than the facts of nature are the focus of the study. He argues that in making mind an object of study in the attempt to discover the essence of humanity the philosopher is engaged in a worthless science. In Ferrier's view consciousness is the distinctive feature of a self. If a philosopher objectifies her mind, making it the object of study, she deprives it of consciousness which must remain with herself, the subject. This shows that mind is neither identical to oneself nor a fit subject for a science of man. He also utilizes common language to make his case. Mind, he asserts, is never identified with the self in common language as demonstrated by the expression 'my mind'. Here, the ego and the mind are presented as different entities; the mind is possessed by the ego. Ferrier allows that the mind may be considered as "a convenient generic term expressing the sum-total of the sensations, passions, intellec-

---

[6] This is a surprising choice of word given that he develops his own metaphysics and in a later article ('Reid and the Philosophy of Common Sense') he promotes 'metaphysics' as opposed to 'psychology' (by which he means Reid's 'science of mind').

tual states, etc., by which the human being is visited"[7] thereby avoiding the obvious retort that if 'my mind' disproves the identity of self and mind it also shows that there are two entities: an ego and a mind. It does not controvert ordinary language to suggest that 'my mind' is shorthand for the sum of all sensations, passions, etc. ... or, in a word, experience. Here, he also begins to develop his own notion of the self, which he asserts exists in inverse proportion to 'mind'. Whenever experiences are all-consuming the self is lessened and *vice versa*, when consciousness is strong the force of a sensation or passion is weakened. He develops this argument further in Part IV when he elaborates on the causal forces acting upon human beings. The 'I' is presented as opposed to the enslaving forces of sensation and the passions.

Towards the end of Part III he considers the onset of consciousness. For Ferrier consciousness is not given, instead it is the individual's first act: thinking oneself I makes oneself I. In this way he compares a young child to a parrot, who mimics rather than embodies consciousness. Therefore, the pre-conscious human being, as he later discusses in Part V, exists only *for others*. The beginning of consciousness signals the first act and the presence of the will. After the onset of consciousness the human becomes a self and finally acts. Thereafter freedom, morality and responsibility are possible. In this way, the individual is not merely acted upon but rather becomes a self and exists *for oneself*.

In Part IV Ferrier provides his first clear statement of idealism and connects it to a defence of Descartes' *cogito ergo sum*. The ego is the first instance in which the notion and the reality are identical: by thinking oneself I one becomes a self and so the act of knowing oneself and being a self are one and the same. Concurrently, consciousness becomes an act of negation; the reality of the self is immediately opposed to everything else that is not oneself. In this way Ferrier's account of self-consciousness as an act of negation is reminiscent of Hegel's view of the opposition between the I and the not-I.

The final selection from this series of articles comes from Part VI. Here, he sets himself apart from the enlightenment project of developing a 'science of man'. For Ferrier systematic consciousness is the true model for philosophy. Additionally, he describes the connec-

---

[7] 'An Introduction to a Philosophy of Consciousness', Part II, Chapter II.

tion between consciousness and morality; morality requires freedom and is the sole preserve of free, conscious beings.

The selection from the 1842 article 'Berkeley and Idealism' provides an account of Ferrier's idealism as inspired by and originating from a reworking of Berkeley's philosophy. In this way he differs from later British Idealists who, as previously mentioned, were largely influenced by Kant and the German Idealists. Ferrier describes Berkeley's philosophy as the forerunner to absolute idealism: "His genius was the first to swell the current of that mighty stream of tendency towards which all modern meditation flows, the great gulf-stream of Absolute Idealism."[8] He reiterates Berkeley's own argument that idealism is the metaphysical position that is in accordance with common sense. In this way, just as Berkeley did before him, Ferrier, perhaps counter-intuitively, contends that the common man is on the side of idealism. Given that the philosophy of common sense developed by Reid and his followers fills the chronological gap between Berkeley and Ferrier, in doing so he at once echoes Berkeley's own account and also indirectly criticises Reid's attempt to reconcile philosophy and common sense. He proceeds by arguing that Berkeley never denied the existence of the external world. Rather, he argues that Berkeley's philosophy upholds the laws of thought by showing that it is impossible to conceive of the noumenal world; all thought is necessarily phenomenal. Yet, Ferrier allows that Berkeley's account is undeveloped in one respect, and he believes that it is this oversight which has allowed his detractors to accuse him of being a subjective idealist. Specifically, he holds that Berkeley overlooks the phenomenal status of non-existence. According to Ferrier, it is not only the existence of things that depend upon thinkers but also the *non-existence* of things. Hence, non-existence is also a known concept which depends upon thinkers. In this way, he hopes to dismiss a misleading objection to idealism and dispel a philosophical myth. First, in showing that non-existence lies within the phenomenal world, he dismisses a central concern about idealism: the charge that the world would cease to exist without some percipient being. In order to consider the annihilation of the world a percipient being is required; non-existence does not lessen the central feature of idealism—the interdependency of thought and reality. Secondly, he reiterates Berkeley's point that the world-as

---

[8] 'Berkeley and Idealism'.

it-is-in-itself is unthinkable and denies the existence and conceivability of noumena; everything that can be thought of is phenomenal: things, nothing, etc. ... Thus, the very notion of a noumenon is nonsensical at best. In this way, he shifts the debate from ontology to epistemology; before we can ask what exists we must first consider what is knowable. For Ferrier it is the laws of thought that are the primary concern of metaphysics.

The purpose of 'Reid and the Philosophy of Common Sense' (1847) was to review Hamilton's collected edition of Reid's works. Ferrier shows his disdain for the project as one that is beneath the brilliant mind of his friend. However, despite such grandstanding, this article offers an informative contrast between two approaches to epistemology: 1) the 'psychologists' by which Ferrier means Reid and anyone who pursues the 'science of man' and 2) the 'metaphysicians', or in other words, Ferrier's own approach. His focus here is the perception of matter. Ferrier contends that the psychological approach breaks down the perception of matter into constituent parts: the perceiver and the matter perceived. In this way, the psychologist cannot avoid representationism; there are two objects of knowledge here: oneself as the immediate object of perception and matter, which is the remote object of perception that is known mediately through one's perception of it. He instead advocates in favour of the metaphysical approach or absolute idealism. In such a system 'the perception of matter' is an indivisible unit, which cannot be broken down thereby preventing the possibility of representationism.

The *Institutes of Metaphysic* perhaps lacks the lucidity of some of his earlier articles yet this shows the fullest development of his idealism. Indeed, here he purports to provide a *complete* system of metaphysics. The structure differs from his other works as he follows Spinoza's deductive method in the hopes of providing a wholly necessary system.

The first section, the Epistemology, starts with a single axiom from which the rest of his system is purportedly derived. The selections that have been chosen mainly include only the propositions and their subsequent demonstrations. In the original *Institutes* all propositions are followed by 'counter-arguments' that Ferrier summarily dismisses. In most cases these have not been included to avoid repetition from other readings. Nevertheless, a few larger selections have been chosen, specifically Propositions I, III and IV. Proposition I states that: "Along with whatever any intelligence knows; it must, as the ground or condition of its knowledge, have some cognisance of *itself*." This represents the beginning of Ferrier's Epistemology and he calls it 'The Primary Law or Condition of all Knowledge.' The presence of the ego signifies the existence of *some* knowledge and conversely, when there is an absence of the ego, knowledge is impossible. In this way, Ferrier contends that consciousness is the feature, which is common to and thereby, links all knowledge. After the primary proposition, by using the method of deduction, he works through twenty-two propositions. The important conclusion that he derives from the primary proposition is that a synthesis of subject-*with*-object is the minimum unit of cognition.[9] He says that this union is the *absolute* in cognition. A key consequence that follows from this and sets him apart from the common sense philosophers and Kant is that matter *per se*, as an object abstracted from a subject, is inconceivable.[10]

In the Epistemology Ferrier outlines the basic structure of any unit of knowledge: some subject in synthesis with some object. However, he has not yet determined what cannot be known. His intention is to determine what exists but he cannot move straight from the Epistemology to the Ontology in the event that what exists is identical to what is unknown. Consequently, Ferrier says that before we can develop a theory of being we must determine the nature and scope of ignorance. This is slightly misleading as we discover that the extent of knowledge is of small concern to Ferrier; his primary interest is the laws of thought. In the second section of his *Institutes* he provides a theory of ignorance and he calls this the Agnoiology. He does not comment on the extent of knowledge, although he suggests that the extent of our ignorance is most likely considerable. But, the amount of knowledge or ignorance a percipient being possesses is beside the point. What Ferrier argues is that we can only know or be ignorant of a subject in synthesis with an object. In Proposition III of the Agnoiology he says: "We can only be ignorant of what can possibly be known; in other words, there can be an ignorance only of that of which there can be a knowledge." This renders both selves-in-themselves and things-in-themselves outwith the boundary of

---

[9] See *Institutes of Metaphysic*, Section I, Proposition III.
[10] See *Institutes of Metaphysic*, Section I, Proposition IV.

conceivability; we can neither know nor be ignorant of them without violating the laws of cognition.

After his Epistemology and Agnoiology he sets out his theory of being in the final section of the *Institutes*: the Ontology. And, it is in the Ontology that the significance of his earlier sections becomes apparent. He contends that the laws of existence are in accordance with the laws of knowledge. In the Ontology he argues that absolute existence must be either that which is the object of knowledge, that which is the object of ignorance or that which is neither the object of knowledge nor ignorance. The first two options are equivalent, as laid out in his Epistemology and Agnoiology; the object of either knowledge or ignorance is some subject in synthesis with some object. In this way, the inclusion of a theory of ignorance in Ferrier's *Institutes* is essential for the development of his idealism and the connection between the knowable and reality. The third option, that which is neither the object of knowledge nor ignorance is equivalent to the unknowable and he calls this the contradictory. In keeping with his previous two sections, the contradictory includes subjects-in-themselves and things-in-themselves; both of which are fundamentally unknowable by all intelligences. He concludes that absolute existence cannot be the contradictory it must be either that which we know or that which we are ignorant of: subject-*with*-object. He resolves his *Institutes* with a form of idealism that is suggestive of Berkeley's spiritual idealism. For Ferrier, any specific instance of absolute existence, some self in synthesis with some object, is contingent. In order to avoid subjective idealism the world cannot depend on such contingencies. Therefore, he asserts that there is one necessary absolute existence: a supreme being in synthesis with everything infinitely.

Scottish Philosophy: the Old and the New (1856) is a more polemical work than Ferrier's other philosophical writings. It was published shortly after he was rejected in his bid to achieve the Chair of Logic and Metaphysics at Edinburgh University. In it he provides a defence of his *Institutes of Metaphysic* from the specific attacks made on him during this process and he contends that his philosophy, whilst different from Reid's, is part of a peculiarly Scottish tradition of philosophy.

VI

Ferrier is an fascinating figure in the history of Scottish and British Philosophy. He offers an idealist innovation of Scottish philosophy, acting as a transitional figure between the old Scottish philosophy of the common sense philosophers and the later idealists, whose prevalence during the decades prior to the turn of the twentieth century suggest that they were the new Scottish philosophers. In the formation of his idealist metaphysics Ferrier provides a critique of Reid and a reappraisal of Berkeley that are of interest to the historian of philosophy. Moreover, the quality of his philosophical arguments in his articles on consciousness and his account of ignorance render Ferrier's philosophy worthy of greater examination than it has been generally accorded.

II

'An Introduction to the Philosophy of Consciousness'

SELECTION 1
PART II OF PHILOSOPHY OF CONSCIOUSNESS

CHAPTER I.

We intended at the outset that these papers should be as little of a controversial character as possible. But a mature consideration of the state in which psychology, or the science of man, stands throughout Europe generally, and in this country in particular, leads us to deviate considerably from our original plan. We find, too, that we cannot clear out a way for the introduction of our own doctrines, without displacing, or at least endeavoring to displace, to a very great extent, the opinions usually held on the subject we are treating of. And, besides all this, we are sensible that, without having gone far enough, or completely made good our point, we have yet committed ourselves so far already in our previous strictures on the prevailing doctrine of "Mind," that there is no drawing back for us now. We must either be prepared to corroborate and illustrate our argument by many additional explanatory statements, or to incur the stigma of leaving it very incomplete, and, as many may think, very inconclusive. In order, therefore, to escape the latter of these alternatives, we will do our best to embrace and comply with the former of them. Such being our reasons, we now *nail our colors to the mast*, and prepare ourselves for a good deal of polemical discussion on the subject of "the human mind." And the first point to be determined is: What is the exact question at issue?

That man is a creature who displays many manifestations of reason, adapting means to the production of ends in a vast variety of ways; that he is also susceptible of a great diversity of sensations, emotions, passions, etc., which, in one form or another, keep appearing, disappearing, and reappearing within him, with few intermissions, during his transit from the cradle to the grave, is a fact which no one will dispute. This, then, is admitted equally by the ordinary metaphysician and by us. Further, the metaphysician postulates, or lays down, "mind," and not "body," as the substance in which these phenomena inhere; and this may readily enough be admitted to him. "Mind," no doubt, is merely an hypothesis, and violates one of the fundamental axioms of science, that, namely, which has been called the principle of philosophical parsimony: *Entia non sunt multiplicanda præter necessitatem*.[1] The necessity in this case has cer-

---

[1] That is, *Entities are not to be multiplied without necessity;* or, in other words, unless it should appear that the phenomena observed cannot possibly inhere in any *already admitted* entity. Dugald Stewart's reasoning on this subject is curious, not because the argument, or that which it regards, is of the smallest interest or importance in itself, but as exhibiting the grossest misconception of the question that ever was palmed off upon an unwary reader. "Matter" must be owned to be *first in the field*. We are conversant and intimate with it long before we know anything about "mind." When the immaterialist or mentalist, then, comes forward, it is his business either to displace matter entirely, substituting "mind" in the place of it; or else to rear up alongside of it, this, the antagonist entity for which he contends. If he attempts the former, he involves himself in a mere play of words. If he maintains that all the *material* phenomena are in fact *mental* phenomena, he does nothing but quibble. The author of the 'Natural History of Enthusiasm' has grievously mistaken the potency of this position. [See The *physical* (!) theory of another life, p. 14.] It is plain, we say, that in this case the immaterialist resolves himself into a mere innovator upon the ordinary language of men. He merely gives the name of "mental" to that which other people have chosen to call "material." The *thing* remains precisely what it was. If, on the other hand, he embraces the latter of the alternatives offered to him, and, without supplanting matter, maintains "mind" to be co-ordinate with it, then he is bound to show a *necessity* for his "multiplication of entities." He is bound to prove that the phenomena with which he is dealing are incompatible with, or cannot possibly inhere in, the entity already in the field. But how is such a proof possible or even conceivable? Let us see what the immaterialist makes of it. It is his object to prove by reasoning that a certain series of phenomena cannot inhere in a certain admitted substance "matter," and must therefore be referred to a different substance "mind." Now all reasoning is either *a priori* or *a posteriori*. If he reasons in the former of these ways, he forms *a priori* such a conception of matter that it would involve a contradiction to suppose that the phenomena occasioning the dispute should inhere in it; he first of all fixes for himself a notion of matter, as of something with which certain phenomena are incompatible, something in which they cannot inhere; and then from this conception he deduces the inference that these phenomena are incompatible with matter, or cannot inhere in it—a *petitio*

tainly never been made manifest. Nevertheless the hypothesis may be admitted, inasmuch as neither the admission nor the rejection of it is of the smallest conceivable importance. Like Dugald Stewart, we reject the question as to the entity in which the admitted phenomena inhere, as altogether unphilosophical; but he and we reject it upon very different grounds. He, indeed, rejected it because he did not consider it at all a true psychological question; and we do the same. But further than this, we now give, what he never gave or dreamt of giving, the *reason* why it cannot be viewed as a psychological question; which reason is this, that the very phenomena themselves, inherent, or supposed to be inherent, in this entity, do not, properly speaking, or otherwise than in the most indirect manner possible, constitute any part of the *facts* of psychology, and therefore any discussion connected with them, or with the subject in which they may inhere, is a discussion extraneous and irrelevant to the real and

principii almost too glaring to require notice. Or does he reason upon this question *a posteriori*? In this case he professes to found upon no *a priori* conception of matter, but to be guided entirely by experience. But experience can only inform us what phenomena do or do not inhere in any particular substance; and can tell us nothing about their abstract compatibility or incompatibility with it. We may afterwards infer such compatibility or incompatibility if we please, but we must first of all know what *the fact is*, or else we may be abstractly arguing a point one way, while the facts go to establish it in the opposite way. In reasoning, therefore, from experience, the question is not, *Can* certain phenomena inhere in a particular substance, or can they *not*? but we must first of all ask and determine this: *Do* they inhere in it, or do they *not*? And this, then, now comes to be the question with which the immaterialist, reasoning *a posteriori*, has to busy himself. Is the negative side of this question to be admitted to him without proof? Are we to permit him to take for granted that these phenomena *do not* inhere in matter? Most assuredly not. He must prove this to be the case, or else he accomplishes nothing; and yet how is it possible for him to prove it? He can only prove it by showing the phenomena to be incompatible with matter; for if he once admits the phenomena to be compatible with matter, then his *postulatum* of mind is at once disqualified from being advanced. He has given up the attempt to make manifest that *necessity* for "mind," which it was incumbent upon him to show.

It is, therefore, absolutely necessary to the very life of his argument that he should stickle for the incompatibility of these phenomena with matter. To prove that these phenomena *do not* inhere in matter, he must show that they *cannot* inhere in it. This is the only line of argument which is open to him. But then how is he to make good this latter point? We have already seen the inevitable and powerless perplexity in which he lands himself in attempting it. He must, as before, adopt one of two courses. He must either recur to his old *a priori* trick of framing for himself, first of all, such a conception of matter, that it would be contradictory to suppose the phenomena capable of inhering in it, and then of deducing their incompatibility or contradictoriness from this conception—a mode of proof which certainly shows that the phenomena cannot inhere in his proper science. Further, he rejected the question as one which was *above* the powers of man: we scout it as one which is immeasurably *beneath* them. He refused to acknowledge it because he considered the human faculties weakly incompetent to *it*: we scorn it, because, knowing what the true business and aim of psychology is, we consider *it* miserably incompetent to *them*. In short, we pass it by with the most supreme indifference. Let the metaphysician, then, retain "the human mind" if he will, and let him make the most of it. Let him regard it as the general complement of all the phenomena alluded to. Let him consider it their subject of inherence if he pleases, and he will find that there is no danger of our quarreling with him about *that*. We will even grant it to be a convenient generic term expressing the sum-total of the sensations, passions, intellectual states, etc., by which the human being is visited.

---

conception of matter, but which by no means proves that they cannot inhere in matter itself. Or he may follow, as before, an *a posteriori* course. But here, too, we have already shown that such a procedure is impossible, without his taking for granted the very point in dispute. We have already shown that, in adhering to experience, the immaterialist must first of all go and ascertain *the fact* respecting these phenomena — *do* they inhere in matter, or do they *not* — before he is entitled to predicate that they *cannot* inhere in it, lest while he is steering his argument in one direction, *the fact* should be giving him the lie in another. We sum up our statement thus: He wishes to prove that certain phenomena *cannot* inhere in matter. In proving this he is brought to postulate the fact that these phenomena *do not* inhere in matter; and then, when pressed for a proof of this latter fact, he can only make it good by reasserting that they *cannot* inhere in matter, in support of which he is again forced to recur to his old statement that they *do not* inhere in matter, an instance of circular reasoning of the most perfect kind imaginable. Thus the immaterialist has not given us, and cannot possibly give us, any argument at all upon the subject. He has not given us the proof which the "necessity" of the case called for, and which, in admitting the principle of parsimony, he pledged himself to give as the only ground upon which his postulation of a new substance could be justified. He has, after all, merely supplied us with the statement that certain phenomena *do not* inhere in matter, which is quite sufficiently met on the part of the materialist, by the counter statement that these phenomena *do* inhere in matter. In struggling to supply us with more than this, his reason is strangled in the trammels of an inexorable *petitio principii*, from which it cannot shake itself loose: while the materialist looks on perfectly quiescent. All this, however, Mr. Stewart totally misconceives. He speaks as if the materialist (of course we mean such as understand and represent the argument rightly) took, or were called upon to take, and *active* part in this discussion. He imagines that the *onus probandi*, the task of *proving* the phenomena to inhere in matter, and of *dis*proving "mind," lay upon his shoulders. He talks of the "scheme of materialism" ('Elements,' p. 4), as if the scheme of materialism, supposing that there is one, did not exist, merely *because* the scheme of

But the metaphysician does not stop here. He will not be satisfied with this admission. He goes much further, and demands a much greater concession. By "mind" he does not mean merely to express the aggregate of the "states;" that is, of the sensations, feelings, etc., which the human being may or may not be conscious of; but, somehow or other, he blends and intertwines consciousness (or the notion of self, self-reference) with these "states," and considers this fact as their necessary, essential, invariable, or inextricable accompaniment. He thus vests in mind, besides its own states, passions, sensations, etc., the fact of the consciousness of these, and the being to whom that consciousness belongs; thus constituting "mind" into *the man*, and making the one of these terms convertible with the other.

Now here it is that we beg leave to enter our protest. We object most strongly to this doctrine as one which introduces into psychology a "confusion worse confounded;" as one which, if allowed to prevail, must end in obliterating everything like science, morality, and even man himself, as far as his true and peculiar character is concerned; substituting in place of him a machine, an automaton, of which the law of causality composes and regulates the puppet-strings.

This, then, is the precise point at issue between us: The metaphysician wishes to make "mind" constitute and monopolize *the whole*

immaterialism cannot, as we have seen, bring itself into existence. If the immaterialist cannot (as we have proved he cannot, logically) set up the entity of mind as a habitation for certain houseless phenomena, will he not permit the materialist charitably to give them shelter in the existing entity of matter? Surely this is a stretch of philosophical intolerance, on the part of the immaterialist, not to be endured. He cannot house these phenomena himself, nor will he permit others to house them. Before concluding this note, which has already run too far, we may point out to the logical student another instance of Mr. Stewart's vicious logic contained in the paragraph referred to. We will be short. "Mind and matter," says he, "considered as objects of human study, are *essentially* different," that is, are *different in their essence*. Now turn to the last line of this paragraph, and read: "We are totally *ignorant* of the *essence of either*." That is to say, being totally ignorant of the essence of two things, we are yet authorized in saying that these two things are essentially different, or different in their essence. Now, difference being in the opinion of most people the condition of knowledge, or, in other words, our knowledge of a thing being based upon the difference observed between it and other things, and our ignorance of a thing being generally the consequence of its real or apparent identity with other things, it appears to us that our ignorance of the essence of these two things (if it did not altogether disqualify us from speaking) should rather have induced us to say that they were essentially the same; or, at any rate, could never justify us in predicating their *essential* DIFFERENCE as Mr. Stewart has done. If we know nothing at all about their essence, how can we either affirm or deny anything with respect to that essence?

man; we refuse to admit that "mind" constitutes any part of the *true and real* man whatsoever. The metaphysician confounds the *consciousness of* a "state of mind," and the being to whom this consciousness belongs, with the "state of mind" itself. Our great object is to keep these two distinctly and vividly asunder. This distinction is one which, as shall soon be shown, is constantly made both by common sense and by common language, a consideration which throws the presumption of truth strongly in our favor. It is one which appears to us to constitute the great leading principle upon which the whole of psychology hinges, one without the strict observance of which any science of ourselves is altogether impossible or null.

We are still, then, quite willing to vest in "mind" all the "states" of mind. But the fact of the consciousness of these states, the notion of himself as the person to whom this consciousness belongs, we insist in vesting in *the man*, or in that being who calls himself "I;" and in this little word expresses compendiously *all* the facts which really and truly belong to him. The question in dispute, and which has to be decided between the metaphysician and ourselves, may be thus worded: He wishes to give everything unto "mind," while we wish to give unto mind the things which are mind's , and unto man the things which are man's. If we can succeed in making good our point, psychology will be considerably lightened — lightened of a useless and unmarketable cargo which has kept her almost *lockfast* for many generations, and which she ought never to have taken on board; for our very first act will be to fling "mind" with all its lumber overboard, and, busying ourselves exclusively with *the man* and *his* facts, we shall see whether the science will not *float* them. But our first problem is to vindicate and make good the distinction we have pointed out.

Before going further, let us make use of an illustration, which will, perhaps, be of some preliminary assistance in rendering our meaning, together with the point at issue still more distinct and manifest to the reader. The mountains, let us say, which the eye beholds are the *objects* of its vision. In the same way the passions, sensations, "states of mind," etc., which the man is, or may be, conscious of, are the *objects* of his consciousness, of his conscious self. But no one ever supposes that the *fact* of vision is the same as the *objects* of vision. The former appertains to the eye; the latter constitute the mountains seen. The *objects* of vision may exist and do exist without the *fact* of vision, and do not create or enforce this fact as their necessary and invariable accompaniment. To make no discrimination between these two things would be confessedly in the highest degree absurd. It is just the same with regard to the *fact* of consciousness and the *objects* of consciousness. The *fact* of consciousness belongs to the man himself, to that being which calls itself "I;" and this, truly speaking, is all that belongs to him. The *objects* of consciousness, namely, man's passions, sensations, etc., are not, properly speaking, his at all. The fact and notion of self do not necessarily or always accompany them. They may be referred to "mind," or to what you please. They are indeed within the man's control, and it is his duty to control them. But this is not because they *are* himself, but only because they are *not* himself; because they are *obscurations* of himself. You may call them the *false* man if you choose; but if they were the *true* man, where would be the truthfulness of that mighty truth which says that the man waxes just in proportion as he makes his passions and his sensual feelings wane? How could this be the case if the man himself were identical with his passions and his desires? Can a creature live and thrive by suspending its own animation? Is it conceivable that a being should increase and strengthen in proportion as it is weakened and diminished? To return to our illustration: the point of it is this — the *objects* of consciousness, namely, the passions, emotions, etc., and Reason itself, might perfectly well exist (and in animals do exist) without any one being conscious of them, or combining with them the notion of self, just as the objects of vision exist without any eye perceiving them: and the *fact* of consciousness, or the fact that a being is conscious of these states, is just as distinct from the states themselves as the fact that the eye *does* behold mountains is distinct from the mountains which it beholds. These two things, then, the fact and the object, are in both cases distinctly separate. In the case of the eye and its objects they are never confounded; but in the case of consciousness and its objects we venture to affirm that the metaphysician has invariably confounded them. Our great primary aim is to remedy this confusion; to establish the fact of consciousness (and the being to whom it belongs) as something quite aloof from, and transcending, the objects of consciousness, namely, mind and all its states, and then to confine our science entirely to the elucidation of this fact, which will be found to be pregnant with many other facts, and with many mighty results, neglecting the *objects* of it as of little importance or of none.

There is one ground, however, still left open to the metaphysician, which he may consider his impregnable stronghold or inner fortress, and which, if he can maintain it, will certainly enable him to set our strictures at defiance, and successfully to defend his tenets against all our objections. We are quite willing that he should entrench himself in this strong citadel, and, with his permission, we will place him fairly within it with our own hands, to stand or to fall. The metaphysician, fully admitting the distinction we have been insisting on, may say, "But this discrimination is itself a mere analysis of mind. The 'state' of which the being is conscious is mind; and the *fact* of consciousness, with the being to whom it belongs, is also mind. In a word, both terms or factors of the analysis are mind. Mind in a state of dualism perhaps; *two* minds, if you choose to call them so; but still susceptible of synthesis, still capable of having the one of them added to the other of them; and hence, though *two*, still capable of being united, and of being viewed in the amalgamation of *one*. Therefore," continues he, "mind, view it as you please, analyze it, or make what discriminations within it you like, is still rightly to be regarded as constituting the real and complete man, and as monopolizing the whole of that which is truly he."

If this argument be valid, we must own ourselves completely foiled, and the fight is done. For it be true that the distinction we are contending for be merely a dead analytical discrimination, and not a real and wonder-working antithesis, a vital antagonism in human nature which, practically operating, brings about all the good and evil of man and of society; and which, working ceaselessly throughout all time, as well as in the individual breast, increases in energy the longer it maintains itself, marking distinctly the progress of the species, and advancing it on and on from that which it once was to that which it now is, and to that which it shall yet be: if it be not, we say, a distinction of this kind, but merely an inoperative "analysis of mind," then we give it up as virtually void, as altogether insignificant and unworthy of a further thought.

But our whole system proceeds upon the reality and vitality of this distinction. It founds itself not upon any principle arising out of an analysis of mind; not upon any distinction made *within* mind; but upon a real antithesis to be established between what belongs, or may be admitted to belong to mind, and what does not and cannot belong to it; and therefore we will not yield up this distinction by owning it to be analytical at all. We allow the metaphysician to take all man's passions, sensations, emotions, states, or whatever else he may choose to call them, and refer them to "mind," making this the *object* of his research. But when he attempts to lay hands on the fact of consciousness, and to make "mind" usurp this fact together with the being to whom this fact belongs, we exclaim, "hold! Hitherto shalt thou come, and no farther; here shall thy weak hypothesis be stayed." If he resists, the question must be put to the proof. Can the fact of consciousness, together with the man himself, be conceived of as vested in the *object* called "mind," as well as the sensations, passions, etc., which have been admitted to be vested therein? or must not this fact and the man himself be held *transcendent* to this object, and incapable of being objectified, or conceived of as an object at all? Unless we can make out this latter point, we shall fail in realizing, in its truth and purity, the only fact with which, in our opinion, as we have already said, psychology ought to busy itself, namely, the fact of consciousness.

We have now, then, brought the question to its narrowest possible point. Can the fact of consciousness, together with our conscious selves, be conceived of as vested in the *object* called "the human mind"? It was to prove the negative side of this question, and thereby to support a conclusion which forms the very life and keystone of our system, that the argument contained in a former part of this discussion was intended; and the reader may, perhaps, be now placed in a situation which will enable him to perceive its drift more clearly. We will recapitulate it very shortly, and in somewhat different words from those formerly used.

An *object* is that which is either *really* or *ideally* different from ourselves; or in other words, is either different in itself, or is conceived of as different by us. Suppose, now, that the metaphysician makes use of the expression of common sense and ordinary language, "my mind." He here certainly appears, at first sight, to lay down a *real* discrimination between himself and his mind. Whatever he may *intend* to say, he clearly *says* that there are *two* of them, namely, his mind and himself, the "I" (call it the *ego*), possessing it. In this case, "mind" may contain what it likes, but the *consciousness* of what it contains certainly remains with the *ego*. In this case mind is *really* destitute of consciousness. Does the metaphysician disclaim this view of the matter? Does he say that mind is really himself, and is only *ideally* an object to him. Then we answer, that in this case mind is *ideally* divested of consciousness, and if the metaphysician thinks otherwise, he imposes upon himself. For how can he make it contain consciousness without first of all ideally replacing within it himself, the *ego* which he had ideally severed from it. But if he does make this reinvestment, mind (his object) at once vanishes from the scene; for none of us can attribute consciousness *directly* to another; we can only attribute it directly to another by becoming it, and if we become it, it ceases to be another; it becomes we, that is to say, nothing but the *ego* is left, and we have no *object* either ideally or really before us. The dilemma to which the philosophers of mind are reduced is this: *unless* they attribute consciousness to mind, they leave out of view the most important and characteristic phenomenon of man; and *if* they attribute consciousness to mind, they annihilate the *object* of their research, in so far as the whole extent of this fact is concerned.

So much in the shape of mere abstract reasoning upon this question. It appears to us that our point is now in a fair way of being completely made out. We think that, as far as mere reasoning can do it, we have succeeded in extricating the fact of consciousness from the oppressive and obscuring envelopment of "the human mind." But our views, their correctness, and their application, still require to be brought out and enforced by many explanations and observations *of fact*. We now, then, descend to various statements, illustrations, and practical considerations which will probably be still more plain and convincing than anything we have yet said. These, however, we reserve for the following chapter.

CHAPTER II.

One of the fundamental and soundest canons of philosophy is this: never violently to subvert, but to follow gently through all its windings, any fact submitted to us by common sense, and never harshly to obliterate the language in which any such fact is expressed, or precipitately to substitute in place of it another expression drawn probably from some mushroom theory, and more consonant, as we may think, with truth, because apparently of a more cultivated cast. The presumption is, that the first expressions are right, and truly denote the fact; and that the secondary language, if much opposed to these, is the offspring of a philosophy erroneously reflective. In short, if we neglect the canon pointed out, the risk of our missing the real facts and running into false speculation is extreme. For common sense, being instinctive or nearly so, rarely errs; and its expressions, not being matured by reflection, generally contain within them, though under very obscure forms, much of the deep truth and wisdom of revelations. What though its facts and its language may often be to us, like the mirage to travelers in the desert, for a time an illusive and disappointing thing? Still let us persevere in the pursuit. The natural mirage is often the most benign provision which Heaven, in its mercy, could call up before the eyes of the wanderers through barren wastes. Ceaselessly holding out to them the promise of blessed gratification, it thus attracts onwards and onwards, till at length they really reach the true and water-flowing oasis, those steps which, but for this timely and continual attraction, would have sunk down and perished in despair amid the un-measurable sands. And spread over the surface of common life there is a moral mirage analogous to this, and equally attractive to the philosopher thirsting after truth. In pursuing it we may be often disappointed and at fault, but let us follow it in faithful hope, and it will lead us on and on unto the true and living waters at last. If we accept in a sincere and faithful spirit the facts and expressions of common sense, and refrain from tampering unduly with their simplicity, we shall perhaps find, like those fortunate ones of old who, opening hospitable doors to poor wearied wayfarers, unwittingly entertained angels, that we are harboring the divinest truths of philosophy in the guise of these homely symbols.

It is comparatively an easy task to exclude such facts and such expressions from our consideration, and then within closed doors to arrive at conclusions at variance with common sense. But this is not the true business of philosophy. True philosophy, meditating a far higher aim and a far more difficult task than this, throws wide her portals to the entrance of all comers, come disguised and unpromising as they may. In other words, she accepts, as given, the great and indestructible convictions of our race, and the language in which these are expressed: and in place of denying or obliterating them, she endeavors rationally to explain and justify them; recovering by reflection steps taken in the spontaneous strength of nature by powers little more than instinctive, and seeing in clear light the operation of principles which, in their primary acts, work in almost total darkness.

Common sense, then, is the problem of philosophy, and is plainly not to be solved by being set aside, but just as little is it to be solved by being taken for granted, or in other words, by being allowed to remain in the primary forms in which it is presented to our notice. A problem and its solution are evidently not one and the same thing; and hence, common sense, the problem of philosophy, is by no means identical, in the first instance at least, with the solution which philosophy has to supply (a consideration which those would do well to remember who talk of the "philosophy of common sense," thus confounding together the problem and the solution). It is only after the solution has been affected that they can be looked upon as identical with each other. How then is this solution to be realized? How is the conversion of common sense into philosophy to be brought about? We answer, by accepting completely and faithfully the facts and expressions of common sense as given in their primitive obscurity, and then by construing them without violence, without addition, and without diminution into clearer and more intelligible forms.

In observance and exemplification, then, of this rule, let us now take up an expression frequently made use of by common sense, and which, in the preceding chapter, we had occasion to bring forward, that expression, to wit, constantly in the mouth of every one, "my mind," or let it be "my emotion," "my sensation," or any similar mode of speech; and let us ask, What does a man, thus talking the ordinary language of common life, precisely mean when he employs these expressions? The metaphysician will tell us that he does *not* mean what he says. We affirm that he *does* mean what he says. The metaphysician will tell us that he does not really make, or intend to make, any discrimination or sundering between *himself* and his "mind;" or we should rather say his "state of mind." We affirm that he both intends to make such a separation, and does make it. The metaphysician declares that by the expression "my emotion" the man merely means that there is *one* of them, namely, "emotion," that this is himself (the being he calls "I"), and contains and expresses every fact which this latter word denotes; and in making this averment the metaphysician roughly subverts and obliterates the language of the man. We, however, reverencing the canon we have just laid down, refrain from doing this gross violence to his expressions, because, if we were guilty of it, we should consider ourselves upon the point of falling into great errors, and of confounding a most essential distinction which has not escaped the primitive and almost instinctive good sense of all mankind, the *genus meta-physicorum* excepted. This tribe will not admit that in using the expression, for instance, "my sensations," the man regards himself as standing aloof from his sensations: or at any rate they hold that such a view on the part of the man is an erroneous one. They will not allow that the man himself and the fact of consciousness stand on the *outside* of the sphere of the "states of mind" experienced: but they fetter him down *within* the circle of these states, and make him and consciousness identical with them.

In opposition to this, the ordinary psychological doctrine, we, for our part, prefer to adhere to the language of common sense; believing that this represents the facts faithfully and truly, while the formulas of metaphysics misrepresent them grievously. We affirm that the natural man, in using the words "my mind," expresses and intends to express what is, and what he feels to be, *the fact*—namely, that his conscious self, that which he calls "I" (*ego*), is not to be confounded, and cannot be confounded, with his "mind," or the "states of mind," which are its objects. Let us observe, he merely views "mind," and uses this word, as a term expressing the aggregate or general assemblage of these states, and connects with it no hypothesis respecting its substance. On the other hand, to the *ego* he never thinks of applying the epithet "my." And why not? Simply because it *is* he; and if mind also was he, he never would dream of applying the word "my" to it either. The *ego* is he, not something which he possesses. He therefore never attempts to *objectify* it, because it will not admit of this. But he can talk rightly and intelligibly of "my sensations;" that is to say, he can tell us that this *ego* is visited by various sensations, because he feels that the *ego*, that is, himself, is different from these sensations. At any rate, he never, of his own accord, confounds himself and his sensations or states of mind together. He never in his natural state, uses the word "mind" as convertible with the word "I;" and if he did so, he would not be intelligible to his species. They would never know that he meant himself; and simply for this reason, that the fact of self-reference or consciousness is not contained or expressed in the word "mind," and cannot, indeed, be denoted by any word in the *third* person. It has been reserved for the "metaphysics of mind" to introduce into thought and language a confusion which man's natural understanding has always steered clear of.

We have found, then, that this distinction between the man himself (that called *ego*) and the states of mind which he is conscious of, obtains in the language of common sense, and we do not feel ourselves entitled to subvert or to neglect it. But to leave it precisely as we found it, would be to turn it to no account whatsoever, and would allow the metaphysician still to triumph in our failure to accomplish what we have declared to be the true end and business of philosophy. The distinction is espoused by common sense, and is thrown out on the very surface of ordinary language: therefore the presumption that it is correct is in its favor; but it still remains to be philosophically vindicated and made good. Let us, then, accept it faithfully as given; and gently construing it into a clearer form, let us see whether every fact connected with it under its philosophic aspect will not prove it to be the most important and valid of all possible discriminations.

To mark this distinction, this conviction and expression of common sense, by a philosophical formula, let us suppose a line terminating in two opposite poles. In the one of these we will vest "mind," that is, the whole assemblage of the various states or changes experienced — all the feelings, passions, sensations etc., of man; and in the other of them we will vest the fact of consciousness, and the man himself calling himself "I." Now we admit, in the first instance, that these two poles are mere postulates, and that our postulation of them can only be justified and made good that they are mutually repulsive; by the fact that there is a reciprocal antithesis or antagonism between them, and between all that each of them contains: or, in other words, we must be borne out by the fact, that an increase of intensity at the one pole is always compensated by a corresponding decrease of intensity at the other pole, and *vice versa*. For if, on the contrary, it should appear that these two poles agree and act so harmoniously together, that the vividness experienced at the one pole (say that in which sensation, etc., reside) is answered by a proportional vividness at the opposite pole of consciousness; and that a depression at this latter pole again takes place in accordance with a diminished intensity at the former pole: in short, if it should appear that these two poles, instead of mutually extinguishing, mutually strengthen each other's light, then we must own that the antithesis we are endeavoring to establish is virtually void and erroneous; that sensation and consciousness are really identical, and that the *two* poles are in fact not *two*, but only *one*. In a word, we will own that the distinction we have been all along fighting for does not exist, and that the ordinary doctrine of psychology upon this head is faultless, and beyond dispute.

This point, however, is not to be settled by speculation, or by abstract reasoning. What says *the fact*? The fact is notorious to everyone except metaphysicians, who have seldom paid much attention to this or any other fact, that the degree of our consciousness or self-reference always exists in an inverse ratio to the degree of intensity of any of our sensations, passions, emotions, etc.; and that consciousness is never so effectually depressed, or, perhaps, we may say, never so totally obliterated within us, as when we are highly transported by the vividness of any sensation, or absorbed in the violence of any passion. While, on the other hand, returning consciousness, or increasing self-reference, has always the effect of deadening the sensation and suspending the passion, until at length, when it reaches its *ultimatum*, the sensation or passion becomes totally extinct. This is decidedly the fact, and there is no denying it. Look at a human being immersed in the swinish gratifications of sense. See here how completely the man is lost in the animal. Swallowed up in the pleasurable sensations of his palate, he is oblivious of everything else, and consciousness sinks into abeyance for a time. The sensation at the one pole monopolizes him, and therefore the consciousness at the other pole does not come into play. He does not think of himself; he does not combine the notion of himself with the sensation, the enjoyment of which is enslaving him. Again, look at another man shaken by wrath, as a tree is shaken by the wind. Here, too, the passion reigns paramount, and everything else is forgotten. Consciousness is extinguished; and hence the expression of the poet, *Ira brevis furor est*—"Rage is a brief insanity"—is strictly and pathologically true; because consciousness, the condition upon which all sanity depends, is for the time absent from the man. Hence, too, the ordinary phrase, that rage transports a man *out of himself*, is closely and philosophically correct. Properly interpreted, it means that the man is taken completely out of the pole where consciousness abides, and vested entirely in the opposite pole where passion dwells; or rather we should say that *as a man* he is extinct, and lives only *as a machine*. In both of these cases the men lose their personality. They are played upon by a foreign agency.

"Infortunati nimium sua si *mala* norint!"

But as yet they know not how mean and how miserable they are. Consciousness must return to them first, and only they themselves can bring it back; and when it does return, the effect of its very first approach is to lower the temperature of the sensation and of the passion. The men are not now wholly absorbed in the state that prevailed at the sensual and passionate pole. The balance is beginning to right itself. They have originated an act of their own, which has given them some degree of freedom; and they now begin to look down upon their former state as upon a state of intolerable slavery; and ever as this self-reference of theirs waxes, they look down upon that state as more and more slavish still, until at length, the balance being completely reversed and lying over on the other side, consciousness is again enthroned, the passion and the sensation are extinguished, and the men feel themselves to be completely free.

The first general expression, then, of this great law (which, however, may require much minute attention to calculate all its subordinate forces and their precise balances) is this: When passion, or any state of mind at the one pole, is at its *maximum*, consciousness is at its *minimum*, this *maximum* being sometimes so great as absolutely to extinguish consciousness while it continues; and, *vice versa*, when consciousness is at its *maximum*, the passion, or whatever the state of mind at the opposite pole may be, is at its *minimum*, the *maximum* being in this case, too, sometimes so great as to amount to a total suspension of the passion, etc. What important consequences does the mere enunciation of this great law suggest! In particular, what a firm and intelligible basis does it afford to the great superstructure of morality! What light does it carry down into the profoundest recesses of duty! Man's passions may be said to be the origin of all human wickedness. What more important fact, then, can there be than this, that the very act of consciousness, simple as it may seem, brings along with it, to a considerable extent, the suspension of any passion which may be tyrannizing over us; and that, as the origination of this act is our own, so is it in our own power to heighten and increase its luster as we please, even up to the highest degree of self-reflection, where it triumphs over passion completely? These matters, however, shall be more fully unfolded when we come to speak of the *consequences* of the fact of consciousness.[2]

---

[2] Dr. Chalmers has a long chapter in his Moral Philosophy (Chap. II.) on the effect which consciousness has in obliterating the state of mind upon which it turns its eye. But to what account does he turn his observation of this fact? He merely notices it as attaching a *peculiar* difficulty to the study of the phenomena of mind. It does indeed. It attaches *so* peculiar a difficulty to the study of these phenomena, that we wonder the Doctor was not led by this consideration to perceive that these

SELECTION 2
FROM PART III OF PHILOSOPHY OF CONSCIOUSNESS

CHAPTER III.

The first question with which we are to be engaged is this: When does consciousness come into operation? And we ask, first of all, Is man *born* conscious, or is he conscious during several (be their number greater or less) of the earlier months, we may say years, of his existence? We answer, No: for if he were, then he would remember, or at least some individuals of the species would remember, the day of their birth and the first year or years of their infancy. People in general recollect that of which they were conscious. But perhaps it may be objected that a man, or that many men, may forget, and often do forget, events of which they were conscious. True; but it is absolutely impossible, and at variance with universal experience, that *everybody* should forget that of which *everybody* was conscious. If the whole human race were conscious at the day of their birth, and during their earliest childhood, it is altogether inconceivable but that *some of them* at least should remember those days and their events. But *no one* possesses any such remembrance; and therefore the inference is irresistible that man is not born conscious, and does not become conscious until some considerable period after his birth. Let

---

phenomena were no longer the real and important facts of the science; but that the fact of consciousness, together with the consequences it brought along with it, and nothing else, truly was so. Again, on the other hand, this fact attaches so peculiar *a facility* to the study of morality, that we are surprised the Doctor did not avail himself of its assistance in explaining the laws and character of duty. But how does Dr. Chalmers "get quit of this difficulty"? If the phenomena of mind disappear as soon as consciousness looks at them, how do you think he obviates the obstacle in the way of science? Why, by emptying human nature of consciousness altogether; or, as he informs us, "by adopting Dr. Thomas Brown's view of consciousness, who makes this act to be," as Dr. Chalmers says, "a brief act of memory." Whether this means that consciousness is a short act of memory, or an act of memory following shortly after the "state" remembered, we are at a loss to say; but, at any rate, we here have consciousness converted into memory. For we presume that there is no difference in kind, no distinction at all between an act of memory which is brief, and an act of memory which is not brief. Thus consciousness is obliterated. Man is deprived of the notion of himself. He no longer is a self at all, or capable of any self-reference. From having been a person, he becomes a mere thing; and is left existing and going through various acts of intelligence, just like the animals around him, which exist and perform many intelligent acts without being aware of their existence, without possessing any personality, or taking any account to themselves of their accomplishments.

this conclusion then be noted, for we may be required to make some use of it hereafter.

If, then, man is not conscious at his birth, or until sometime after it has elapsed, at what period of his life does consciousness manifest itself? To ascertain this period we must seek for some vital sign of the existence of consciousness. It is possible that, before the true and real consciousness of the human being displays itself, there are within him certain obscure prefigurations or anticipations of the dawning phenomenon; and therefore it may not be practicable to fix in the precisest and strictest manner its absolute point of commencement. Still, compared with the actual rise and development of consciousness, these dim and uncertain preludes of it are even more faint and indistinct than are the first feeble rays which the sun sends up before him, compared with the glory which fills heaven and earth when the great luminary himself bursts above the sea. This parallel is certainly not perfect, because the sun, though below the horizon, nevertheless exists; but an unapparent consciousness is zero, or no consciousness at all. Consciousness, no doubt, keeps ever gaining in distinctness, but there is certainly a period when it is an absolute blank, and then there is an epoch at which it exists and comes forth distinctly into the light; an epoch so remarkable that it may be assumed and fixed as the definite period when the true existence and vital manifestation of consciousness commences. Our business now is to point out and illustrate this epoch.

It is a well-known fact that children, for some time after they acquire the use of language, speak of themselves *in the third person*, calling themselves John, Tom, or whatever else their names may be. Some speak thus for a longer, others for a shorter period; but all of them invariably speak for a certain time after this fashion. What does this prove, and how is it to be accounted for?

In the first place, it proves that they have not yet acquired the notion of their own personality. Whatever their intellectual or rational state may in other respects be, they have not combined with it the conception of *self*. In other words, it proves that as yet they are unconscious. They as yet exist merely *for others*, not *for themselves*.

In the second place, how is the origin of the language, such as it is, which the child makes use of, to be explained? It is to be accounted for upon exactly the same principle, whatever this may be, as that which enables the parrot to be taught to speak. This principle may be called imitation, which may be viewed as a modification of the great law of association, which again is to be considered as an illustration of the still greater law of cause and effect; and under any or all of these views it is not to be conceived that intelligence is by any means absent from the process. The child and the parrot hear those around them applying various names to different objects, and, being imitative animals, acting under the law of causality, they apply these names in the same manner: and now mark most particularly the curious part of the process, how they follow the same rule when speaking of themselves. They hear people calling them by their own names in the third person, and not having any notion of themselves, not having realized their own personality, they have nothing else for it than to adhere, in this case too, to their old principle of imitation, and to do towards themselves just what others do towards them; that is to say, when speaking of themselves they are unavoidably forced to designate themselves by a word in the third person; or, in other words, to speak of themselves as if they were *not* themselves.

So long, then, as this state of things continues, the human being is to be regarded as leading altogether mere animal life, as living completely under the dominion and within the domain of nature. The law of its whole being is the law of causality. Its sensations, feelings of every kind, and all its exercises of reason, are mere effects, which again in their turn are capable of becoming causes. It cannot be said to be without "mind," if by the attribution of "mind" to it we mean that it is subject to various sensations, passions, desires, etc.; but it certainly is without consciousness, or that notion of self, that realization of its own personality, which, in the subsequent stages of its existence, accompanies these modifications of its being. It is still entirely the creature of instinct, which may be exactly and completely defined as *unconscious reason*.

It is true that the child at this stage of its existence often puts on the semblance of the intensest selfishness; but to call it selfish, in the proper sense of the word would be to apply to it a complete misnomer. This would imply that it stood upon moral ground, whereas its being rests as yet upon no moral foundations at all. *We* indeed have a moral soil beneath our feet. And this is the origin of our mistake. In us, conduct similar to the child's would be really selfish, *because* we occupy a moral ground, and have realized our own personality; and hence, forgetting the different grounds upon which we and it stand, we transfer over upon it, through a mistaken analogy, or rather upon a false hypothesis, language which would serve to characterize its conduct, only provided it stood in the same situation with us, and like us possessed the notion and reality of itself. The child is driven to the gratification of its desires (prior to consciousness) at whatever cost, and whatever the consequences may be, just as an animal or a machine is impelled to accomplish the work for which it was designed; and the desire dies only when gratified, or when its natural force is spent, or when supplanted by some other desire equally blind and equally out of its control. How can we affix the epithet selfish, or any other term indicating either blame or praise, to a creature which as yet is not a *self* at all, either in thought, in word, or deed? For let it be particularly noted that the notion of self is a great deal more than a mere notion, — that is to say, it possesses far more than a mere logical value and contents — it is absolutely genetic or creative. *Thinking* oneself "I" *makes* oneself "I;" and it is only *by thinking* himself "I" that a man *can* make himself "I;" or, in other words, change an unconscious thing into that which is now a conscious self. Nothing else will or can do it. So long as a Being does *not* think itself "I," it does not and cannot become "I." No other being, no being except itself, can make it "I." More, however, of this hereafter.

But now mark the moment when the child pronounces the word "I," and knows what this expression means. Here is a new and most important step taken. Let no one regard this step as insignificant, or treat our mention of it lightly and superciliously; for, to say the least of it, it is a step the like of which in magnitude and wonder the human being never yet took, and never shall take again, throughout the whole course of his rational and immortal career. We have read in fable of Circæan charms, which changed men into brutes; but here in this little monosyllable is contained a truer and more potent charm, the spell of an inverted and un-fabulous enchantment, which converts the *feral* into the *human* being. The origination of this little monosyllable lifts man out of the natural into the moral universe. It places him, indeed, upon a perilous pre-eminence, being the assertion of nothing less than his own absolute independence. He is now no longer a paradisiacal creature of blind and unconscious good. He has fallen from that estate by this very assertion of his independence; but, in compensation for this, he is now a conscious and a moral creature, knowing evil from good, and able to choose the latter even when he embraces the former; and this small word of one letter, and it alone, is the talisman which has effected these mighty changes — which has struck from his being the fetters of the law of causality, and given him to breathe the spacious atmosphere of absolute freedom; thus rendering him a moral and accountable agent, by making him the first cause or complete originator of all his actions.

If we reflect for a moment upon the origin and application of the word "I," as used by the child, we shall see what a remarkable contrast exists between this term and any other expression which he employs; and how strikingly different its origin is from that of all these expressions. We have already stated that the child's employment of language previous to his use of the word "I," may be accounted for upon the principle of imitation, or that at any rate it falls to be considered as a mere illustration of the general law of cause and effect. He hears other people applying certain sounds to designate certain objects; and when these objects or similar ones are presented, or in any way recalled, to him, the consequence is that he utters the same sounds in connection with their presence. All this takes place, very naturally, under the common law of association. But neither association, nor the principle of imitation, nor any conceivable modification of the law of cause and effect, will account for the child's use of the word "I." In originating and using this term, he reverses, or runs counter to all these laws, and more particularly performs a process diametrically opposed to any act of imitation. Take an illustration of this: A child hears another person call a certain object "a table;" well, the power of imitation naturally leads him to call the same thing, and any similar thing, "a table." Suppose, next, that the child hears this person apply to himself the word "I:" In this case, too, the power of imitation would naturally (that is to say, letting it operate here in the same way as it did in the case of the table) lead the child to call that man "I." But is this what the child does? No. As soon as he becomes conscious, he ceases, so far at least as the word "I" is concerned, to be an imitator. He still applies the word "table" to the objects to which other people apply that term; and in this he imitates them. But with regard to the word "I," he applies this expression to a thing totally different from that which he hears all other people applying it to. They apply it to themselves, but he does not apply it *to them*, but *to himself*; and in this he is not an imitator, but the absolute originator of a new notion, upon which he now, and henceforth, takes up his stand, and which leads him on in the career of a destiny most momentous, and altogether anomalous and new.

In opposition to this view is it objected that in the use of the word "I" the child may still be considered an imitative creature, inasmuch as he merely applies to himself a word which he hears other people applying to themselves, having borrowed this application of it from them? Oh! vain and short-sighted objection! As if this very fact did not necessarily imply and prove that he has first of all originated within himself the notion expressed by the word "I" (namely, the notion of his conscious self), and thereby, and thereby only, has become capable of comprehending what *they* mean by it. In the use and understanding of this word every man must be altogether *original*. No person can *teach* to another its true meaning and right application; for this reason, that no two human beings ever use it, or ever can use it, in the same sense or apply it to the same being: a true but astounding paradox, which may be thus forcibly expressed. Every one rightly calls himself by a name which no other person can call him by without being convicted of the most outrageous and almost inconceivable insanity. The word "I" in *my* mouth as applied to *you* would prove me to be a madman. The word "I" in *your* mouth as applied to *me* would prove you to be the same. Therefore, I cannot by any conceivability teach you what it means, nor can you teach me. We must both of us originate it first of all independently for ourselves, and then we can understand one another. This may be put to the actual test if anyone is curious to prove it. Let any man teach a parrot to say "I" (it meaning thereby itself), and we pledge ourselves to un-write all that we have written upon this topic.[3]

We have now, then, brought this question to a conclusion; besides having opened up slightly and incidentally a few collateral views

---

[3] It will not do to say that man is capable of forming the notion expressed by the word "I," in consequence of the reason with which he has been endowed, and that the parrot and other animals are not thus capable of forming it in consequence of their inferior degree of intelligence. We have treated of this point at some length in the first part of our discussion. Let us now, however, make one remark on the subject. It is plain that an increase or a deficiency of reason can only cause the creature in which it operates to accomplish its ends with greater or less exactness and perfection. Reason in itself runs straight, however much its volume may be augmented. Is it said that this consciousness, this self-reference, this reflex fact denoted by the word "I," is merely a peculiar inflection which reason takes in man, and which it does not take in animals? True; but the smallest attention shows us that reason only takes this peculiar inflection in consequence of falling in with the fact of consciousness: so that instead of reason accounting for consciousness, instead of consciousness being the derivative of reason, we find that it is consciousness which meets reason, and gives it that peculiar turn we have spoken of, rendering it and all its works referable to ourselves. It is not, then, reason which gives rise to consciousness, but it is the prior existence of consciousness which makes reason *human* reason.

'An Introduction to the Philosophy of Consciousness' 35

connected with other problems, we have returned a distinct answer to the question. When does consciousness come into operation? Sensation, passion, reason, etc., all exist as soon as the human being is born, but *consciousness* only comes into existence when he has originated within him the notion and the reality denoted by the word "I." Then only does he begin to exist *for himself*. In our next paper we shall proceed to the discussion of the most important, but at the same time most difficult, question in all psychology, *How* does consciousness come into operation?

SELECTION 3

FROM PART IV OF PHILOSOPHY OF CONSCIOUSNESS

CHAPTER II.

We have already[4] had occasion to establish and illustrate the radical distinction between consciousness on the one hand, and sensation on the other, or any other of those "states of mind," as they are called, of which we are cognizant. We showed that consciousness is not only distinct from any of these states, but it is diametrically opposed, or placed in a direct antithesis, to them all. Thus, taking for an example, as we have hitherto done, the smell of a rose, it appears that so long as the sensation occasioned by this object remains moderate, consciousness, or the realization of self in union with the feeling, comes into play without any violent effort. But, suppose the sensation is increased until we almost

"Die of a rose, in aromatic pain,"

then we affirm that the natural tendency of this augmentation is to weaken or obliterate consciousness, which, at any rate, cannot now maintain its place without a much stronger exertion. We do not say that this loss of self-possession, or possession *of self*, always happens even when human sensations are most immoderate; but we affirm that in such circumstances there is a natural tendency in man to lose his consciousness or to have it weakened; and that when he retains it, he does so by the counteracting exercise of an *unnatural*, that is, of a free and moral power; and we further maintain that this tendency or law, or fact of humanity, which is fully brought to light when our

[4] See Part II, Ch. II.

sensations, emotions, etc., are rendered very violent, clearly proves that there is at bottom a vital and ceaseless repugnancy between consciousness and all these "states of mind," even in their ordinary and more moderate degrees of manifestation, although the equipoise then preserved on both sides may render it difficult for us to observe it. Had man been visited by much keener sensations, and hurried along by much stronger passions, and endowed with a much more perfect reason, the realization of his own personality, together with the consequences it involves, would then have been a matter of much greater difficulty to him than it now is; perhaps it would have amounted to an impossibility. Even as it is, nothing can be more wonderful than that he should evolve this antagonist power in the very heart of the floods of sensation which, pouring in upon all sides, are incessantly striving to overwhelm it; and secure in its strength, should ride, as in a lifeboat, amid all the whirlpools of blind and fatalistic passion, which make the life of every man here below a sea of roaring troubles.

We now avail ourselves of the assistance of this antagonism, which has thus been established *as fact* by experience, in order to displace the false fact generally, we might say universally, assumed in our current metaphysics—namely, that consciousness, or the fact and notion denoted by the word "I," comes into manifestation at the bidding, and under the influence, of the objects which induce the sensations accompanying it.

One fact admitted on all hands is, that our sensations are caused by certain objects presented to our senses; another fact *assumed* on all hands is, that our *consciousness of* sensations falls under the same law, and is likewise induced by the presence of these objects. But consciousness and sensation are each other's opposites, and exist as thesis and antithesis; therefore, according to this doctrine, we find two contradictory effects attributed at the same moment to the same cause, and referred to the same origin, just as if we were to affirm that the same object is at the same moment and in the same place the cause at once of light and of the *absence* of light, or that the sun at one and the same instant both ripens fruit and *prevents* it from ripening. To illustrate this by our former example (for a variety of illustrations adds nothing to the clearness of an exposition), let us suppose a sentient being to experience the smell of a rose. So long as this being's state is simply sentient, its sensation is absorbing, effective, and complete; but as soon as consciousness, or the realization of self, blends with this feeling, it from that moment becomes weaker and less perfect. It is no longer pure and unalloyed, and consequently its integrity is violated, and its strength in some degree impaired; yet, according to our ordinary psychologists, the same object, namely, the rose, which induces the strength of the sensation, also brings along with it that suspension or weakening of the sensation which consciousness is. We are called upon to believe that the same cause at the same moment both produces and destroys a particular effect, a creed too contradictory and unintelligible to be easily embraced when thus plainly exposed. If a particular object induces a particular sensation, surely the suspension of that sensation, or, in other words, the consciousness which impairs it, and prevents it from being all-absorbing, cannot be induced by the same cause. And, besides, if our consciousness depended on our sensations, passions, or any other of our "states of mind," would not its light kindle, and its energy wax in proportion as these were brightened and increased? We have seen, however, that the reverse of this is the case, and that consciousness never burns more faintly than during man's most vivid paroxysms of sensation and of passion.

This argument, which is, however, rather a fact presented to us by experience than an inference, entirely disproves the dependency of man's consciousness upon the external objects which give birth to his sensations. It thus radically uproots that false fact by which man is made the creature and thrall of causality in his intercourse with the outward world, and the passive recipient of its impressions. At the same time, the displacement of this false fact opens up to us a glimpse of that great truth, the view and realization of which it has hitherto obstructed, the liberty of man. In order to get a nearer and clearer prospect of this grand reality, let us extirpate still more radically the spurious fact we have been dealing with, until not a fiber of it remains to shoot forth anew into sprouts of error.

CHAPTER III.

The earliest speculators among mankind were, as we have before remarked, mere naturalists or *physici*. They looked at everything and conceived everything under the law of cause and effect. After a time, when speculation began to be directed upon man, or became what is now termed "metaphysical," this law still continued to be regarded as supreme, and the spirit of the old method was carried on into the new research. But as no instance of causality could be conceived without the existence of a thing *operated on*, as well as of a thing *operating*, they were forced to postulate something in man (either physical or hyperphysical) for the objects of external nature to act upon. Thus, in order to allow the law of causality an intelligible sphere of operation, and at the same time to lift man out of the mire of a gross materialism, they devised or assumed a certain spiritualized or attenuated substance called "mind," endowed with certain passive susceptibilities as well as with various active powers; and this hypothetical substance, together with all the false facts and foolish problems it brings along with it, has been permitted to maintain its place, almost without challenge, in all our schools of philosophy down to the present hour; so completely has psychological science in general taken the color and imbibed the spirit of physical research.

> "Ut multis nota est naturæ causa latentis;
> At sua qui noscat pectora rarus adest."

It is time, however, that this substance, and the doctrines and facts taught in connection with it, were tested in a more rigorous and critical spirit, not, indeed, upon their own account, but on account of those greater and more important truths whose places they have usurped. How, then, do we propose testing this substance? In this way. The word "mind" is exceedingly remote and ambiguous, and denotes—nobody knows what. Let us then substitute in place of it that much plainer expression which everybody makes use of, and in some degree, at least, understands—the expression "I" or "me;" and let us see how mind, with its facts and doctrines, will fare when this simple, unpretending, and un-hypothetical word is employed in its place.

"External objects take effect upon mind, and perception is the result." This doctrine lies at the very threshold of our ordinary metaphysics, and forms the foundation-stone upon which their whole superstructure is erected. But is it true? Let us come to a more distinct understanding of it by changing it into the following statement, and we shall see what gross though deep-lurking falsities are brought to light by the alteration. Let us say "external objects take effect upon *me*, and perception is the result." We now then ask, To what period of our life is this proposition meant to have reference? Does the philosopher of "mind" answer that it may be applied to us during any period, from first to last, of our existence? Then we tell him in return that, in that case, the doctrine is certainly false, for it is not the fact that things take effect upon "me" at the birth or during the earlier years of that particular Being which *afterwards* becomes "I," there being at that time no "me" at all in the case; no "me" *for* things to take effect upon, as was proved in the preceding problem, where it was shown that no man is born conscious, or, in other words, that no man is born "I." It is true that things take effect, from the very first, upon that particular Being which, *after a time and after a certain process*, becomes "I." But this particular Being was not "I" at its birth, or until a considerable time after it had elapsed; and, therefore, the proposition, "things take effect upon *me*," is seen to be untrue when applied to one period of human life at least, and thus the *ego*, or that which, in the case of each individual man, is "I;" or, in other words, his true being is liberated from the control of the law of causality, during the earlier stages at least of his existence, in the most conclusive and effectual way possible, namely, by showing that at that time this "I" has no manner of existence or manifestation whatsoever.

Does the philosopher of mind, giving up this point, maintain that the proposition quoted has, at any rate, a true and intelligible application to us in our grown or advanced condition? Then we tell him that, in that case, the affirmation or dogma is altogether *premature*; because, before it can be admitted, he is bound to explain to us how the particular Being given and contemplated, which was not "I" or "me" at first, became converted into "me." Before any subsequent averment connected with this "me" can be listened to, it is first of all incumbent upon him, we say, to point out to us how this conversion is brought about; to explain to us the origin and significance of this "I," the circumstances out of which it arose; for, as we have already said, the particular Being which now appropriates it was certainly not sent into the world a born or readymade "I."

Suppose, then, that the metaphysician should say that this Being becomes "I" under the law of causality, and beneath the action of the external objects which produce impressions upon it, then we would like to know how it happened that these outward objects, which induced the human Being's sensations at the very first did not cause him to become "I" *then*. When he was first born he was just as sensitive as he ever was afterwards, no doubt more so, but for long his sensations continued pure and unalloyed. After a time, however, they were found to be combined with the notion and reality of self, a new notion and reality altogether. The human Being has now become *ego*; from a *thing* he has become a *person*. But what new circumstances were there in his sensations, or their exciting causes, by which they brought about this new fact and phasis of existence? The metaphysician cannot answer us. He must admit that the sensations and their causes remain, after the manifestation of the *ego*, precisely what they were before it came into existence, and, therefore, that they can never account for its origin.

But we have already, in the preceding chapter, disproved still more effectually the fact that the *ego* comes into existence in consequence of the influence of external objects. We there showed that consciousness not only does not manifest itself in obedience to their action, but that it actually tends to be suppressed and obliterated thereby. Now consciousness is the very essence and origin of the *ego*; consciousness creates the *ego*; without consciousness no man would be "I." Therefore the *ego* is also exempt from the influences of outward objects, and manifests itself, and maintains its place, not *in consequence*, but *in spite* of them. Consciousness develops and preserves itself by refusing to take part or identify itself with the sensation, passion, or whatever it may be that is striving to enslave the man; and the *ego*, which is but the more personal and vital expression of consciousness, exists merely by refusing to imbibe the impressions of external things. Thus, so far is it from being true that outward objects take effect upon *me*, that "I," in truth, only *am* by resisting and refusing to be impressed by their action.

When an effect, or impression, is produced on any substance, whether it be motion, as in the case of a struck billiard-ball, or sensation, as in the case of animals and men, the substance impressed is either conscious of the impression, as is the case with men, or unconscious of it, as is the case with animals and billiard-balls. If it be unconscious of the impression, then, being filled and monopolized by the same, it never rises above it, but, yielding to its influence, it becomes altogether the slave of the law of causality, or of the force that is working on it. But if this substance be conscious of the impression made upon it, then it is absolutely necessary, in the eye of reason, that a portion of this being should stand aloof from the impression, should be exempt from the action of the object causing it; in short, should resist, repel, and deny it in the exercise of a free activity; otherwise, like animals and inferior things, being completely absorbed and monopolized by the influence present to it, it would no more be able to become conscious of it than a leaf can comprehend the gale in which it is drifting along, or the tiger the passion which impels him to slake his burning heart in blood. It is obvious that the point in man at which he becomes aware of his impressions must be free from these impressions, and must stand out of their sphere, otherwise it would be swallowed up by them, and nothing save the impressions would remain. But man is not made up of mere impressions—passions, sensations, "states of mind," or whatever they may be. He is not engulfed and borne along in their vortices. There is a point from which he looks down upon them all, and knows himself to be free. He stands within a circle more impregnable than enchanter's ring; a circle which, however much they may assault it, they cannot overpass: and this point or circle of freedom, this true life of humanity, is that which, in the case of each man, is "I."

This view disposes of a question which has been ever regarded as forming the *opprobrium* of metaphysics. We allude to the problem respecting the mode and nature of the intercourse which takes place between the external universe and man, or, as metaphysicians say, "Mind." This question is now given up, not because it has been solved, not because it is regarded as too contemptible and irrelevant to be entertained by speculative philosophy, but (pro pudor!) because it is considered insoluble, inscrutable, and beyond the limits of the human faculties. Oh, ye metaphysicians! Ye blind leaders of the blind! How long will ye be of seeing and understanding that there is no communication at all between man in his true Being and the universe that surrounds him, or that, if there be any, it is the communication of *non*-communication? Know ye not that ye are what ye are only on account of the antagonism between you and it; that ye perceive things only by resisting their impressions, by denying them, not in word only, but also in vital deed; that your refusal to be acted upon by them constitutes your very personality and your very perception of them; that this perception arises not in consequence of the union, but in consequence of the *dis*union between yourselves and matter; and, in fine, that your consciousness, even in its simplest acts, so far from being in harmony and keeping with the constitution of nature, is the commencement of that grand disruption between yourselves and the world, which perhaps ye will know more about before ye die?

Of all difficult entails to be broken through, the most difficult is the entail of false facts and erroneous opinions. If, however, the foregoing observations be attended to, we trust we have done something to cut off speculators yet unborn from their inheritances of error. Of all the false facts involved in the "science of the human mind," the greatest is this, that, starting from the assumption of "mind" as a given substance, we are thereby led to believe that the *ego* or central and peculiar point of humanity comes into the world *ready-made*. In opposition to this belief, the true fact is that the *ego* does *not* thus come into the world, but that the being which is now "I" was *not* "I" at first, but became "I" after a time and after a process, which it is the business of the philosopher to explain. Various other fictitious facts spring out of this tap-root of error. Thus, if we start from mind as a given substance, we, of course, are compelled to make this, in the first instance, passive, and only active through a species of reaction. But the *ego* is never passive. Its being is pure act. To hold it passive is to hold it annihilated. It is forever acting against the fatalistic forces of nature. Its free and antagonist power shows itself equally to the eye of reflection in our simplest perceptive as in our highest moral acts. It lives and has a being only in so far as it refuses to bow under the yoke of causality; and whenever it bends beneath that yoke, its life and all its results are gone.[5]

One word to those who imagine that the *ego* is merely a variety of expression signifying nothing more than the proper name of the person employing it. There cannot be a greater philosophical error than to conceive that the non-manifestation of the *ego* is merely a verbal or logical defect, and that the reality of it may exist in a being where the notion of it is wanting. Yet this appears to us to be one of the commonest errors in psychology. Metaphysicians undisciplined by reflection, when contemplating the condition of a young child, and observing its various sensitive, passionate, or rational states, are prone, in the exercise of an unwarranted imagination, also to invest it with a personality, with consciousness; in short, with that which, in their own case, they call "I," transferring over upon it this notion and reality which exist only for them. For the child all this while does not think itself "I," and therefore it does not in reality become "I." It

---

[5] "The false facts of metaphysics" ought to form no inconsiderable chapter in the history of philosophy. Those specified are but a few of them; but they are all that we have room for at present. To state, almost in one word, the fundamental error we have noticed in the text, we should say, that the whole perversion and falsity of the philosophy of man are owing to our commencing with a *substance*, "mind," and not with an *act*, the act or fact of consciousness.

'An Introduction to the Philosophy of Consciousness' 43

never can become "I" through *their* thinking. The "I" they think for it is a spurious and non-existent "I." To become "I" in reality, it must think itself "I," which it has not yet done. But what do we mean precisely by saying that the *notion* of "I" creates the *reality* of "I"? This we can best explain by a digression into the history of philosophy, and by rescuing a once famous dogma from the undeserved contempt into which it has generally fallen.

CHAPTER IV.

The Cartesian philosophy is said to commence by inculcating a species of wide and deep-searching skepticism; and its fundamental and favorite tenet is that *Cogito, ergo sum*, which is now so universally decried. But abandoning altogether its written dogmas and formulas, let us only return upon them after we have looked forth for ourselves into the realities of things.

When a man sees and thinks a mountain, it is obvious that his thought does not create the mountain. Here, then, the thought and the reality are not identical; nor does the one grow out of the other. The two can be separated, and, in point of fact, stand apart, and are quite distinct. In this case, then, it requires some degree of faith to believe that the notion and the reality correspond. It is evident that there is a sort of flaw between them which nothing but the cement of Faith can solder; a gap which no scientific ingenuity has ever been able to bridge; in short, that here there is a chink in the armor of reason which skepticism may take advantage of if it chooses; for the reality of the mountain being independent of the notion of the mountain, the notion may also be independent of the reality, and, for anything that can be shown to the contrary, may have been induced by some other cause. In short, the notion, even when the mountain appears present before us, may possibly exist without any corresponding reality, for it clearly does not create that reality.

In looking out, then, for a sure and certain foundation for science, we must not build upon any tenet in which a distinction between our thought and its corresponding reality is set forth (as, for example, upon any proposition expressing the real existence of an external world), for here skepticism might assail us, possibly with success; but we must seek for some subject of experience, between the notion of which and the reality of which there is no flaw, distinction, or interval whatsoever. We must seek for some instance in which the thought of a certain reality actually creates that reality; and if we can find such an instance, we shall then possess an *inconcussum quid* which will resist forever all the assaults of skepticism.

But no instance of this kind is to be found, as we have seen, by attaching our thoughts to the objects of the universe around us. Our *thinking* them does not *make* them realities. If they are realities, they are not so in consequence of our thoughts; and if they are not realities, unreal they will remain in spite of our thoughts. Let us turn from the universe, then, and look to ourselves, "I." Now here is an instance in which there is no distinction or sundering between the notion and the reality. The two are coincident and identical, or rather, we should say, the one (that is, the notion "I") creates and enforces the other (that is, the reality "I"); or, at any rate, this appears to be the best way of logically exhibiting the two. Between the notion and the reality in this case skepticism can find no conceivable entrance for the minutest point of its spear. Let any man consult his own experience whether, the notion "I" being given, the reality "I" must not also necessarily be present; and also whether, the reality being present, the notion must not also accompany it. Let him try to destroy or maintain the one without also destroying or maintaining the other, and see whether he can succeed. Succeed he easily may in the case of any other notion and reality. The word mountain, for instance, denotes both a notion and a reality. But the notion may exist perfectly well without the reality, and the reality without the notion. The notion, "I," however, cannot exist without the reality "I," and the reality cannot exist without the notion "I," as any one may satisfy himself by the slightest reflection.

Here, then, we have found the instance we were seeking for. What is the notion "I"? It is consciousness or the notion of self. What is the reality "I"? It is simply "I." Connect the two together in a genesis which makes the one arise out of the other, and you have the famous fundamental position of the Cartesian philosophy, *Cogito, ergo sum*, a formula which is worthy of respect, for this reason, if for no other, that by it the attention of psychologists was first distinctly directed to the only known instance in which a notion and a reality are identical and coincident, in which *a thought* is the same as *a thing*.

But, by means of the dogma, *Cogito, ergo sum*, was it not the design of Descartes to prove his own existence? Take our word for it, no such miserable intention ever entered into his head. His great object, in the first place, was emphatically to signalize the very singular and altogether anomalous phenomenon we have spoken of, namely, the identity in man of thought and reality, and then to found upon this point as on a rock which no conceivable skepticism could shake; and, in the second place, he attempted to point out the genesis of the *ego*, in so far as it admitted of logical exposition. *Cogito, ergo sum*, I am conscious, therefore I am; that is, consciousness, or the *notion* of "I," takes place in a particular Being, and the *reality* of "I" is the immediate result. The *ergo* here does not denote a mere logical inference from the fact of consciousness, but it points to a genetic or creative power in that act.

"Consciousness created you, that is to say, you created yourself; did you?" we may here imagine an opponent of Descartes to interpose.

"No," replies Descartes; "I did not create myself, in so far as my mere existence is concerned. But, in so far as I am an *ego*, or an existence *as a self*, I certainly did create myself. By becoming conscious, I, in one sense, actually created myself."

"But," says the other, "must you not have existed before you could become conscious, and in order to become conscious?"

"Certainly," answers Descartes, "some sort of being must have existed *before* my consciousness, but it was only *after* consciousness that that being became *I*".

"Do you then cease to be whenever you cease to be conscious?"

To this question Descartes answers both yes and no. "As an existing being," says he, "fulfilling many purposes of creation, I certainly do not cease to exist when I cease to be conscious; but as an 'I' (ego), I certainly am no more the moment consciousness leaves me. Consciousness made me from a *thing*, a *self*; that is, it lifted me up from existing merely *for others*, and taught me to exist also *for myself*. My being as an *ego* depends upon, and results from my consciousness, and therefore, as soon as my consciousness is taken away, my existence as an *ego* or self vanishes. The being heretofore called 'I' still exists, but not as 'I.' It lives only for others, not for itself; not as a self at all, either in thought or in deed."

CHAPTER V.

But though we have seen that consciousness is the genesis or origin of the *ego*, and that without the former the latter has no existence, we have yet to throw somewhat more light on consciousness itself, and the circumstances in which it arises.

Let thyself float back, oh reader! as far as thou canst in obscure memory into thy golden days of infancy, when the light of thy young life, rising out of unknown depths, scattered away death from before its path, beyond the very limits of thought; even as the sun beats off the darkness of night into regions lying out of the visible boundaries of space. In those days thy light was single and without reflection. Thou wert one with nature, and, blending with her bosom, thou didst drink in inspiration from her thousand breasts. Thy consciousness was faint in the extreme, for as yet thou hadst but slightly awakened *to thyself*; and thy sensations and desires were nearly all-absorbing. Carry thyself back still farther into days yet more "dark with excess of light," and thou shalt behold, through the visionary mists, an earlier time, when thy consciousness was altogether null; a time when the discrimination of thy sensations into *subject* and *object*, which seems so ordinary and inevitable a process to thee *now*, had not taken place, but when thyself and nature were enveloped and fused together in a glowing and indiscriminate synthesis. In these days thy state was indeed blessed, but it was the blessedness of bondage. The earth flattered thee, and the smiling heavens flattered thee into forgetfulness. Thou wert nature's favorite, but at the same time her fettered slave.

But thy destiny was to be free; to free thyself, to break asunder the chains of nature, to oppose thy will and thy strength to the universe, both without thee and within thee, to tread earth and the passions of earth beneath thy feet; and thy first step towards this great consummation was to dissolve the strong, primary, and natural synthesis of sensation. In the course of time, then, that which was originally *one* in the great unity of nature, became *two* beneath the first exercise of a reflective analysis. Thy sensation was now divided into *subject* and *object*; that is, thyself and the universe around thee. Now, for the first time, wert thou "I."

Wouldst thou re-examine thy sensation as it exists in its primary synthetic state? Then look at it; what is it but a pure unmixed sensation, a sensation and *nothing more*? Wouldst thou behold it, in thy own secondary analysis of it? then, lo! how a new element, altogether transcending mere sensation, is presented to thee, the element or act of negation; that is, as we shall show, of freedom.

Sensation in man is found to be, first of all, a unity, and at this time there is no *ego* or *non-ego* at all in the case; but afterwards it becomes a duality, and then there is an *ego* and a *non-ego*. But, in the latter case, it is obvious that very different circumstances are connected with sensation, and very different elements are found along with it, than are found in it when it is a unity: there is, for instance, the fact of negation, the *non* which is interposed between the subject and the object; and there are also, of course, any other facts into which this one may resolve itself.

Moreover, it is evident that, but for this act of negation or division, there would be no *ego*, or *non-ego*. Take away this element, and the sensation is restored to its first unity, in which these, being un-discriminated, were virtually non-existent. For it is obvious that, unless a man discriminates himself as "I" from other things, he does not exist as "I." The *ego* and the *non-ego*, then, only are by being discriminated, or by the one of them being denied (not in thought or word only, but in a primary and vital act) of the other. But consciousness also is the discrimination between the *ego* and the *non-ego*; or, in other words, consciousness resolves itself, in its clearest form, into an act of negation.

In order, then, to throw the strongest light we can on consciousness, we must ascertain the value and import, and, if possible, the origin of this act of negation, this fundamental energy and vital condition upon which the peculiar being of humanity depends. And, first of all, we must beg the reader (a point we have had occasion to press upon him before) to banish from his mind the notion that this negation is a mere logical power, or form, consisting of a thought and a word. Let him endeavor to realize such a conception of it as will exhibit it to him as a vital and energetic deed by which he brings himself into existence, not indeed as a Being, but as that which he calls "I." Let him consider that, unless this deed of negation were practiced by him he *himself* would not be here; a particular Being would, indeed, be here: but it is only by denying or distinguishing itself from other things that that being becomes a self—*himself*. Unless this discrimination took place, the Being would remain lost and swallowed up in the identity or uniformity of the universe. It would be only *for others*, not *for itself*. Self, in its case, would not emerge.

Am I, then, to say that "I" have been endowed by some other Being with this power of sundering myself, during sensation, from the objects causing it; am I to say that this capability has been given "me"? *Given me*! Why, I was not "I" until *after* this power was exerted; how then could it have been given "me"? There was no "me" to give it to. I became "I" only by exercising it; and *after* it had been exerted, what would be the advantage of supposing it given to me *then*, I having it already? If, then, I suppose this power given to "me" *before* it is exerted, I suppose it given to that which does not as yet exist to receive it; and if I suppose it given to me *after* it is exerted, *after* I have become "I," I make myself the receiver of a very superfluous and unnecessary gift.

But suppose it should be said that this power, though not, properly speaking, given to "me," is yet given to that particular Being which afterwards, in consequence of exercising it, becomes "I," then we answer, that in this case it is altogether a mistake to suppose that this particular Being exercises the power. The power is, truly speaking, exercised by the Being which infused it, and which itself here becomes "I;" while the particular Being supposed to become "I" in consequence of the endowment, remains precisely what it was, and does not, by any conceivability, become "I." One Being may, indeed, divide and sunder another Being from other objects; but this does not make the latter Being "I." In order to become "I" it must sunder *itself* from other things by *its own* act. Finally, this act of negation, or, in other words, consciousness, is either derived or un-derived. If it is derived, then it is the consciousness of the Being from whom it is derived, and not mine. But I am supposing it, and it is admitted to be, *mine*, and not another Being's, therefore it must be un-derived; that is to say, self-originated and free.

A particular Being becomes "I" in consequence of exercising this act of negation. But this act must be that Being's own; otherwise, supposing it to be the act of another Being, it would be that other Being which would become I, and not the particular Being spoken of. But it was this particular Being, and no other, which was supposed to become I, and therefore the act by which it became so must have been its own; that is, it must have been an act of pure and absolute freedom.

In this self-originated act there is no passivity. Now every pure and un-derived act, of course, implies and involves the presence of will of the agent. If the act were evolved without his will it would be the act of another Being. In this act of negation, then, or, in other words, in perception and consciousness, Will has place. Thus, though man is a sentient and passionate creature, without his will, he is not a conscious, or percipient being, not an *ego*, even in the slightest degree, without the concurrence and energy of his volition.

Thus early does human will come into play; thus profoundly down in the lowest foundations of the *ego* is its presence and operation to be found.

SELECTION 4
PART V OF PHILOSOPHY OF CONSCIOUSNESS

CHAPTER I

The question of Liberty and Necessity has been more perplexed and impeded in its solution by the confounding of a peculiar and very important distinction, than by all the other mistakes and oversights burdened upon it besides. The distinction to which we allude is one which ought to be constantly kept in mind, and followed out as a clue throughout the whole philosophy of man; the distinction, namely, between one's existence *for others*, and one's existence *for oneself*; or, in other words, the distinction between unconscious and conscious existence. This distinction, we remark, is very commonly confounded; that is to say, the separate species of existence specified, instead of being regarded as *two*, are generally regarded as only *one*; and the consequence is, that all the subsequent conclusions of psychology are more or less perplexed and vitiated by this radical entanglement, and more particularly is the great question just mentioned involved in obscurity thereby, and, to all appearance, doomed to revolve in the weary rounds of endless and barren speculation. We have already, in various parts of this discussion, endeavored to establish a complete distinction between these two kinds of being; and now, with a view of throwing some light on the intricate question of Liberty and Necessity, not derived from *reasoning*, but from immediate *fact*, we proceed to illustrate and enforce this discrimination more strenuously than ever.

What, then, is our existence *for others*; and in what respect is it to be taken into account in a scientific estimate of ourselves? A little reflection will explain to us what it is, together with all its actual or possible accompaniments.

It will be admitted that except in man there is no consciousness anywhere throughout the universe. If, therefore, man were deprived of consciousness, the whole universe, and all that dwell therein, would be destitute of that act. Let us suppose, then, that this deprivation actually takes place, and let us ask, What difference would it make in the general aspect and condition of things? As far as the objects of the external universe, animals and so forth, are concerned, it would confessedly make none; for all these are without consciousness at any rate, and therefore cannot be affected by its absence. The stupendous machinery of nature would move round precisely as heretofore. But what difference would the absence of consciousness make in the condition of man? Little or none, we reply, in the eyes of a *spectator ab extra*. In the eyes of a Being *different* from man, and who regards him, we shall suppose, from some other sphere, man's on-goings *without* consciousness would be the same, or nearly the same, as they were *with* consciousness. Such a Being would occupy precisely the same position towards the unconscious man as the conscious man at present holds towards the unconscious objects of creation; that is to say, man would still exist for this Being, and for him would evolve all his varied phenomena. We are not to suppose that man in this case would be cut off from any of those sources of inspiration which make him a rational, a passionate, a sentient, and an imaginative creature. On the contrary, by reason of the very absence of consciousness, the flood-gates of his being would stand wider than before, and let in upon him stronger and deeper currents of inspiration. He would still be visited by all his manifold sensations, and by all the effects they bring along with them; he would still be the creature of pleasure and of pain; his emotions and desires would be the same as ever, or even more overwhelming; he would still be the inspired slave of all his soft and all his sanguinary passions; for, observe, we are not supposing him deprived of any of these states of being, but only of the consciousness, or reference to self, of them—only of that notion and reality of self which generally accompanies them; a partial curtailment perfectly conceivable, and one which sometimes actually takes place; for instance, in that abnormal condition of humanity denominated somnambulism. In the case we are supposing, then, man's reason or intelligence would still be left to him. He would still be a mathematician like the bee, and like the beaver a builder of cities. He might still, too, have a language and a literature of a certain kind, though destitute, of course, of all allusions and expressions of a conscious or personal character. But the "Goddess" or the "Muse" might and would still infuse into his heart the gift of song; and then an unconscious Homer, blind in soul as well as blind in sight, filled by the transmitted power of some foreign *afflatus*, might have sung the wrath of an unconscious Achilles, and the war waged against Troy by heroic somnambulists from Greece. For poetry represents the derivative and unconscious, just as philosophy represents the free and conscious, elements of humanity; and is itself, according to every notion of it entertained and expressed from the earliest times down to the present, an inspired or fatalistic development, as is evident from the fact, that all great poets, in the exercise of their art, have ever referred away their power from themselves to the "God," the "Goddess," the "Muse," or some similar source of inspiration always foreign to themselves.[6] "*Est Deus*," says the poet,

"Est Deus in nobis, agitante calescimus illo."

Listen also to the testimony of our own Milton, who, in one of his elegies, gives voice to the belief that he owed his genius to the spring, and, like a tree in the budding woods, was wont to blossom into song beneath the vivifying spirit of that genial time. "*Fallor?*" he asks,

"Fallor? an et nobis redeunt in carmina vires,
Ingenuiumque mihi *munere veris adest*?"[7]

The sublimest works of intelligence, then, are quite possible, and may be easily conceived to be executed without any consciousness of them on the part of the apparent and immediate agent. Suppose man to be actuated throughout his whole nature by the might of some foreign agency; and he may realize the most stupendous operations, and yet remain in darkness, and incognizant of them all the while. A cognizance of these operations certainly does not necessarily go hand in hand with their performance. What is there in the workings of human passion that consciousness should necessarily accompany it, anymore than it does the tossings of the stormy sea? What is there in the radiant emotions which issue forth in song, that consciousness should naturally and necessarily accompany them, anymore than it does the warbling and the dazzling verdure of the sun-lit woods? What is there in the exercise of reason, that consciousness should inevitably go along with it, anymore than it accompanies the mechanic skill with which the spider spreads his claggy snares? There is obviously nothing. The divorce, then, between consciousness, and all these powers and operations, may be conceived

---

[6] Hence the truth of the common saying, *Poeta nascitur, non fit*; an adage which is directly reversed in the case of the philosopher, *Philosophus fit, non nascitur*.
[7] Miltoni Poemata. Elegia quinta. In adventum Veris.

as perfectly complete; and this conception is all that is here necessary for the purposes of our coming argument.

Existence, then, together with all the powers and operations just indicated, might be truly predicated of man, even in his unconscious state. And even more than this might be affirmed of him. We could not, indeed, with propriety, say (the reason of which will appear by-and-by) that man, without consciousness, would be invested in any degree with a moral character. Yet even here, according to the moral philosophy of Paley and his school, in which morality is expounded as the mere adaptation of means to ends in the production of the social welfare, which adaptation might be perfectly well effected without any consciousness on the part of man, just as bees and other animals adapt means to ends without being aware of what they are about; according to this view, man, although unconscious, would still be a moral creature. Neither, without consciousness, would man possess laws in the proper sense of the word; but here, too, according to the Hobbesian doctrines which make law to consist in the domination or supremacy of force, and the power of a supreme magistrate all that is necessary to constitute it, man might, in every respect, be considered a finished legislator, and a creature living under laws.

But it is time to turn these preliminary observations to some account. Let us now, then, ask, depriving man of consciousness, What is it we actually leave him, and what is it we actually deprive him of? We leave him all that we have said. We leave him existence, and the performance of many operations, the greatest, as well as the most insignificant. But the existence thus left to him, together with all its phenomena, is, we beg it may be observed, only *one* species of existence. It is a peculiar kind of existence which must be noted well, and discriminated from existence of *another* species which we are about to mention. In a word, it is existence merely *for others*. This is what we leave man when we suppose him divested of consciousness.

And now we again ask, depriving man of consciousness, What do we really deprive him of? and we answer, that we totally deprive him of existence *for himself*; that is, we deprive him of that kind of existence in which alone *he* has any share, interest, or concern; or, in other words, by emptying him of consciousness, we take away from him altogether his personality, or his true and proper being. For of what importance is it to *him* that he should exist *for others*, and, for them, should evolve the most marvelous phenomena, if he exists not *for himself*, and takes no account of the various manifestations he displays? What reality can such a species of existence have for him? Obviously none. What can it avail a man to be and to act, if he remains all the while without consciousness of his Being and his actions? In short, divested of consciousness, is it not plain that a man is no long "I," or self, and, in such circumstances, must not his existence, together with all its on-goings, be, in so far as *he* is concerned, absolutely zero, or a blank?

Thus existence becomes discriminated into two distinct species, which, though they may be found together, as they usually are in man, are yet perfectly separate and distinguishable; existence, namely, for others, and existence for oneself. Recapitulating what we have said, this distinction may be established and explained thus, in a very few words: Deprive man of consciousness, and in one sense you do *not* deprive him of existence, or of any of the vigorous manifestations and operations of existence. In one sense, that is, *for others*, he exists just as much as ever. But in another sense, you *do* deprive him of existence as soon as you divest him of consciousness. In this latter sense he now ceases to exist; that is, he exists no longer *for himself*. He is no longer that which was "I," or self. He has lost his personality. He takes no account of his existence, and therefore his existence, as far as he is concerned, is virtually and actually null. But if there were only one species, and one notion of existence, it is impossible that man, when denuded of consciousness, should both exist and not exist, as we have shown he does. If existence were of one kind only, it would be impossible to reconcile this contradiction, which is yet seen to be perfectly true, and an undeniable matter of fact. The conclusion, therefore, is inevitable and irresistible, that existence is not of one, but of two kinds; existence, to wit, for others, and existence for ourselves; and that a creature may possess the former without possessing the latter, and that, though it should loss the latter by losing consciousness, it may yet retain the former, and "live and breathe and have a being in the eyes of others."

Does someone here remark that consciousness is not our existence, but is merely the *knowledge of* our existence? Then we beg such a person to consider what would become of his existence, *with respect to him*, if he were deprived of the knowledge of it. Would it not be, in so far as he was concerned, precisely on the footing of a nonentity? One's knowledge, therefore, or consciousness of existence, is far more than *mere* consciousness of existence. It is the actual ground of a species of existence itself. It constitutes existence for oneself, or personal existence; for without this consciousness a man would possess no personality, and each man's personality is his true and proper being.

Having divided existence, then, into two distinct kinds, the next question is, To what account do we propose turning the discrimination? If it is of no practical use in removing difficulties and in throwing light upon the obscurer phenomena of man, it is worthless, and must be discarded as a barren and mere hair-splitting refinement. What application, then, has it to the subjects we are engaged in discussing; and, in particular, what assistance does it afford us in clearing up the great fact of Human Liberty, that key-stone in the arch of humanity, without which all our peculiar attributes, morality, responsibility, law, and justice, loosened from their mighty span would fall from their places, and disappear forever in the blind abysses of Necessity?

In availing ourselves, then, of the assistance of this distinction, and in applying it to our purposes, the first circumstance connected with it which attracts our attention is the following *fact*, deserving, we may be permitted to say, of very emphatic notice; that while the one of these species of existence precedes the act of consciousness, the other of them *follows* that act. Our existence for others is antecedent, but our existence for ourselves is *subsequent* to the act of consciousness. Before a child is conscious, it exists for others; but it exists for itself only *after* it is conscious. Prior to consciousness, or in the absence of that act, man is a one-sided phantasmagoria; vivid on the side *towards others* with all the colors, the vigorous on-goings, the accomplishments, and the reality of existence; but on the other side, the side where he himself should be, but is not yet, what is there? a blank; utter nothingness. But, *posterior* to consciousness, and in consequence of it, this vacuity is filled up, new scenery is unfolded, and a new reality is erected on the blank side behind the radiant pageant. The man himself is now there. The one-sided existence has become doubled. He no longer exists merely for others; he exists also for himself, a very different, and, for him, a much more important matter.

Existence for oneself, then, personal existence, or, in other words, that species of Being which alone properly concerns man, is found not to precede, but to follow the act of consciousness; therefore the next *fact* of humanity to which we beg to call very particular attention is this: that man, properly speaking, *acts* before he *exists*; for consciousness is, as we have already shown, and will show still further, a pure act, and partakes in no degree of the nature of a passion. At the same time, the proof that consciousness is of this character will convince us that it cannot have its origin in the first-mentioned and given species of existence, which we have called existence for others, or existence without consciousness. But this is not the place for that proof. It will be attempted by-and-by.

This fact, that man *acts* before he truly and properly *exists*, may perhaps at first sight appear rather startling, and may be conceived to be at direct variance with what are called "the laws of human thought;" for it may be said that these laws compel us to conceive man *in Being* before we can conceive him *in act*. But if it should be really found to be thus at variance with these laws, our only answer is, that facts are "stubborn things," and that we do not care one straw for the laws of human thought when they contradict the facts of experience; and a fact of experience we maintain it to be (let people conceive or not as they please or can), that man's true *Being* follows and arises out of man's *act*, that man, properly speaking, cannot be said to *be* until he *acts*; that consciousness is an act, and that our proper existence, being identical and convertible with our personality, which results from consciousness, is not the antecedent but the consequent of that act.

Need we say anything further in enforcement and illustration of this very extraordinary fact? Every man will admit that his true Being is that which for him is "I." Now suppose no man had ever thought himself "I," would he ever have become "I," or possessed a proper personal Being? Certainly not. It is only after thinking oneself "I," and in consequence of thinking oneself "I," that one becomes "I." But thinking oneself "I" is an act, the act of consciousness. Therefore the act of consciousness is anterior to the existence of man, therefore man is in Act before he is truly and properly in Being; or, in other words, he performs an act before he has an existence (i.e., *a standing out*) for himself.

But how can man *act* before he *is*? Perhaps we cannot perfectly explain the *How*, but we can state, and have stated the *That*, namely, that the fact is so. But at the same time we beg it to be understood that it is only in one sense that this is true. We would not be misunderstood. We here guard ourselves from the imputation of saying that in every sense man is absolutely a nonentity before he acts, or that he actually creates his Being. This we are very far indeed from affirming. Prior to the act of consciousness, he possesses, as we have said, an existence in the eyes of others; and this species of existence is undoubtedly *given*. Anterior to this act, the foundations of his Being are wonderfully and inscrutably laid. He is a mighty machine, testifying his Creator's power. But at this time being destitute of consciousness, we again maintain that he is destitute of personality, and that therefore he wants that which constitutes the true reality and proper life of humanity. We maintain, further, that this personality, realized by consciousness, is a new kind of existence reared up upon the ground of that act; that, further, there was no provision made in the old *substratum* of unconscious Being for the evolution of this new act; but that, like the fall of man (with which perhaps it is in some way connected), it is an absolutely free and un-derived deed, self-originated, and entirely exempt from the law of causality; and, moreover, in its very essence, the antagonist of that law. This we shall endeavor to make out in the following chapters; and if we can succeed in showing this act to be primary original and free, of course it will follow that the Being which results from it must be free likewise. But, whether we succeed or not, we at any rate think that, having shown fully that the thought "I" precedes and brings along with it the reality or existence "I," and that this thought "I" is an act, we have now said enough to establish this important truth in psychology, that man, when philosophizing concerning himself, does not do well to commence with the contemplation, or with any consideration of himself *as a Being* (we say this with an especial eye to the substance and doctrine of "Mind"), for his proper Being is but a secondary articulation in his actual development, and therefore ought to form but a secondary step in his scientific study of himself, and ought to hold but a subordinate place in his regard. But he ought to commence with the contemplation of himself *as an act* (the act of consciousness), for this is, in reality, his true and radical beginning; and, therefore, in speculation he ought to follow the same order; and, copying the living truth of things in his methodical exposition of himself, should take this act as the primary commencement or starting-point of his philosophical researches. Such, in our opinion, is the only true method of psychological science.

SELECTION 5
FROM PART VI OF PHILOSOPHY OF CONSCIOUSNESS

CHAPTER I.

Philosophy has long ceased to be considered a valid and practical discipline of life. And why? Simply because she commences by assuming that man, like other natural things, is a passive creature, ready-made to her hand; and thus she catches from her object the same inertness which she attributes to him. But why does philosophy found on the assumption that man is a being who comes before her ready shaped, hewn out of the quarries of nature, fashioned into form, and with all his lineaments made distinct, by other hands than his own? She does so in imitation of the physical sciences; and thus the inert and lifeless character of modern philosophy is ultimately attributable to her having degenerated into the status of a physical science.

But is there no method by which vigor may yet be propelled into the moribund limbs of philosophy; and by which, from being a dead system of theory, she may be renovated into a living discipline of practice? There is, if we will but reflect and understand that the course of procedure proper to the physical sciences—namely, the assumption that their objects and the facts appertaining to these objects lie before them *ready-made*—is utterly inadmissible in true philosophy, is totally at variance with the scope and spirit of a science which professes to deal *fairly* with the phenomena of Man. Let us endeavor to point out and illustrate the deep-seated contradistinction between philosophical and physical science, for the purpose, more particularly, of getting light thrown upon the moral character of our species.

When an inquirer is engaged in the scientific study of any natural object, let us say, for instance, of water and its phenomena, his contemplation of this object does not add any new phenomenon to the facts and qualities already belonging to it. These phenomena remain the same, without addition or diminution, whether he studies them or not. Water flows downwards, rushes into a vacuum under the atmospheric pressure, and evolves all its other phenomena, whether man be attending to them or not. His looking on makes no difference as far as the nature of the water is concerned. In short, the number and character of its facts continue altogether uninfluenced by his study of them. His science merely enables him to classify them, and to bring them more clearly and steadily before him.

But when man is occupied in the study of the phenomena of his own natural being, or, in other words, is philosophizing, the case is very materially altered. Here his contemplation of these phenomena *does* add a new phenomenon to the list already under his inspection: it adds, namely, the new and anomalous phenomenon that he *is* contemplating these phenomena. To the old phenomena presented to him in his given or ready-made being, for instance, his sensations, passions, rational and other states, which he is regarding, there is added the supervision of these states; and this is itself a new phenomenon belonging to him. The very fact that man contemplates or makes a study of the facts of his being, is itself a fact which must be taken into account; for it is one of his phenomena just as much as any other fact connected with him is. In carrying forth the physical sciences, man very properly takes no note of his contemplation of their objects; because this contemplation does not add, as we have said, any new fact to the complement of phenomena connected with these objects. Therefore, in sinking this fact, he does not suppress any fact to which they can lay claim. But in philosophizing, that is, in constructing a science of himself man cannot suppress this fact without obliterating one of his own phenomena; because man's contemplation of his own phenomena is itself a new and separate phenomenon added to the given phenomena which he is contemplating.

Here, then, we have a most radical distinction laid down between physics and philosophy. In ourselves, as well as in nature, a certain given series of phenomena is presented to our observation, but in studying the objects of nature, we add no new phenomenon to the phenomena already there; whereas, on the contrary, in studying ourselves we *do add* a new phenomenon to the other phenomena of our being; we add, to wit, the fact that we are thus studying ourselves. Be this new phenomenon important or unimportant, it is, at any rate, evident that in it is violated the analogy between physics and philosophy, between the study of man and the study of nature. For what can be a greater or more vital distinction between two sciences or disciplines than this; that while the one contributes nothing to the making of its own facts, but finds them all (to use a very familiar colloquialism) *cut and dried* beneath its hand, the other creates, in part at least, its own facts, supplies to a certain extent, and by its own free efforts, as we shall see, the very materials out of which it is constructed?

But the parallel between physics and philosophy, although radically violated by this new fact, is not totally subverted; and our popular philosophy has preferred to follow out the track where the parallel partially holds good. It is obvious that two courses of procedure are open to her choice. Either, following the analogy of the natural sciences, which of themselves add no new fact to their objects, she may attend exclusively to the phenomena which she finds in man, but which she has no hand in contributing; or else, breaking loose from that analogy, she may direct her attention to the novel and un-paralleled phenomenon which she, of herself, has added to her object, and which we have already described. Of these two courses, philosophy has chosen to adopt the former — and what has been the result? Surely all the ready-made phenomena of man have been, by this time, sufficiently explored. Philosophers, undisturbed, have pondered over his passions; unmoved they have watched and weighed his emotions. His affections, his rational states, his sensations, and all the other ingredients and modifications of his natural framework have been rigidly scrutinized and classified by them; and, after all, what have they made of it? What sort of a picture have their researches presented to our observation? Not the picture of a man; but the representation of an automaton, that is what it cannot help being; a phantom dreaming what it cannot but dream; an engine performing what it *must* perform; an incarnate reverie; a weathercock shifting helplessly in the winds of sensibility; a wretched association machine, through which ideas pass linked together by laws over which the machine has no control; anything, in short, except that free and self-sustained center of un-derived, and therefore responsible activity, which we call *Man*.

If such, therefore, be the false representation of man which philosophy invariably and inevitably pictures forth whenever she makes common cause with the natural sciences, we have plainly no other course left than to turn philosophy aside from following their analogy, and to guide her footsteps upon a new line and different method of inquiry. Let us, then, turn away the attention of philosophy from the facts which she does *not* contribute to her object (viz., the ready-made phenomena of man); and let us direct it upon the new fact which she *does* contribute thereto, and let us see whether greater truth and a more practical satisfaction will not now attend her investigations.

The great and only fact which philosophy, of herself, adds to the other phenomena of man, and which nothing but philosophy can add, is, as we have said, the fact that man *does* philosophize. The fact that man philosophizes is (so often as it takes place) as much a human phenomenon as the phenomenon, for instance, of passion is, and therefore cannot legitimately be overlooked by an impartial and true philosophy. At the same time, it is plain that philosophy creates and brings along with her this fact of man; in other words, does not find it in him ready made to her hand; because, if man did not philosophize, the fact that he philosophizes would, it is evident, have no manner of existence whatsoever. What, then, does this fact which philosophy herself contributes to philosophy and to man, contain, embody, and set forth, and what are the consequences resulting from it?

The act of philosophizing is the act of systematically contemplating our own natural or given phenomena. But the act of contemplating our own phenomena, *unsystematically*, is no other than our old friend, the act of consciousness; therefore the only distinction between philosophy and consciousness is, that the former is with system, and the latter without it. Thus, in attending to the fact which philosophy brings along with her, we find that consciousness and philosophy become identified; that philosophy is a systematic or studied consciousness, and that consciousness is an unsystematic or unstudied philosophy. But what do we here mean by the words *systematic* and *unsystematic*? These words signify only a greater and a less degree of clearness, expansion, strength, and exaltation. Philosophy possesses these in the higher degree, our ordinary consciousness in the lower degree. Thus philosophy is but a clear, an expanded, a strong, and an exalted consciousness; while, on the other hand, consciousness is an obscurer, a narrower, a weaker, and a less exalted philosophy. Consciousness is philosophy nascent; philosophy is consciousness in full bloom and blow. The difference between them is only one of degree, and not one of kind; and thus all conscious men are to a certain extent philosophers, although they may not know it.

But what comes of this? Whither do these observations tend? With what purport do we point out, thus particularly, the identity in kind between philosophy and the act of consciousness? Reader! if thou has eyes to see, thou canst not fail to perceive (and we pray thee mark it well) that it is precisely in this identity of philosophy and consciousness that the merely *theoretical* character of philosophy disappears, while, at this very point, her ever-living character, as a *practical* disciplinarian of life, bursts forth into the strongest light. For consciousness is no dream, no theory; it is no lesson taught in the schools, and confined within their walls; it is not a system remote from the practical pursuits and interests of humanity; but it has its proper place of abode upon the working theatre of living men. It is a real, and often a bitter struggle on the part of each of us against the fatalistic forces of our nature, which are at all times seeking to enslave us. The causality of nature, both without us, and especially within us, strikes deep roots, and works with a deep intent. The whole scheme and intention of nature, as evolved in the causal nexus of creation, tend to *prevent* one and all of us from becoming conscious, or, in other words, from realizing our own personality. First come our sensations, and these monopolize the infant man; that is to say, they so fill him that there is no room left for his personality to stand beside them; and if it does attempt to rise, they tend to overbear it, and certainly for a time they succeed. Next come the passions, a train of even more overwhelming sway, and of still more flattering aspect; and now there is even less chance than before of our ever becoming personal beings. The causal, or enslaving powers of nature, are multiplying upon us. These passions, like our sensations, monopolize the man, and cannot endure that anything should infringe their dominion. So far from helping to realize our personality, they do everything in their power to keep it aloof or in abeyance, and to lull man into oblivion — *of himself*. So far from coming into life, our personality tends to disappear, and, like water torn and beaten into invisible mist by the force of a whirlwind, it often entirely vanishes beneath the tread of the passions. Then comes reason; and perhaps you imagine that reason elevates us to the rank of personal beings. But looking at reason *in itself*, that is, considering it as a straight, and not as a reflex act,[8] what has reason done, or what can reason do for man (we speak of kind, and not of degree, for man may have a higher degree of it than animals), which she has not also done for beavers and for bees, creatures which, though rational, are yet not personal beings? Without some other power to act as supervisor

---

[8] See Part III, Ch. 3.

of reason, this faculty would have worked in man just as it works in animals: that is to say, it would have operated within him merely as a power of adapting means to ends, without lending him any assistance towards the realization of his own personality. Indeed, being, like our other natural modifications, a state of monopoly of the man, it would, like them, have tended to keep down the establishment of his personal being.

Such are the chief powers that enter into league to enslave us, and to bind us down under the causal nexus, the moment we are born. By imposing *their* agency upon us, they prevent us from exercising *our own*. By filling us with *them*, they prevent us from becoming *ourselves*. They do all they can to withhold each of us from becoming "I." They throw every obstacle they can in the way of our becoming conscious beings; they strive by every possible contrivance, to keep down our personality. They would fain have each of us to take all our activity from them, instead of becoming, each man for himself, a new center of free and independent action.

But, strong as these powers are, and actively as they exert themselves to fulfill their tendencies with respect to man, they do not succeed forever in rendering human personality a non-existent thing.
After a time man proves too strong for them; he rises up against them, and shakes their shackles from his hands and feet. He puts forth (obscurely and unsystematically, no doubt), but still he puts forth a particular kind of act, which thwarts and sets at nought the whole causal domination of nature. Out of the working of this act is evolved man in his character of a free, personal, and moral being. This act is itself man; it is man acting, and man *in act* precedes, as we have seen, man *in being*, that is, in true and proper being. Nature and her powers have now no constraining hold over him; he stands out of her jurisdiction. In this act he has taken himself out of her hands into his own; he has made himself his own master. In this act he has displaced his sensations, and his sensations no longer monopolize him; they have no longer the complete mastery over him. In this act he has thrust his passions from their place, and his passions have lost their supreme ascendancy. And now what is this particular kind of act? What is it but the act of consciousness, the act of becoming "I," the act of placing *ourselves* in the room which sensation and passion have been made to vacate? This act may be obscure in the extreme, but still it is an act of the most *practical* kind, both in itself and in its results; and this is what we are here particularly desirous of having

noted. For what act can be more vitally practical than the act by which we realize our existence as free personal beings? and what act can be attended by a more practical result than the act by which we look our passions in the face, and, in the very act of looking at them, *look them down*?

Now, if consciousness be an act of such mighty and practical efficiency in real life, what must not the practical might and authority of philosophy be? Philosophy is consciousness *sublimed*. If, therefore, the lower and obscurer form of this act can work such real wonders and such great results, what may we not expect from it in its highest and clearest potence? If our unsystematic and undisciplined consciousness be thus practical in its results (and practical to a most momentous extent it is), how much more vitally and effectively practical must not our systematic and tutored consciousness, namely, philosophy, be? Consciousness when enlightened and expanded is identical with philosophy. And what is consciousness enlightened and expanded? It is, as we have already seen, an act of practical antagonism put forth against the modifications of the whole natural man: and what then is philosophy but an act of practical antagonism put forth against the modifications of the whole natural man? But further, what is this act of antagonism, when it, too, is enlightened and explained? What is it but an act of freedom — an act of resistance, by which we free ourselves from the causal bondage of nature — from all the natural laws and conditions under which we were born; and what then is philosophy but an act of the highest, the most essential, and the most practical freedom? But further, what is this act of freedom when it also is cleared up and explained? It turns out to be Human Will; for the refusal to submit to the modifications of the whole natural man must be grounded on a law opposed to the law under which these modifications develop themselves, namely, the causal law, and this opposing law is the law called human will: and what then is philosophy but pure and indomitable will? or, in other words, the most practical of all conceivable acts, inasmuch as will is the absolute source and fountainhead of all real activity. And, finally, let us ask again, what is this act of antagonism against the natural states of humanity? What is this act in which we sacrifice our sensations, passions, and desires, that is, our *false selves*, upon the shrine of our *true selves*? What is this act in which Freedom and Will are embodied to defeat all the enslaving powers of darkness that are incessantly beleaguering us? What is it but morality of the highest, noblest, and most active kind? And, therefore, what is human philosophy, ultimately, but another name for human virtue of the most practical and exalted character?

Such are the steps by which we vindicate the title of philosophy to the rank of a real and practical discipline of humanity. To sum up: we commenced by noticing, what cannot fail to present itself to the observation of everyone, the inert and unreal character of our modern philosophy, metaphysical philosophy as it is called; and we suspected, indeed we felt assured, that this character arose from our adopting, in philosophy, the method of the physical sciences. We, therefore, tore philosophy away from the analogy of physics, and in direct violation of their procedure we made her contemplate a fact which she herself created, and contributed to her object, a fact which she did not *find* there; the fact, namely, that an act of philosophizing was taking place. But the consideration of this fact or act brought us to perceive the identity between consciousness and philosophy, and then the perception of this identity led us at once to note the truly practical character of philosophy. For consciousness is an act of the most vitally real and practical character (we have yet to see more fully how it makes us *moral* beings). It is κατ ἐξοχήν the great practical act of humanity — the act by which man becomes man in the first instance, and by the incessant performance of which he preserves his moral status, and prevents himself from falling back into the causal bondage of nature, which is at all times too ready to reclaim him; and, therefore, philosophy, which is but a higher phase of consciousness, is seen to be an act of a still higher practical character. Now, the whole of this vindication of the practical character of philosophy is evidently based upon her abandonment of the physical method, upon her turning away from the *given* facts of man to the contemplation of a fact which is *not* given in his natural being, but which philosophy herself contributes to her own construction and to man, namely, the act itself of philosophizing, or, in simple language, the act of consciousness. This fact cannot possibly be given: for we have seen that all the given facts of man's being necessarily tend to suppress it; and therefore (as we have also seen) it is, and must be a free and un-derived, and not in any conceivable sense a ready-made fact of humanity.

Thus, then, we see that philosophy, when she gets her due — when she deals fairly with man, and when man deals fairly by her — in short, when she is rightly represented and understood, loses her merely theoretical complexion, and becomes identified with all the best practical interests of our living selves. She no longer stands aloof from humanity, but, descending into this world's arena, she takes an active part in the on-goings of busy life. Her dead symbols burst forth into living realities; the dry rustling twigs of science become clothed with all the verdure of the spring. Her inert tutorage is transformed into an actual life. Her dead lessons grow into man's active wisdom and practical virtue. Her sleeping waters become the bursting fountainhead from whence flows all the activity which sets in motion the currents of human practice and of human progression. Truly, γνῶθι ϱεαυτόν was the sublimest, the most comprehensive, and the most practical oracle of ancient wisdom. *Know thyself*, and, in knowing thyself, thou shalt see that this self is not thy *true* self; but, in the very act of knowing this, thou shalt at once displace this false self, and establish thy true self in its room.

CHAPTER II.

Philosophy, then, has a practical as well as a theoretical side; besides being a system of speculative truth, it is a real and effective discipline of humanity. It is the point of conciliation in which life, knowledge, and virtue meets. In it, fact and duty,[9] or, that which *is*, and that *which ought to be*, are blended into one identity. But the practical character

---

[9] Sir James Mackintosh, and others, have attempted to establish a distinction between "mental" and "moral" science, founded on an alleged difference between fact and duty. They state, that it is the office of the former science to teach us *what is* (quid est), and that it is the office of the latter to teach us *what ought to be* (quid oportet). But this discrimination vanishes into nought upon the slightest reflection; it either incessantly confounds and obliterates itself, or else it renders moral science an unreal and nugatory pursuit. For, let us ask, does the *quid oportet* ever become the *quid est*? Does *what ought to be* ever pass into *what is*, or, in other words, is duty ever realized as fact? If it is, then the distinction is at an end. The *oportet* has taken upon itself the character of the *est*. Duty, in becoming practical, has become a fact. It no longer merely points out something which *ought to be*, it also embodies something which *is*. And thus it is transformed into the very other member of the discrimination from which it was originally contradistinguished; and thus the distinction is rendered utterly void; while "mental" and "moral" science, if we must affix these epithets to philosophy, lapse into one. On the other hand, does the *quid oportet* never, in any degree, become the *quid est*, does duty never pass into fact? Then is the science of morals a visionary, a baseless, and an aimless science, a mere querulous hankering after what can never be. In this case, there is plainly no real or substantial science, except the science of facts, the science which teaches us the *quid est*. To talk now of a science of the *quid oportet*, would be to make use of unmeaning words.

of philosophy, the active part which it plays throughout human concerns, has yet to be more fully and distinctly elucidated.

The great principle which we have all along been laboring to bring out—namely, that human consciousness is, in every instance, an act of antagonism against someone or other of the given modifications of our natural existence—finds its strongest confirmation when we turn to the contemplation of the *moral* character of man. We have hitherto been considering consciousness chiefly in its relation to those modifications of our nature which are impressed upon us *from without*. We here found, that consciousness, when deeply scrutinized, is an act of opposition put forth against our sensations; that our sensations are invaded and impaired by an act of resistance which breaks up their monopolizing dominion, and in the room of the sensation thus partially displaced, realizes man's personality, a new centre of activity known to each individual by the name "I," a word which, when rightly construed, stands as the exponent of our violation of the causal nexus of nature, and of our consequent emancipation therefrom. The complex antithetical phenomenon in which this opposition manifests itself, we found to be the fact of perception. We have now to consider consciousness in its relation to those modifications of our nature which assail us *from within*; and here it will be found, that just as all perception originates in the antagonism between consciousness and our sensations, so all morality originates in the antagonism between consciousness and the passions, desires, or inclinations of the natural man.

We shall see that, precisely as we become *percipient* beings, in consequence of the strife between consciousness and sensation, so do we become *moral* beings in consequence of the same act of consciousness exercised against our passions, and the other imperious wishes or tendencies of our nature. There is no difference in the mode of antagonism, as it operates in these two cases; only, in the one case, it is directed against what we may call our external, and, in the other, against what we may call our internal, modifications. In virtue of the displacement or sacrifice of our sensations by consciousness, each of us becomes "I;" the *ego* is, to a certain extent, evolved; and even here, something of a nascent morality is displayed; for every counteraction of the causality of nature is more or less the development of a free and moral force. In virtue of the sacrifice of our passions by the same act, morality is more fully unfolded; this "I," that is, our personality, is more clearly and powerfully realized, is advanced to a higher potence; is exhibited in a brighter phase and more expanded condition.

Thus we shall follow out a clue which has been too often, if not always, lost hold of in the labyrinths of philosophy, a clue, the loss of which has made inquirers represent man as if he lived in distinct[10] sections, and were an inorganic agglutination of several natures, the percipient, the intellectual, and the moral, with separate principles regulating each. This clue consists in our tracing the principle of our moral agency back into the very principle in virtue of which we become percipient beings; and in showing that in both cases it is the same act which is exerted—an act, namely, of freedom or antagonism against the caused or derivative modifications of our nature. Thus, to use the language of a foreign writer, we shall at least make the attempt to cut our scientific system *out of one piece*, and to marshal the frittered divisions of philosophy into that organic wholeness which belongs to the great original of which they profess, and of which they ought to be the faithful copy; we mean man himself. In particular, we trust that the discovery (if such it may be called) of the principal we have just mentioned, may lead the reflective reader to perceive the inseparable connection between psychology and moral philosophy (we should rather say their essential sameness), together with the futility of all those mistaken attempts which have been often made to break down their organic unity into two distinct departments of "intellectual" and "moral" science.

Another consideration connected with this principle is, that instead of being led by it to do what many philosophers, in order to preserve their consistency, have done—instead of being led by it to observe in morality nothing but the features of a higher self-love, and a more refined sensuality, together with the absence of free-will; we are, on the contrary, led by it to note, even in the simplest act of perception, an incipient self-sacrifice, the presence of a dawning will struggling to break forth, and the aspect of an infant morality beginning to develop itself. This consideration we can only indicate thus briefly; for we must now hurry on to our point.

We are aware of the attempts which have been made to invest our emotions with the stamp and attribute of morality; but, in addition

---

[10] "You may understand," says S. T. Coleridge, "by *insect*, life *in sections*." By this he means that each insect has several centers of vitality, and not merely one; or that it has no organic unity, or at least no such decided organic unity as that which man possesses.

to the testimony of our own experience, we have the highest authority for holding that none of the natural feelings or modifications of the human heart partake in any degree of a moral character. We are told by revelation, and the eye of reason recognizes the truth of the averment, that love itself, that is, *natural* love, a feeling which certainly must bear the impress of morality if any of our emotions do so—we are told by revelation in emphatic terms that such love has no moral value or significance whatsoever. "If ye love them," says our Savior, "which love you, what reward have ye? Do not even the publicans the same?" To love those who love us is natural love; and can any words quash and confound the claim of such love to rank as a moral excellence or as a moral development more effectually than these?

"But," continues the same Divine Teacher, "I say unto you, *Love your enemies;*" obviously meaning, that in this kind of love, as contradistinguished from the other, a new and higher element is to be found, the element of morality, and that this kind of love is a state worthy of approbation and reward, which the other is not. Here, then, we find a discrimination laid down between two kinds of love—love of friends and love of enemies; and the hinge upon which this discrimination turns is, that the character of morality is denied to the former of these, while it is acceded to the latter. But now comes the question, *Why* is the one of these kinds of love said to be a moral state or act, and why is the other not admitted to be so? To answer this question we must look into the respective characters and ingredients of these two kinds of love.

Natural love, that is, our love of our friends, is a mere affair of temperament, and in entertaining it, we are just as passive as our bodies are when exposed to the warmth of a cheerful fire. It lies completely under the causal law; and precisely as any other natural effect is produced by its cause, it is generated and entailed upon us by the love which our friends bear towards us. It comes upon us unsought. It costs us nothing. No thanks to us for entertaining it. It is, in every sense of the word, *a passion*; that is to say, nothing of an *active* character mingles with the modification into which we have been molded. And hence, in harboring such love, we make no approach towards rising into the dignity of free and moral beings.

But the character and groundwork of the other species of love—of our love, namely, of our enemies—is widely different from this. Let us ask what, is the exact meaning of the precept, "Love your enemies?" Does it mean, love them with a *natural* love, love them *as* you love your friends? Does it mean, make your love spring up towards those that hate you, just in the same way, and by the same natural process as it springs up towards those that love you? If it means this, then we are bold enough to say, that it plainly and palpably inculcates an impracticability; for we are sure that no man *can* love his enemies with the same direct natural love as he loves his friends withal; if he ever does love them, it can only be after he has passed himself through some intermediate act which is not to be found in the natural emotion of love. Besides, in reducing this kind of love to the level of a natural feeling, it would be left as completely stripped of its character of morality as the other species is. But Christianity does not degrade this kind of love to the level of a passion, neither does it in this, or in any other case, inculcate an impracticable act or condition of humanity. What, then, is the meaning of the precept, Love your enemies? What sort of practice or discipline does this text, in the first instance at least, enforce? What but this? *Act against your natural hatred of them*, resist the anger you naturally entertain towards them, quell and subjugate the boiling indignation of your heart. Whatever subsequent progress a man may make, under the assistance of divine grace, towards entertaining a *positive* love of his enemies, this *negative* step must be unquestionably take the precedence; and most assuredly such assistance will not be vouchsafed to him, unless he first of all take the initiative by putting forth this act of resistance against that derivative modification of his heart, which, in the shape of hatred, springs up within him under the breath of injury and injustice, just as naturally as noxious reptiles are generated amid the foul air of a charnel-house.

The groundwork, then, of our love of our enemies, the features which principally characterizes it, and the condition which renders it practicable, is an act of resistance exerted against our natural hatred of them; and this it is which gives to that kind of love its moral complexion. Thus, we see that this kind of love, so far from arising out of the cherishing or entertaining of a natural passion, does, on the contrary, owe its being to the sacrifice of one of the strongest passive modifications of our nature; and we will venture to affirm that, without this sacrificial act, the love of our enemies is neither practical nor conceivable; and if this act does not embody the whole of such love, it at any rate, forms a very important element in its composition. In virtue of the tone and active character given to it by this element, the love of our enemies may be called *moral* love, in contradistinction to the love of our friends, which, on account of its purely passive character, we have called natural love.

And let it not be thought that this act is one of inconsiderable moment. It is, indeed, a mighty act, in the putting forth of which man is in nowise passive. In this act he directly thwarts, mortifies, and sacrifices one of the strongest susceptibilities of his nature. He transacts it in the freedom of an original activity, and, most assuredly, nature lends him no helping hand towards its performance. On the contrary, she endeavors to obstruct it by every means in her power. The voice of human nature cries, "By all means, trample your enemies beneath your feet." "No," says the Gospel of Christ, "rather tread down into the dust that hatred which impels you to crush them."

But, now comes another question, What is it that, in this instance, gives a supreme and irreversible sanction to the voice of the Gospel, rendering this resistance of our natural hatred of our enemy *right*, and our non-resistance of that hatred *wrong*?

We have but to admit that freedom, or, in other words, emancipation from the thralldom of a foreign causality, a causality which, ever since the Fall of Man, must be admitted to unfold itself in each individual's case, in a dark tissue of unqualified evil; we have but to admit that the working out of this freedom is the great end of man, and constitutes his true self; and we have also but to admit that whatever conduces to the accomplishment of this end *is right*; and the question just broached easily resolves itself. For, supposing man not to be originally free, let us ask how is the end of human liberty to be attained? Is it to be attained by passively imbibing the various impressions forced upon us from without? Is it to be attained by yielding ourselves up in pliant obedience to the manifold modifications which stamp their molds upon us from within? Unquestionably not. All these impressions and modifications constitute the very badges of our slavery. They are the very trophies of the causal conquests of nature planted by her on the ground where the true man ought to have stood, but where he fell. Now, since human freedom, the great end of man, is thus, contravened by these passive conditions and susceptibilities of his nature, therefore, it is that they are wrong. And, by the same rule, an act of resistance put forth against them is right, inasmuch as an act of this kind contributes, every time it is exerted, to the accomplishment of that great end.

'An Introduction to the Philosophy of Consciousness'   71

Now, looking to our hatred of our enemies, we see that this is a natural passion which is most strongly forced upon us by the tyranny of the causal law; therefore it tends to obliterate and counteract our freedom. But our freedom constitutes our true and moral selves; it is the very essence of our proper personality: therefore, to entertain, to yield to this passion, is wrong, is moral death, is the extinction of our freedom, of our moral being, however much it may give life to the natural man. And, by the same consequence, to resist this passion, to act against it, to sacrifice it, is right, is free and moral life, however much this act may give the death-stroke to our natural feelings and desires.

But how shall we, or how do we, or how can we, act against our hatred of our enemies? We answer, simply by becoming conscious of it. By turning upon it a reflective eye (a process by no means agreeable to our natural heart), we force it to faint and fade away before our glance. In this act we turn the tables (so to speak) upon the passion, whatever it may be, that is possessing us. Instead of its possessing us, we now possess it. Instead of our being in its hands, it is now in our hands. Instead of its being our master, we have now become its; and thus is the first step of our moral advancement taken; thus is enacted the first act of that great drama in which demons are transformed into men. In this act of consciousness, founded, as we have elsewhere seen, upon will, and by which man becomes transmuted from a natural into a moral being, we perceive the prelude or dawning of that still higher regeneration which Christianity imparts, and which advances man onwards from the precincts of morality into the purer and loftier regions of religion. We will venture to affirm that this consciousness, or act of antagonism, is the ground or condition, in virtue of which that still higher dispensation is enabled to take effect upon us, and this we shall endeavor to make out in its proper place. In the meantime to return to our point: —

In the absence of consciousness, the passion (of hatred, for instance) reigns and ranges unalloyed, and goes forth to the fulfillment of its natural issues, unbridled and supreme. But the moment consciousness comes into play against it, the colors of the passion become less vivid, and its sway less despotic. It is to a certain extent dethroned and sacrificed even upon the first appearance of consciousness; and if this antagonist manfully maintain its place, the scepter of passion is at length completely wrested from her hands:

and thus consciousness is a moral act, is the foundation stone of our moral character and existence.

If the reader should be doubtful of the truth and soundness of this doctrine, namely, that consciousness (whether viewed in its own unsystematic form, or in the systematic shape which it assumes when it becomes philosophy) is an act which of itself tends to put down the passions, these great, if not sole, sources of human wickedness; perhaps he will be willing to embrace it when he finds it enforced by the powerful authority of Dr. Chalmers.

"Let there be an attempt," says he, "on the part of the mind to study the phenomena of anger, and its attention is thereby transferred from the cause of the affection to the affection itself; and, so soon as its thoughts are withdrawn from the cause, the affection, *as if deprived of its needful aliment*, dies away from the field of observation. There might be heat and indignancy enough in the spirit, so long as it broods over the affront by which they have originated. But whenever it proposes, instead of looking outwardly at the injustice, to look inwardly at the consequent irritation, it instantly becomes cool."[11]

We have marked certain of these words in italics, because in them Dr. Chalmers appears to account for the disappearance of anger before the eye of consciousness in a way somewhat different from ours. He seems to say that it dies away because "deprived of its needful aliment," whereas we hold that it dies away in consequence of the antagonist act of consciousness which comes against it, displacing and sacrificing it. But, whatever our respective theories may be, and whichever of us may be in the right, we agree in the main point, namely, as to the *fact* that anger *does* vanish away in the presence of consciousness; and therefore this act acquires (whatever theory we may hold respecting it) a moral character and significance, and the exercise of it becomes an imperative duty; for what passion presides over a wider field of human evil and of human wickedness than the passion of human wrath? And, therefore, what act can be of greater importance than the act which overthrows and puts an end to its domineering tyranny?

The process by which man becomes metamorphosed from a natural into a moral being, is precisely the same in every other case: it is invariably founded on a sacrifice or mortification of someone or

---

[11] "Moral Philosophy," pp. 62, 63.

other of his natural desires, a sacrifice which is involved in his very consciousness of them whenever that consciousness is real and clear. We have seen that moral love is based on the sacrifice of natural hatred. In the same way, generosity, if it would embody any morality at all, must be founded on the mortification of avarice or some other selfish passion. Frugality, likewise, to deserve the name of a virtue, must be founded on the sacrifice of our natural passion of extravagance or ostentatious profusion. Temperance, too, if it would claim for itself a moral title, must found on the restraint imposed upon our gross and gluttonous sensualities. In short, before any condition of humanity can be admitted to rank as a moral state, it must be based on the suppression, in whole or in part, of its opposite. And, finally, courage, if it would come before us invested with a moral grandeur, must have its origin in the unremitting and watchful suppression of fear. Let us speak more particularly of Courage and Fear.

What is natural courage? It is a passion or endowment possessed in common by men and by animals. It is a mere quality of temperament. It urges men and animals into the teeth of danger. But the bravest animals and the bravest men (we mean such as are emboldened by mere natural courage) are still liable to *panic*. The game-cock, when he has once turned tail, cannot be induced to renew the fight; and the hearts of men, inspired by mere animal courage, have at times quailed and sunk within them, and, in the hour of need, this kind of courage has been found to be a treacherous passion.

But what is *moral* courage? What is it but the consciousness of Fear? Here it is that the struggle and the triumph of humanity are to be found. Natural courage faces danger, and perhaps carries itself triumphantly through it, perhaps not. But moral courage faces fear, and in the very act of facing it puts it down: and this is the kind of courage in which we would have men put their trust; for if fear be vanquished, what becomes of danger? It dwindles into the very shadow of a shade. It is a historical fact (to mention which will not be out of place here), that nothing but the intense consciousness of his own natural cowardice made the great Duke of Marlborough the irresistible hero that he was. This morally brave man was always greatly agitated upon going into action, and used to say, "This little body trembles at what this great soul is about to perform." About this great soul we know nothing, and therefore pass it over as a mere figure of speech. But the trembling of "this little body," that is, the cowardice of the natural man, or, in other words, his want of courage, in so far as courage is a mere affair of nerves, was a fact conspicuous to all. Equally conspicuous and undeniable was the antagonism put forth against this nervous bodily trepidation. And what was this antagonism? What but the struggle between consciousness and cowardice? A struggle by and through which the latter was dragged into light and vanquished; and then the hero went forth into the thickest ranks of danger, strong in the consciousness of his own weakness, and as if *out of very spite* of the natural coward that wished to hold him back, and who rode shaking in his saddle as he drove into the hottest of the fight. Natural courage, depending upon temperament, will quail at times, and prove faithless to its trust; the strongest nerves will often shake, in the hour of danger, like an aspen in the gale; but what conceivable terrors can daunt that fortitude (though merely of a negative character), that indomitable discipline wherewith a man, by a stern and deliberate consciousness of his own heart's frailty, meets, crushes, and subjugates, at every turn, and in its remotest hold, the entire passion of fear?

Human strength, then, has no positive character of its own; it is nothing but the clear consciousness of human weakness. Neither has human morality any positive character of its own; it is nothing but the clear consciousness of human wickedness. The whole rudiments of morality are laid before us, if we will but admit the fact (for which we have Scripture warrant) that all the given modifications of humanity are dark and evil, and that consciousness (which is not a given phenomenon, but a free act) is itself, in every instance, an acting against these states. Out of this strife morality is breathed up like a rainbow between the sun and the storm. Moreover, by adopting these views, we get rid of the necessity of postulating a moral sense, and of all the other hypothetical subsidies to which an erroneous philosophy has recourse in explaining the phenomena of man. Our limits at present prevent us from illustrating this subject more fully; but in our next number we shall show how closely our views are connected with the approved doctrine of man's natural depravity. In order to penetrate still deeper into the secrets of consciousness, we shall discuss the history of the Fall of Man, and shall show what mighty and essential parts are respectively played by the elements of good and evil in the realization of human liberty; and we shall conclude our whole discussion by showing how consonant our speculations are with the great scheme of Christian Revelation.

III

'Berkeley and Idealism'

Among all philosophers, ancient or modern, we are acquainted with none who presents fewer vulnerable points than Bishop Berkeley.[1] His language, it is true, has sometimes the appearance of paradox; but there is nothing paradoxical in his thoughts, and time has proved the adamantine solidity of his principles. With less sophistry than the simplest, and with more subtlety than the acutest of his contemporaries, the very perfection of his powers prevented him from being appreciated by the age in which he lived. The philosophy of that period was just sufficiently tinctured with common sense to pass current with the vulgar, while the common sense of the period was just sufficiently colored by philosophy to find acceptance among the learned. But Berkeley, ingenious beyond the ingenuities of philosophy, and unsophisticated beyond the artlessness of common sense, saw that there was no sincerity in the terms of this partial and unstable compromise; that the popular opinions, which gave currency and credence to the theories of the day, were not the unadulterated convictions of the natural understanding; and that the theories of the day, which professed to give enlightenment to the popular opinions, were not the genuine offspring of the speculative reason. In endeavoring to construct a system in which this spurious coalition should be exposed, and in which our natural convictions and our speculative conclusions should be more firmly and enduringly reconciled, he necessarily offended both parties, even when he appeared to be giving way to the opposite prejudices of each. He overstepped the predilections both of the learned and the

---

[1] 'A Review of Berkeley's Theory of Vision, designed to show the unsoundness of that celebrated speculation.' By Samuel Bailey, author of 'Essays on the Formation and Publication of Opinions,' &c. London: Ridgway. 1842.

unlearned. His extreme subtlety was a stumbling-block in the path of the philosophers; and his extreme simplicity was more than the advocates of common sense were inclined to bargain for.

But the history of philosophy repairs any injustice which may be done to philosophy itself; and the doctrines of Berkeley, incomplete as they appear when viewed as the isolated tenets of an individual, and short as they no doubt fell, in his hands, of their proper and ultimate expression, acquire a fuller and a profounder significance when studied in connection with the speculations which have since followed in their train. The great problems of humanity have no room to work themselves out within the limits of an individual mind. Time alone weaves a canvas wide enough to do justice to their true proportions; and a few broad strokes is all that the genius of any one man, however gifted, is permitted to add to the mighty and illimitable work. It is therefore no reproach to Berkeley to say that he has left his labors incomplete; that he was frequently misunderstood, that his reasonings fell short of their aim, and that he perhaps failed to carry with him the unreserved and permanent convictions of any one of his contemporaries. The subsequent progress of philosophy shows how much the science of man is indebted to his researches. He certainly was the first to stamp the indelible impress of his powerful understanding on those principles of our nature, which, since his time, have brightened into imperishable truths in the light of genuine speculation. His genius was the first to swell the current of that mighty stream of tendency towards which all modern meditation flows, the great gulf-stream of Absolute Idealism.

The peculiar endowment by which Berkeley was distinguished, far beyond his predecessors and contemporaries, and far beyond almost every philosopher who has succeeded him, was the eye he had *for facts*, and the singular pertinacity with which he refused to be dislodged from his hold upon them. The fact, the whole fact, and nothing but the fact, was the clamorous and incessant demand of his intellect, in whatever direction it exercised itself. Nothing else, and nothing less, could satisfy his intellectual cravings. No man ever delighted less to expatiate in the regions of the occult, the abstract, the impalpable, the fanciful, and the unknown. His heart and soul clung with inseparable tenacity to the concrete realities of the universe; and with an eye uninfluenced by spurious theories, and un-perverted by false knowledge, he saw directly into the very life of things. Hence he was a speculator in the truest sense of the word; for speculation is not the art of devising ingenious hypotheses, or of drawing subtle conclusions, or of plausibly maneuvering abstractions. Strictly and properly speaking, it is the power of seeing true facts, and of *unseeing* false ones; a simple enough accomplishment to all appearance, but nevertheless one which, considered in its application to the study of human nature, is probably the rarest, and, at any rate, has been the least successfully cultivated, of all the endowments of intelligence.

What a rare and transcendent gift this faculty is, and how highly Berkeley was endowed with it, will be made more especially apparent when we come to speak of his great discoveries on the subject of vision. In the meantime, we shall take a survey of those broader and more fully developed doctrines of Idealism to which his speculations on the eye were but the tentative herald or preliminary stepping-stone.

People who have no turn for philosophic research are apt to imagine that discussions on the subject of matter are carried on for the purpose of proving something, either *pro* or *con*, concerning the existence of this disputed entity. No wonder, then, that they should regard the study of philosophy as a most frivolous and inane pursuit. But we must be permitted to remark that these discussions have no such object in view. Matter and its existence is a question about which they have no direct concern. They are entirely subservient to the far greater end of making us acquainted with our own nature. This is their sole and single aim; and if such knowledge could be obtained by any other means, these investigations would certainly never have encumbered the pages of legitimate inquiry. But it is not so to be obtained. The laws of thought can be discovered only by vexing, in all its bearings, the problem respecting the existence of matter. Therefore, to those interested in these laws, we need make no further apology for disturbing the dust which has gathered over the researches on this subject of our country's most profound, but most misrepresented, philosopher.

Berkeley is usually said to have denied the existence of matter; and in this allegation there is something which is true, combined with a great deal more that is false. But what *is* matter? *That* is matter, said Dr. Johnson, once upon a time, kicking his foot against a stone; a rather peremptory explanation, but, at the same time, one for which Berkeley, to use the Doctor's own language, would have *hugged* him. The great Idealist certainly never denied the existence of matter in the sense in which Johnson understood it. As the touched, the seen, the heard, the smelled, and the tasted, he admitted and maintained its existence as readily and completely as the most illiterate and unsophisticated of mankind.

In what sense, then, was it that Berkeley denied the existence of matter? He denied it not in the sense in which the multitude understood it, but solely in the sense in which *philosophers*[2] understood and explained it. And what was it that philosophers understood by matter? They understood by it an occult something which, in itself, is *not* touched, *not* seen, *not* heard, *not* smelled, and *not* tasted; a phantom-world lying behind the visible and tangible universe, and which, though constituting in their estimation the sum and substance of all reality, is yet never itself brought within the sphere or apprehension of the senses. Thus, under the direction of a misguided imagination, they fancied that the sensible qualities which we perceive in things were copies of other occult qualities of which we have no perception, and that the whole sensible world was the unsubstantial representation of another and real world, hidden entirely from observation, and inaccessible to all our faculties.

Now it was against this metaphysical phantom of the brain, this crotchet-world of philosophers, and against it alone, that all the attacks of Berkeley were directed. The doctrine that the realities of things were not made for man, and that he must rest satisfied with their mere appearances, was regarded, and rightly regarded by him, as the parent of skepticism,[3] with all her desolating train. He saw that philosophy, in giving up the reality immediately within her grasp, in favor of a reality supposed to be less delusive, which lay beyond the limits of experience, resembled the dog in the fable, who, carrying a piece of meat across a river, let the substance slip from his jaws, while, with foolish greed, he snatched at its shadow in the stream. The dog lost his dinner, and philosophy let go her secure hold upon the truth. He therefore sided with the vulgar, who recognize no distinction between the reality and the appearance of objects, and, repudiating the baseless hypothesis of a world existing unknown and unperceived, he resolutely maintained that what are

---

[2] Berkeley's Works: 'Of the Principles of Human Knowledge,' sec. 35, 37, 56. First Dialogue, vol. i. pp. 110, 111. Second Dialogue, vol. i. p. 159. Third Dialogue, vol. i. p. 199, 222. Ed. 1820.
[3] 'Principles of Human Knowledge,' sec. 86, 87.

called the sensible shows of things are in truth the very things themselves.

The precise point of this polemic between Berkeley and the philosophers, is so admirably stated in the writings of David Hume, that we feel we cannot do justice to the subject without quoting his simple and perspicuous words; premising, however, that the arch-skeptic had his own good reasons for not doing full justice to his great forerunner. Nothing indeed was further from his intention than the wish that the world should know the side which, in this controversy, Berkeley had so warmly espoused. Had he furnished this information, he would have frustrated the whole scope of his own observations.

"Men," says Hume, "are carried by a natural instinct or prepossession to repose faith in their senses. When they follow this blind and powerful instinct of nature, they always suppose the *very images* presented to the senses *to be* the external objects, and never entertain any suspicion that the one are nothing but representations of the other. But this universal and primary opinion of all men is soon destroyed by the slightest philosophy, which teaches us that nothing can ever be present to the mind *but an image or perception*. So far, then, we are necessitated by reasoning to contradict or depart from the primary instincts of nature, and to embrace a new system with regard to the evidence of our senses. But here philosophy finds herself extremely embarrassed, when she would justify this new system, and obviate the cavils and objections of the skeptics. She can no longer plead the infallible and irresistible instinct of nature, for that led us to a quite different system, which is acknowledged fallible and even erroneous. And to justify this pretended philosophical system by a chain of clear and convincing argument, or even any appearance of argument, exceeds the power of all human capacity." Then follows the famous skeptical dilemma which was never, before or since, so clearly and forcibly put. "Do you," he continues (firstly), "follow the instinct and propensities of nature in assenting to the veracity of sense? But these lead you to believe that the *very perception or sensible image is the external object*." (Then, secondly), "Do you *disclaim this principle* in order to embrace a more rational opinion, that the perceptions are *only representations* of something external? You here depart from your natural propensities and more obvious sentiments; and yet are not able to satisfy your reason, which can never find any convincing argument from experience to prove that the perceptions are connected with any external objects."[4]

Now, when a man constructs a dilemma, it is well that he should see that both of its horns are in a condition to gore to the quick any luckless opponent who may throw himself upon either of their points. But Hume had only tried the firmness and sharpness of the second horn of this dilemma; and certainly its power of punishing had been amply proved by the mercilessness with which it had lacerated, during every epoch, the body of speculative science. But he had left untried the temper of the other horn. In the triumph of his overweening skepticism, he forgot to examine this alternative antler, no doubt considering its aspect too menacing to be encountered even by the most foolhardy assailant. But the horn was far less formidable than it looked. Berkeley had already thrown himself upon it, and though he did not find it to be exactly a cushion of down, he was not one whit damaged in the encounter. "*I* follow," says he, embracing the first of the alternatives, "*I* follow the instincts and prepossessions of nature. "*I* assent to the veracity of sense, and *I* believe that the very perception or sensible image *is* the external object, and on no account whatever will I consent 'to disclaim this principle.' Your philosophy, your more rational opinions, your system of representation, your reasonings which, you say, necessitate me to depart from my primary instincts, all these I give, without reservation, to the winds. And now, *what do you make of me*?[5] And if he had answered thus, as he would undoubtedly have done had he been alive, for such a reply is

---

[4] Hume's Philosophical Works, vol. iv. pp. 177, 178, 179. Ed. 1826. We have abridged the passage, but have altered none of Hume's expressions.

[5] *Vide* Berkeley's Works, vol. i. pp. 182, 200, 203,—If the anachronism were no objection, a very happy and appropriate motto for Berkeley's works would be—
"Spernit *Humum* fugiente penna."
—Horace, Od. iii. 2, 24.

David Hume, however, was a very great man—great as a historian, as every one admits; but greater still as a philosopher; for it is impossible to calculate what a blank, but for him, the whole speculative science of Europe for the last seventy years would have been. If the reader wishes to see the character of his writings, and the scope of the sceptical philosophy fairly appreciated, we beg to refer him to an article in the 'Edinburgh Review' (Vol. LII. p. 196 *et icq.*, Art. 'Philosophy of Perception'), written by Sir William Hamilton, and which, in our opinion, contains more condensed thought and more condensed learning than are to be found in any similar number of pages in our language, on any subject whatever. It gives us great pleasure to see that the writings of this distinguished philosopher, extracted from the ' Edinburgh Review,' have been translated into French (Paris, 1840) by M. Peisse, a very competent translator, who has prefixed to the work an introduction of his own, not unworthy of the profound disquisitions that follow.

in harmony with the whole spirit of his philosophy, we do not, indeed, see what Hume, with all his subtle dialect, could have made of him. But the champion of common sense, he alone who could have foiled the prince of skeptics at his own weapons, was dead,[6] and the cause had fallen into the hands of Dr. Reid, a far easier customer, who, when he could not avoid both horns of the dilemma, preferred to encounter the second, as apparently the less mischievous of the two.

The first great point, then, on which Berkeley differed from the ordinary philosophical doctrine, and sided with the vulgar, is that he contended, with the whole force of his intellect, for the inviolable identity of objects and the appearances of objects. The external world *in itself*, and the external world in relation *to us*, was a philosophic distinction which he refused to recognize. In his creed, the substantive and the phenomenal were one. And, though he has been accused of sacrificing the substance to the shadow, and though he still continues to be charged, by every philosophical writer, with reducing all things to ideas in the mind, he was guilty of no such absurdity, at least when interpreted by the spirit, if not by the letter of his speculations. Nay, the very letter of his philosophy, in general, forestalls, and bears him up against, all the cavils of his opponents. His own words, in answer to these allegations, are the following. "No," says he, addressing his antagonist Hylas, who is advocating the common opinion of philosophers, and pressing against him the objections we have spoken of, "No, I am not for changing things into ideas, but rather *ideas* into *things*; since those immediate objects of perception, which, according to you, are only appearances of things, *I* take to be the real things themselves."

"Things!" rejoins Hylas; "you may pretend what you please; but it is certain you leave us nothing but the empty forms of things, the outside of which only strikes the senses."

"What you," answers Berkeley, "what *you* call the empty forms and outside of things, seem to *me* the very things themselves.... We both, therefore, agree in this, that we perceive only sensible forms;

---

[6] *Was dead.* This is not precisely true, for Hume's 'Treatise of Human Nature,' from which the above extract is taken, was published in 1739, and Berkeley did not die until 1753. But we explain it by saying that Hume's work fell dead-born from the press, and did not attract any degree of attention until long after its publication, and when at length, after a lapse of many years, the proper time for answering it arrived, on account of the general notoriety which it had suddenly obtained, that then Berkeley was no more.

but herein we differ, you will have them to be *empty appearances*, I, *real beings*. In short, you do *not* trust your senses, *I do*."[7]

So far, then, there does not appear to be much justice in the ordinary allegation, that Berkeley discredited the testimony of the senses, and denied the existence of the material universe. He merely denied the distinction between things and their appearances, and maintained that the thing *was* the appearance, and that the appearance *was* the thing. But this averment brings us into the very thick of the difficulties of the question. For does it not imply that the external world exists *only* in so far as it is perceived, that its *esse*, as Berkeley says, is *percipi*; that its existence is its being perceived, and that, if it were not perceived, it would not exist? At first sight the averment certainly does imply something very like all this; therefore, we must now be extremely cautious how we proceed.

We have already remarked that Berkeley, in vindicating the cause of common sense, frequently appeared to overshoot the mark, and to give vent to opinions which somewhat staggered even the simplest of the vulgar, and seemed less reconcilable with the obvious sentiments of nature than the philosophical doctrines themselves which they were brought forward to supplant. And the opinion now stated is the most startling of these tenets, and one which, to all appearance, is calculated rather to endamage than to help the cause which it is intended to support. But, in advancing it, Berkeley knew perfectly well what he was about; and though he is far from having fenced it with all the requisite explanations, and though he did not succeed in putting it in a very clear light, or in giving it an adequate and ultimate form of expression, or in obviating all the cavils and strong objections to which it was exposed, or in sounding the depths of its almost unfathomable significance; still he felt, with the instinct of a prophet, that it was a stronghold of impregnable truth, and that in resting on it he was treading on a firm footing of fact which could never be swept away. Time, and the labors of his successors, have done for him what the span of one man's life—and span too, we may say, of one man's intellect, capacious as his undoubtedly was—prevented him doing for himself.

We shall admit, then, that Berkeley holds that matter has no existence independently of mind, that mind, if entirely removed, would involve in its downfall the absolute annihilation of matter. And

---

[7] Berkeley's Works, vol. i. p. 201. Ed. 1820.

admitting this, we think, at the same time, that we can afford a perfectly satisfactory explanation of so strange and difficult a paradox, and resolve a knot which Berkeley was the first to loosen, but which he certainly did not explicitly untie. The question is, Supposing ourselves away or annihilated, would the external world continue to exist as heretofore, or would it vanish into nonentity? But the terms of this question involve a preliminary question, which must first of all be disposed of. Mark what these terms are; they are comprised in the words, "*supposing ourselves away or annihilated.*" But *can* we suppose ourselves away or annihilated? If we can, then we promise to proceed at once to give a categorical answer to the question just put. But if we cannot, then the prime condition of the question not being purified, the question itself has not been intelligibly asked; and therefore it cannot expect to receive a rational or intelligible answer. Should this be found to be the case, it will be obvious that we have been imposing upon ourselves, and have only mistakenly imagined ourselves to be asking a question which in truth we are *not* asking.

Can we, then, conceive ourselves removed or annihilated? is this thought a possible or conceivable supposition? Let us try it by the test of experience, by hypothetically answering the original question, *in the first place*, in the affirmative, and by saying that, although we conceive ourselves and all percipient beings annihilated, still the great universe of matter would maintain its place as firmly and as faithfully as before. We believe, then, that were there no eye actually present to behold them, the sky would be as bright, and the grass as green, as if they were gazed upon by ten million witnesses; that, though there were no ear present to hear them, the thunder would roar as loudly, and the sea sound as tempestuously as before; and that the firm-set earth, though now deserted by man, would remain as solid as when she resisted the pressure of all the generations of her children. But do we not see that, in holding this belief, we have violated, at the very outset, the essential conditions of our question? We bound ourselves to annihilate the percipient in thought, to keep him ideally excluded from the scene, and having done this, we professed ourselves ready to believe and maintain that the universe would preserve its place and discharge its functions precisely the same as heretofore. But in thinking of the bright sky, and of the green grass, and of the loud thunder, and of the solid earth, we have *not* kept him excluded from the scene, but have brought back in thought the very percipient being whom we supposed, but most erroneously supposed, we had abstracted from his place in the creation. For what is this brightness and this greenness but an ideal vision, which cannot be thought of unless man's eyesight be incarnated with it in one inseparable conception? Nature herself, we may say, has so *beaten up together* sight and color, that man's faculty of abstraction is utterly powerless to dissolve the charmed union. The two (supposed) elements are not two, but only one, for they cannot be separated in thought even by the craft of the subtlest analysis. It is God's synthesis, and man cannot analyze it. And further, what is the loud thunder, and what is the sounding sea, without the ideal restoration of the hearing being whom we professed to have thought of as annihilated? And finally, what is the solidity of the rocks and mountains but that which is conceived to respond to the touch and tread of some human percipient, ideally restored to traverse their unyielding and everlasting heights?

Perhaps the reader may here imagine that we are imposing a quibble both on ourselves and him, and that though we may not be able to conceive ourselves *ideally* removed, yet that we are perfectly able to conceive ourselves *actually* removed out of the universe, leaving its existence unaltered and entire; but a small degree of reflection may satisfy him that this distinction will not help him in the least. For, what is this universe which the reader, after conceiving himself, as he thinks, *actually* away from it, has left behind him un-mutilated and entire? We ask him to tell us something about it. But when he attempts to do so, he will invariably find the constitution of his nature to be such that, instead of being able to tell us anything about *it*, he is compelled to revert to a description of his own human perceptions of it, perceptions which, however, ought to be left altogether out of the account; for what he is bound to describe to us is the universe itself, abstracted from all those impressions of it which were supposed to be non-existent. But this is what it is impossible for him to describe. A man declares that if he were annihilated the universe would still exist. But what universe would still exist? The bright, the green, the solid, the sapid, the odoriferous, the extended, and the figured universe would still exist. Certainly it would. But this catalog comprises the series of your perceptions of the universe, and this is not what we want; this is precisely what you undertook *not* to give us. In mixing up the thought of these perceptions with the universe, professedly thought to exist independently of them, you have transgressed the stipulated terms of the question, the conclusion from which is that, in supposing yourself annihilated, you did *not* suppose yourself annihilated, you took yourself back into being in the very same breath in which you puffed yourself away into nonentity.

We must here beg to guard ourselves most particularly against the imputation of having said that, in thinking of the external universe, man thinks *only* of his own perceptions of it; or that, when he has it actually present before him, he is conscious *only* of the impressions which it makes upon him. This is a doctrine very commonly espoused by the idealistic writers. It is a tempting trap into which they have all been too prone to fall; and Berkeley himself, and a man as great as he, Fichte, have not altogether escaped the snare. But it cuts up the very roots of genuine speculative idealism, and controverts the first and strongest principle on which it rests. This principle, we may remind the reader, is that the thing *is* the appearance, and that the appearance *is* the thing; that the object *is* our perception of it, and that our perception of it *is* the object; in short, that these two are convertible ideas, or, more properly speaking, are one and the same idea. But this use of the word *only* implies that we possess a faculty of abstraction, in virtue of which we are able to distinguish between objects and our perceptions of objects, between things and the appearances of things, a doctrine which, if admitted (and admit it we must, if we use the word *only* in the application alluded to above), would leave this as the distinction between realism and idealism, that whereas the former separates objects from our perceptions of them for the purpose of *preserving* the objects, the latter separates the two for the purpose of *annihilating* the objects. And the truth is that this is precisely the distinction between spurious realism and spurious idealism. They both found upon the assumed capability of making this abstraction, only they differ, as we have said, herein, that the one makes it in order to preserve the objects and the other in order to destroy them. But genuine idealism, looking only to the fact, and instructed by the unadulterated dictates of common sense, denies altogether the capability of making the abstraction, denies that we can separate in thought objects and perceptions *at all*; and hence this system has nothing whatever to do either with the preservation or with the destruction of the material universe; and hence, too, it is identical, in its length, and in its breadth, and in its whole significance, with genuine un-perverted realism, which just as stoutly refuses to acknowledge the operation of this pretended faculty. Let us beware, then, of maintaining that man, in his intercourse with the external universe, has *only* his own perceptions or impressions to deal with. It was this unwary averment which gave rise to the systems, on the one hand, of subjective idealism, with all its hampering absurdities; and, on the other hand, of hypothetical realism, with all its unwarrantable and unsatisfying conclusions.

To return to our question. It seems certain, then, that the question, Would matter exist if man were annihilated? cannot be intelligently asked, when we consider it as answered in the affirmative, because it is clear that its terms cannot be complied with. Conceiving the universe to remain entire, we cannot conceive ourselves as abstracted or removed from its sphere. We think ourselves back, in the very moment in which we think ourselves away.

But, *in the second place,* suppose that we attempt to answer the question in the negative, and to maintain that the material universe would no longer exist if we and all percipient beings were annihilated; how will this hypothetical conclusion help us out of the difficulty which hampers the very enunciation of the problem? We are aware that this is the favorite conclusion of idealism as commonly understood, and it is a conclusion not altogether un-countenanced by the reasoning of Berkeley himself. But still the form of idealism which espouses any such conclusion is unguarded and shortsighted in the extreme. The ampler and more wary system refuses to have anything to do with it; for this system sees that, when the question is attempted to be answered in the negative, the conditions of its statements are not one whit more faithfully discharged than they were when a reply was supposed to be given to it in the affirmative. For let us try the point. Let us say that, man being annihilated, there would no longer be any external universe; that is to say, that there would be universal colorlessness, universal silence, universal impalpability, universal tastelessness, and so forth. But universal colorlessness, universal silence, universal impalpability, universal tastelessness, and so forth, are just as much phenomena requiring, in thought, the presence of an ideal percipient endowed with sight and hearing and taste and touch, as their more positive opposites were phenomena requiring such a percipient. Non-existence itself is a phenomenon requiring a percipient present to apprehend it, just as much as existence is. No external world is no more no external world without an ideal percipient, than an external world is an external world without an ideal percipient. Therefore, in saying that there would be no external world if man were annihilated, we involve ourselves in precisely the same incapacity of rationally enunciating the question as we did in the former case. We are compelled to bring back in thought our very percipient selves, whom we declared we had conceived of as annihilated. In neither case can we adhere to the terms of the question; in neither case can we construe it intelligibly to our own minds; and therefore the question is unanswerable, not because it cannot be answered, but because it cannot be asked.

Now for the great truth, to which these observations are the precursor. We have already taken occasion to remark that discussions of the kind we are engaged in, are carried on, not for the sake of any conclusion we may arrive at with respect to the existence or the non-existence of the material universe, but solely for the sake of the laws of human thought which may be evolved in the course of the research. Now, the conclusion to which we are led by the train of our present speculation is this, that no question and no proposition whatever can for a moment be entertained which involves the supposition of our annihilation. It is an irreversible law of human thought, that no such idea can be constructed to the mind by any effort of the understanding, or rationally articulated by any power of language. We cannot, and we do not think it; we only *think that we think it*. And upon the basis of this law and upon it alone, independently of revelation, rests the great doctrine of our immortality. The fear of death is a salutary fear, and the thought of death is a salutary thought, not because we can really think the thought or really entertain the fear, but only because we *imagine* that we can do so. This imagination of ours (we say it with the deepest reverence) is a gracious imposition practiced upon us by the Author or our nature, for the wisest and most benevolent of purposes. We *appear* to ourselves to be able to realize the thought and the fear, and this it is which drives us back so irresistibly into the busy press of life, and weds us so passionately to its rosy forms; we *are* not able to realize the thought or the fear, and this it is which makes us secretly to rejoice "in the sublime attractions of the grave." Woe to us, if we could indeed think of death! In the real thought of it we should be already dead, but in the mere illusive imagination of the thought we are already an immortal race. We have nothing to wait for; eternity is even now within us, and time, with all its vexing troubles, is no more.[8]

But to return to Berkeley. What then is the precise position in which he has left the question respecting man and the material universe? He maintains, as we have said, that matter depends entirely for its existence upon mind. And in this opinion we cordially agree with him. But we must be allowed to widen very amply the basis of his principle, otherwise, on account of the doctrine thus professed, we feel well assured that our friends would be disposed to call our sanity in question. Berkeley's doctrine amounts to this, that there are trees, for instance, and houses in the world, because they are either seen, and so forth, or thought of *as seen*, and so forth. But here his groundwork is far too narrow, for it seems to imply this, that there would be no trees and no houses *unless* they were seen, or thought of as seen. It is therefore exposed to strong objections and misconstructions. The realist may laugh it to scorn by saying, "Then, I suppose, there are no trees and no houses when there is no man's mind either seeing or thinking of them!" But broaden the basis of the idealistic principle, and see how innocuous this objection falls to the ground; affirm that in the case of *every* phenomenon, that is, even in the case of the *phenomenon of the absence of all phenomena*, a subject-mind must be thought of as incarnated with the phenomenon, and the cavil is at once obviated and disarmed. The realist expects the idealist, in virtue of his principle, taken in its narrower significance, to admit that when the percipient neither sees, nor thinks of seeing, trees and houses, there would be no such thing as these objects. But the idealist, instructed by his principle in its wider significance, replies, "No, my good sir; no-trees and no-houses (*i.e.*, space empty of trees and houses) is a phenomenon, just as much as trees and houses themselves are phenomena; and as such it can no more exist without being seen or thought of as seen than any other phenomenon can. Therefore, if I were to admit that, in the total absence and oblivion of the percipient there would be no-trees and no-houses in a particular place, I should be guilty of the very error I am most anxious to avoid, and which it is the aim of my whole system to guard people against committing; I should merely be substituting *other* phenomena in lieu

---

[8] Wordsworth's little poem, entitled 'We are Seven,' illustrates this great law of human thought—the natural inconceivability of death; and hence, simple as its character may be, it is rooted in the most profound and recondite psychological truth.

of those which had disappeared; I should merely be placing the phenomenon of no-object in the room of the phenomenon of object, and, in maintaining (as you seem to expect I should) that the former might exist without being seen or thought of as seen, while the latter might not so exist, I should be giving a direct contradiction to my whole speculation: I should be chargeable with holding that *some* phenomena are independent and irrespective of a percipient mind either really or ideally present to them, and that *others* are not; whereas my great doctrine is, that *no* phenomena, not even, as I have said, the phenomenon of the absence of all phenomena, are thus independent or irrespective." It appears to us that Berkeley's principle requires to be enlarged in some such terms as these; and being so, we think that it is then proof against all cavils and objections whatsoever. It is perfectly true that the existence of matter depends entirely on the presence, that is, either the real or the ideal presence, of a conscious mind. But it does not follow from this that there would be *no-matter* if no such conscious mind were present or thought of as present, because *no-matter* depends just as much upon the real or the ideal presence of a conscious mind. Thus are spiked all the cannon of false realism; thus all her trenches are obliterated, all her supplies cut off, and all her resources rendered unserviceable. This, too, we may add, is the flank of false idealism turned, and her forces driven from their ground, while absolute real idealism, or the complete conciliation of common sense and philosophy, remains in triumphant possession of the field.

Now we think that this mode of meeting the question respecting mind and matter, and of clearing its difficulties, is infinitely preferable to that resorted to by some philosophers, in which they make a distinction between what they call the *primary* and what they call the *secondary* qualities of matter; holding that the latter are purely subjective affections, or impressions existing only in ourselves; and that the former are purely objective elements, constituting the very existence of things. As this is a very prevalent and powerfully supported opinion, we cannot pass it by without some notice. But in our exposure of its futility we shall be very brief. All the secondary qualities, colors, sounds, tastes, smells, heat, hardness, everything, in short, which is an *affection of sense*, may be generalized at one sweep into *our mere* knowledge of things. But the primary qualities, which are usually restricted to extension and figure, and which constitute, it is said, the objective or real essence of things, and which are entirely independent of us, into what shall they be generalized? Into what but into this? into the *knowledge* of something, which exists in things over and above *our mere* knowledge of things. It is plain enough that we cannot generalize them into pure, objective existence in itself; we can only generalize them into a *knowledge* of pure objective existence. But such a knowledge, that is to say, a knowledge of something existing in things, over and above our *mere* knowledge of them, is not one whit less *our* knowledge, and is not one whit more *their* existence, than the other more subjective knowledge designated by the word *mere*. Our knowledge of extension and figure is just as little these real qualities themselves, as our affection of color is objective color itself. Just as little we say, and just as much. You (we suppose ourselves addressing an imaginary antagonist), you hold that our knowledge of the secondary qualities is not these qualities themselves; but we ask you, Is, then, our knowledge of the primary qualities these qualities themselves? This you will scarcely maintain; but perhaps you will say, Take away the affection of color, and the color no longer exists; and we retort upon you, Take away the knowledge of extension, and the extension no longer exists. This you will peremptorily deny, and we deny it just as peremptorily; but why do both of us deny it? Just because both of us have subreptitiously restored the knowledge of extension in denying that extension itself would be annihilated. The knowledge of extension *is* extension, and extension *is* the knowledge of extension. Perhaps, in continuation, you will say, we have our own ideas, the secondary qualities are in truth our own ideas; but that besides these we have an idea of something existing externally to us which is *not an idea*, and that this something forms the aggregate of the primary qualities. Admitted! But is this idea of something which is not an idea, in any degree *less an idea* than the other ideas spoken of? We should like to be informed in what respect it is so. Depend on it, the primary qualities must be held to stand on precisely the same footing as the secondary, in so far as they give us any information respecting real objective existences. In accepting the one class the mind may be passive, and in accepting the other class she may be active; but that distinction will not bring us one hair's-breadth nearer to our mark. If the one class is subjective, so is the other; if the one class is objective, so is the other; and the conciliating truth is, that both classes are at once subjective *and* objective. In fine, we thus break the neck of the distinction. There is a world as it exists in relation *to us*: true. And there is the same world as it exists *in itself*, and in non-relation to us: true also. But, the world as it exists in relation to us, is just *one* relation in which the world exists in relation to us; and the world as it exists in itself and in non-relation to us, is just *another* relation in which the world exists in relation to us.

Some readers may perhaps imagine that in making this strong statement we are denying the real objective existence, the primary qualities, the *noumena*, as they are sometimes called, of things. But we are doing no such thing. Such a denial would lead us at once into the clueless labyrinths of subjective idealism, which is a system we altogether repudiate. All that we deny is *the distinction* between the primary and the secondary qualities, between the noumena and the phenomena; and we deny this distinction, because we deny the existence of the faculty (the faculty of abstraction) by means of which we are supposed to be capable of making it. This certainly is no denial, but rather an affirmation, of the primary qualities of real objective existence, and it places us upon the secure and impregnable ground of real objective idealism, a system in which knowledge and existence are identical and convertible ideas.

IV

'Reid and the Philosophy of Common Sense'

In entering on an examination of the system of Dr. Reid, we must ask first of all, what is the great problem about which philosophers in all ages have busied themselves most, and which consequently must have engaged, and did engage, a large share of the attention of the champion of Common Sense? We must also state the *fact* which gives rise to the problem of philosophy.

The perception of a material universe, as it is the most prominent fact of cognition, so has it given rise to the problem which has been most agitated by philosophers. This question does not relate to the existence of the fact. The existence of the perception of matter is admitted on all hands. It refers to the nature, or origin, or constitution of the fact. Is the perception of matter simple and indivisible, or is it composite and divisible? Is it the ultimate, or is it only the penultimate, *datum* of cognition? Is it a relation constituted by the concurrence of a mental or subjective, and a material or objective element; or do we impose upon ourselves in regarding it as such? Is it a state or modification of the human mind? Is it an effect that can be distinguished from its cause? Is it an event consequent on the presence of real antecedent objects? These interrogations are somewhat varied in their form, but each of them embodies the whole point at issue, each of them contains the cardinal question of philosophy. The perception of matter is the admitted fact. The *character* of this fact, that is the point which speculation undertakes to canvass, and endeavors to decipher.

Another form in which the question may be put is this: We all believe in the existence of matter, but what *kind* of matter do we believe in the existence of? Matter *per se*, or matter *cum perception*? If the former, this implies that the given fact (the perception of matter) is compound and submits to analysis; if the latter, this implies that it is simple and defies partition.

Opposite answers to this question are returned by psychology and metaphysic. In the estimation of metaphysic, the perception of matter is the absolutely elementary in cognition, the *ne plus ultra* of thought. Reason cannot get beyond, or behind it. It has no pedigree. It admits of no analysis. It is not a relation constituted by the coalescence of an objective and a subjective element. It is not a state or modification of the human mind. It is not an effect which can be distinguished from its cause. It is not brought about by the presence of antecedent realities. It is positively the FIRST, with no forerunner. The perception-of-matter is one mental word, of which the verbal words are mere syllables. We impose upon ourselves, and we also falsify the fact, if we take any other view of it than this. Thus speaks metaphysic, though perhaps not always with an unfaltering voice.

Psychology, or the science of the human mind, teaches a very different doctrine. According to this science, the perception of matter is a secondary and composite truth. It admits of being analyzed into a subjective and an objective element, a mental modification called perception on the one hand, and matter *per se* on the other. It is an effect induced by real objects. It is not the first *datum* of intelligence. It has matter itself for its antecedent. Such, in very general terms, is the explanation of the perception of matter which psychology proposes.

Psychology and metaphysic are thus radically opposed to each other in their solutions of the highest problem of speculation. Stated concisely, the difference between them is this: psychology regards the perception of matter as susceptible of analytic treatment, and travels, or endeavors to travel, beyond the given fact; metaphysic stops short in the given fact, and there makes a stand, declaring it to be an indissoluble unity. Psychology holds her analysis to be an analysis of things. Metaphysic holds the psychological analysis to be an analysis of sounds, and nothing more. These observations exhibit, in their loftiest generalization, the two counter doctrines on the subject of perception. We now propose to follow them into their details, for the purpose both of eliciting the truth and of arriving at a correct judgment in regard to the reformation which Dr. Reid is supposed to have effected in this department of philosophy.

The psychological or analytic doctrine is the first which we shall discuss, on account of its connection with the investigations of Dr. Reid, in regard to whom we may state, beforehand, our conclusion and its grounds, which are these: that Reid broke down in his philosophy, both polemical and positive, because he assumed the psychological and not the metaphysical doctrine of perception as the basis of his arguments. He did not regard the perception of matter as absolutely primary and simple; but in common with all psychologists, he conceived that it admitted of being resolved into a mental condition and a material reality; and the consequence was, that he fell into the very errors which it was the professed business of his life to denounce and exterminate. How this catastrophe came about we shall endeavor shortly to explain.

Reid's leading design was to overthrow skepticism and idealism. In furtherance of this intention, he proposed to himself the accomplishment of two subsidiary ends,—the refutation of what is called the ideal or representative theory of perception, and the substitution of a doctrine of intuitive perception in its room. He takes, and he usually gets, credit for having accomplished both of these objects. But if it be true that the representative theory is but the inevitable development of the doctrine which treats the perception of matter analytically, and if it be true that Reid adopts this latter doctrine, it is obvious that his claims cannot be admitted without a very considerable deduction. That both of these things are true may be established, we think, beyond the possibility of a doubt.

In the first place, then, we have to show that the theory of a representative perception (which Reid is supposed to have overthrown) is identical with the doctrine which treats the perception of matter analytically; and, in the second, we have to show that Reid himself followed the analytic or psychological procedure in his treatment of this fact, and founded upon the analysis his own doctrine of perception.

First, the representative theory is that doctrine of perception which teaches that, in our intercourse with the external universe, we are not immediately cognizant of real objects themselves, but only of certain mental transcripts or images of them, which, in the language of the different philosophical schools, were termed ideas, representations, phantasms, or species. According to this doctrine we are cognizant of real things, not in and through themselves, but in and through these species or representations. The representations are the immediate or proximate, the real things are the mediate or remote, objects of the mind. The existence of the former is a matter of knowledge, the existence of the latter is merely a matter of belief.

To understand this theory, we must construe its nomenclature into the language of the present day. What, then, is the modern synonym for the "ideas," "representations," "phantasms," and "species," which the theory in question declares to be vicarious of real objects? There cannot be a doubt that the word *perception* is that synonym. So that the representative theory, when fairly interpreted, amounts simply to this, that the mind is immediately cognizant, not of real objects themselves, but *only of its own perceptions of real objects*. To accuse the representationist of maintaining a doctrine more repugnant to common sense than this, or in any way different from it, would be both erroneous and unjust. The golden rule of philosophical criticism is to give every system the benefit of the most favorable interpretation which it admits of.

This, then, is the true version of representationism, namely, that our perceptions of material things and not material things *per se*, are the proximate objects of our consciousness when we hold intercourse with the external universe.

Now, this is a doctrine which inevitably emerges the instant that the analysis of the perception of matter is set on foot and admitted. When a philosopher divides, or imagines that he divides, the perception of matter into two things, perception *and* matter, holding the former to be a state of his own mind, and the latter to be no such state; he does, in that analysis, and without saying one other word, avow himself to be a thoroughgoing representationist. For his analysis declares that, in perception, the mind has an immediate or proximate, and a mediate or remote object. Its perception of matter is the proximate object, the object of its consciousness; matter itself, the material existence, is the remote object—the object of its belief. But such a doctrine is representationism, in the strictest sense of the word. It is the very essence and definition of the representative theory to recognize, in perception, a remote as well as a proximate object of the mind. Every system which does this is necessarily a representative system. The doctrine which treats the perception of matter analytically does this; therefore the analytic or psychological doctrine is identical with the representative theory. Both hold that the perceptive process involves two objects, an immediate and a mediate; and nothing more is required to establish their perfect identity. The analysis of the fact which we call the perception of matter, is unquestionably the groundwork and pervading principle of the theory of a representative perception, whatever form of expression this scheme may at any time have assumed.

Secondly, did Dr. Reid go to work analytically in his treatment of the perception of matter? Undoubtedly he did. He followed the ordinary psychological practice. He regarded the *datum* as divisible into perception and matter. The perception he held to be an act, if not a modification of our minds; the matter he regarded as something which existed out of the mind and irrespective of all perception. Right or wrong, he resolved, or conceived that he had resolved, the perception of matter into its constituent elements, these being a mental operation on the one hand and a material existence on the other. In short, however ambiguous many of Dr. Reid's principles may be, there can be no doubt that he founded his doctrine of perception on an analysis of the given fact with which he had to deal. He says, indeed, but little about this analysis, so completely does he take it for granted. He accepted, as a thing of course, the notorious distinction between the perception of matter and matter itself; and, in doing so, he merely followed the example of all preceding psychologists.

These two points being established — *first*, that the theory of representationism necessarily arises out of an analysis of the perception of matter; and, *secondly*, that Reid analyzed or accepted the analysis of this fact — it follows as a necessary consequence that Reid, so far from having overthrown the representative theory, was himself a representationist. His analysis gave him more than he bargained for. He wished to obtain only one, that is, only a proximate object in perception; but his analysis necessarily gave him two: it gave him a remote as well as a proximate object. The mental mode or operation which he calls the perception of matter, and which he distinguishes from matter itself, this, in his philosophy, is the proximate object of consciousness, and is precisely equivalent to the species, phantasms, and representations of the older psychology; the real existence, matter itself, which he distinguishes from the perception of it, this is the remote object of the mind, and is precisely equivalent to the mediate or represented object of the old psychology. He and the representationists, moreover, agree in holding that the latter is the object of belief rather than of knowledge.

The merits of Dr. Reid, then, as a reformer of philosophy, amount in our opinion to this: he was among the first[1] to *say* and to *write* that the representative theory of perception was false and erroneous, and was the fountainhead of skepticism and idealism. But this admission of his merits must be accompanied by the qualification that he adopted, as the basis of his philosophy, a principle which rendered nugatory all his protestations. It is of no use to disclaim a conclusion if we accept the premises which inevitably lead to it. Dr. Reid disclaimed the representative theory, but he embraced its premises, and thus he virtually ratified the conclusions of the very system which he clamorously denounced. In his language he is opposed to representationism, but in his doctrine he lends it the strongest support by accepting as the foundation of his philosophy an analysis of the perception of matter.

In regard to the *second* end which Dr. Reid is supposed to have overtaken—the establishment of a doctrine of intuitive as opposed to a doctrine of representative perception—it is unnecessary to say much. If we have proved him to be a representationist, he cannot be held to be an intuitionist. Indeed, a doctrine of intuitive perception is a sheer impossibility upon his principles. A doctrine of intuition implies that the mind in perceiving matter has only one, namely, a proximate object. But the analysis of the perception of matter always yields, as its result, a remote as well as a proximate object. The proximate object is the perception, the remote object is the reality. And thus the analysis of the given fact necessarily renders abortive every endeavor to construct a doctrine of intuitive perception. The attempt *must* end in representationism. The only basis for a doctrine of intuitive perception, which will never give way, is a resolute forbearance from all analysis of the fact. Do not tamper with it, and you are safe.

Such is the judgment which we are reluctantly compelled to pronounce on the philosophy of Dr. Reid in reference to its two cardinal

---

[1] *Among the first.* He was not *the* first. Berkeley had preceded him in denouncing most unequivocally the whole theory of representationism. The reason why Berkeley does not get the credit of this is, because his performance is even more explicit and cogent than his promise. He made no phrase about refuting the theory, he simply refuted it. Reid *said* the business, but Berkeley *did* it. The two greatest and most unaccountable blunders in the whole history of philosophy are probably Reid's allegations that Berkeley was a representationist, and that he was an idealist; understanding by the word *idealist*, one who denies the existence of a real external universe. From every page of his writings, it is obvious that Berkeley was neither the one of these nor the other, even in the remotest degree.

claims, the refutation of the ideal theory, and the establishment of a truer doctrine—a doctrine of intuitive perception. In neither of these undertakings do we think that he has succeeded, and we have exhibited the grounds of our opinion. We do not blame him for this: he simply missed his way at the outset. Representationism could not possibly be avoided, neither could intuitionism be possibly fallen in with, on the analytic road which he took.

But we have not yet done with this consideration of the psychological or analytic doctrine of perception. We proceed to examine the entanglements in which reason gets involved when she accepts the perception of matter not in its natural and indissoluble unity, but as analyzed by philosophers into a mental and a material factor. We have still an eye to Dr. Reid. He came to the rescue of reason, how did it fare with him in the struggle?

The analysis so often referred to affords a starting-point, as has been shown, to representationism: it is also the tap-root of skepticism and idealism. These four things hang together in an inevitable sequence. Skepticism and idealism dog representationism, and representationism dogs the analysis of the perception of matter, just as obstinately as substance is dogged by shadow. More explicitly stated, the order in which they move is this: The analysis divides the perception of matter into perception and matter—two separate things. Upon this, representationism declares, that the perception is the proximate, and that the matter is the remote, object of the mind. Then skepticism declares, that the existence of the matter which has been separated from the perception is problematical, because it is not the direct object of consciousness, and is consequently hypothetical. And, last of all, idealism takes up the ball and declares, that this hypothetical matter is not only problematical, but that it is non-existent. These are the perplexities which rise up to embarrass reason whenever she is weak enough to accept from philosophers their analysis of the perception of matter. They are only the just punishment of her infatuated facility. But what has Reid done to extricate reason from her embarrassments?

We must remember that Reid commenced with analysis and that consequently he embraced representationism, in its spirit, if not positively in its letter. But how did he evade the fangs of skepticism and idealism, to say nothing of destroying, these sleuth-hounds which on this road were sure to be down upon his track the moment they got wind of him? We put the question in a less figurative form: When skepticism and idealism doubted or denied the independent existence of matter, how did Reid vindicate it? He faced about and appealed boldly to our instinctive and irresistible *belief* in its independent existence.

The crisis of the strife centers in this appeal. In itself, the appeal is perfectly competent and legitimate. But it may be met, on the part of the skeptic and idealist, by two modes of tactic. The one tactic is weak, and gives an easy triumph to Dr. Reid: the other is more formidable, and, in our opinion, lays him prostrate.

The first Skeptical Tactic. — In answer to Dr. Reid's appeal, the skeptic or idealist may say, "Doubtless we have a belief in the independent existence of matter; but this belief is not to be trusted. It is an insufficient guarantee for that which it avouches. It does not follow that a thing is true because we instinctively believe it to be true. It does not follow that matter exists because we cannot but believe it to exist. You must prove its existence by a better argument than mere belief." This mode of meeting the appeal we hold to be pure trifling. We join issue with Dr. Reid in maintaining that our nature is not rooted in delusion, and that the primitive convictions of common sense must be accepted as infallible. If the skeptic admits that we *have* a natural belief in the independent existence of matter, there is an end to him: Dr. Reid's victory is secure. This first tactic is a feeble and mistaken maneuver.

The second Skeptical Tactic. — This position is not so easily turned. The stronghold of the skeptic and idealist is this: they deny the primitive belief to which Dr. Reid appeals to be *the fact*. It is not true, they say, that any man believes in the independent existence of matter. And this is perfectly obvious the moment that it is explained. Matter in its *independent* existence, matter *per se*, is matter disengaged in thought from all perception of it present or remembered. Now, does any man believe in the existence of such matter? Unquestionably not. No man by any possibility can. What the matter is which man really believes in shall be explained when we come to speak of the metaphysical solution of the problem, perhaps sooner. Meanwhile we remark that Dr. Reid's appeal to the conviction of common sense in favor of the existence of matter *per se*, is rebutted, and in our opinion triumphantly, by the denial on the part of skepticism and idealism that any such belief exists. Skepticism and idealism not only deny the independent existence of matter, but they deny that any man believes in the independent existence of matter. And in this denial they are most indubitably right. For observe what such a belief requires as its condition. A man must disengage in thought, a tree, for instance, from the thought of all perception of it, and then he must believe in its existence thus disengaged. If he has not disengaged, in his mind, the tree from its perception (from its present perception, if the tree be before him; from its remembered perception, if it be not before him), he cannot believe in the existence of the tree disengaged from its perception; for the tree is *not* disengaged from its perception. But unless he believes in the existence of the tree disengaged from its perception, he does not believe in the independent existence of the tree, in the existence of the tree *per se*. Now, can the mind by any effort effect this disengagement? The thing is an absolute impossibility. The condition on which the belief hinges cannot be purified, and consequently the belief itself cannot be entertained.

People have, then, *no belief* in the independent existence of matter; that is, in the existence of matter entirely denuded of perception. This point being proved, what becomes of Dr. Reid's appeal to *this belief* in support of matter's independent existence? It has not only no force, it has no meaning. This second tactic is invincible. Skepticism and idealism are perfectly in the right when they refuse to accept as the guarantee of independent matter a belief which itself has no manner of existence. How can they be vanquished by an appeal to a nonentity?

A question may here be raised. If the belief in question be not the fact, what has hitherto prevented skepticism from putting a final extinguisher on Reid's appeal by *proving* that no such belief exists? A very sufficient reason has prevented skepticism from doing this, from explicitly extinguishing the appeal. There is a division of labor in speculation as well as in other pursuits. It is the skeptic's business simply to deny the existence of the belief: it is no part of his business to exhibit the grounds of his denial. *We* have explained these grounds; but were the skeptic to do this, he would be traveling out of his vocation. Observe how the case stands. The reason why matter *per se* is not and cannot be believed in, is because it is impossible for thought to disengage matter from perception, and consequently it is impossible for thought to believe in the disengaged existence of matter. The matter to be believed in, is not disengaged from the perception, consequently it cannot be believed to be disengaged from the perception. But unless it be believed to be disengaged from the perception, it cannot be believed to exist *per se*. In short, as we have already said, the impossibility of complying with the *condition* of the belief is the ground on which the skeptic denies the *existence* of the belief. But the skeptic is himself debarred from producing these grounds. Why? Because their exhibition would be tantamount to a rejection of the principle which he has *accepted* at the hands of the orthodox and dogmatic psychologist. That principle is the analysis so often spoken of—the separation, namely, of the perception of matter into perception and matter *per se*. The skeptic accepts this analysis. His business is simply to *accept*, not to discover or scrutinize principles. Having accepted the analysis, he then denies that any belief attaches to the existence of matter *per se*. In this he is quite right. But he cannot, consistently with his calling, exhibit the ground of his denial; for this ground is, as we have shown, the impossibility of performing the analysis, of effecting the requisite disengagement. But the skeptic has accepted the analysis, has admitted the disengagement. He therefore cannot now retract: and he has no wish to retract. His special mission, his only object, is to confound the principle which he has accepted by means of the reaction of its consequences. The inevitable consequence which ensues when the analysis of the perception of matter is admitted is the extinction of all belief in the existence of matter. The analysis gives us a kind of matter to believe in to which no belief corresponds. The skeptic is content with pronouncing this to be the fact without going into its reason. It is not his business to correct, by a direct exposure, the error of the principle which the dogmatist lays down, and which he accepts. The analysis is the psychologist's affair; let *him* look to it. Were the skeptic to make it his, he would emerge from the skeptical crisis, and pass into a new stage of speculation. He, indeed, subverts it indirectly by a *reductio ad absurdum*. But he does not *say* that he subverts it; he leaves the orthodox proposer of the principle to find that out.

Reid totally misconceived the nature of skepticism and idealism in their bearings on this problem. He regarded them as habits of thought, as dispositions of mind peculiar to certain individuals of vexatious character and unsound principles, instead of viewing them as catholic eras in the development of all genuine speculative thinking. In his eyes they were subjective crotchets limited to some, and not objective crises common to all who think. He made *personal* matters of them, a thing not to be endured. For instance, in dealing with Hume, he conceived that the skepticism which confronted him in the pages of that great genius was *Hume's* skepticism, and was not the skepticism of human nature at large—was not his own skepticism just as much as it was Hume's. *His* soul, so he thought, was free from the obnoxious flaw, merely because *his* anatomy; shallower than Hume's, refused to lay it bare. With such views it was impossible for Reid to eliminate skepticism and idealism from philosophy. These foes are the foes of each man's own house and heart, and nothing can be made of them if we attack them in the person of another. Ultimately and fairly to get rid of them, a man must first of all thoroughly digest them, and take them up into the vital circulation of his own reason. The only way of putting them back is by carrying them forward.

From having never properly secreted skepticism and idealism in his own mind, Reid fell into the commission of one of the gravest errors of which a philosopher can be guilty. He falsified the fact in regard to our primitive beliefs, a thing which the obnoxious systems against which he was fighting never did. He conceived that skepticism and idealism called in question a fact which was countenanced by a natural belief; accordingly, he confronted their denial with the allegation that the disputed fact, the existence of matter *per se*, was guaranteed by a primitive conviction of our nature. But this fact receives no support from any such source. There is no belief in the whole repository of the mind which can be fitted on to the existence of matter denuded of all perception. Therefore, in maintaining the contrary, Reid falsified the fact in regard to our primitive convictions, in regard to those principles of common sense which he professed to follow as his guide. This was a serious slip. The rash step which he here took plunged him into a much deeper error than that of the skeptic or idealist. They err[2] in common with him in accepting as their starting-point the analysis of the perception of matter. He errs, by himself, in maintaining that there is a belief where no belief exists.

But do not skepticism and idealism doubt matter's existence *altogether*, or deny to it *any* kind of existence? Certainly they do; and in harmony with the principle from which they start they must do this. The *only* kind of matter which the analysis of the perception of matter yields, is matter *per se*. This existence of such matter is, as we have

---

[2] *They err.* This, however, can scarcely be called an error. It is the business of the skeptic at least to accept the principles generally recognized, and to develop their conclusions, however absurd or revolting. If the principles are false to begin with, that is no fault of his, but of those at whose hands he received them.

shown, altogether un-countenanced either by consciousness or belief. But there is no other kind of matter in the field. We must, therefore, either believe in the existence of matter *per se*, or we must believe in the existence of *no* matter whatever. We do not, and we cannot, believe in the existence of matter *per se*; therefore we cannot believe in the existence of matter at all. This is not satisfactory, but it is closely consequential.

But why not, it may be said, why not cut the knot, and set the question at rest, by admitting at once that every man *does*, popularly speaking, believe in the existence of matter, and that he practically walks in the light of that belief during every moment of his life? This observation tempts us into a digression, and we shall yield to the temptation. The problem of perception admits of being treated in *three* several ways: *first*, we may ignore it altogether, we may refuse to entertain it at all; or, *secondly*, we may discuss it in the manner just proposed, we may lay it down as gospel that every man does believe in the existence of matter, and acts at all times upon this conviction, and we may expatiate diffusely over these smooth truths; or, *thirdly*, we may follow and contemplate the subtle and often perplexed windings which reason takes in working her way through the problem — a problem which, though apparently clearer than the noonday sun, is really darker than the mysteries of Erebus. In short, we may *speculate* the problem. In grappling with it we may trust ourselves to the mighty current of *thinking*, with all its whirling eddies, certain that, if our thinking be genuine objective thinking, which deals with nothing but *ascertained* facts, it will bring us at last into the haven of truth. We now propose to consider which of these modes of treating the problem is the best; we shall begin by making a few remarks upon the *second*, for it was this which brought us to a stand, and seduced us into the present digression.

It is, no doubt, perfectly true that we all believe in the existence of matter, and that we all act up to this belief. The truth that "each of us exists;" the truth that "each of us is the same person today that he was yesterday;" the truth that "a material universe exists, and that we believe in its existence;" all these are most important truths, most important things to know. It is difficult to see how we could get on without this knowledge. Yet they are not worth one straw in communication. And why not? Just for the same reason that atmospheric air, though absolutely indispensable to our existence, has no value whatever in exchange; this reason being that we can get, and have already got, both the air and the truths in unlimited abundance for nothing, and thanks to no man. It is not its *importance*, then, which confers upon truth its value in communication. The value of truth is measured by precisely the same standard which determines the value of wealth. This standard is in neither case the importance of the article; it is always its difficulty of attainment, its cost of production. Has *labor* been expended on its formation or acquisition: then the article, if a material commodity, has a value in exchange; if a truth, it has a value in communication. Has no labor been bestowed upon it, and has Nature herself furnished it to every human being in overflowing abundance: then the thing is altogether destitute of exchange-value, whether it be an article of matter or of mind; no man can, without impertinence, transmit or convey such a commodity to his neighbor. If this be the law on the subject (and we conceive that it must be so ruled) it settles the question as to the *second* mode of dealing with the problem of perception. It establishes the point that this method of treating the problem is not to be permitted.

The *first* and *third* modes of dealing with our problem remain to be considered. The first mode ignores the problem altogether; it refuses to have anything to do with it. Perhaps this mode is the best of the three. We will not say that it is not: it is at any rate preferable to the second. But once admit that philosophy is a legitimate occupation, and this mode must be set aside, for it is a negation of all philosophy. Everything depends upon this admission. But the admission is, we conceive, a point which has been already and long ago decided. Men must and will philosophize. That being the case, the only alternative left is, that we should discuss the highest problem of philosophy in the terms of the *third* mode proposed. We have called this the speculative method, which means nothing more than that we should expend upon the investigation the uttermost toil and application of thought; and that we should estimate the truths which we arrive at, not by the scale of their importance, but by the scale of their difficulty of attainment, of their cost of production. *Labor*, we repeat it, is the standard which measures the value of truth as well as the value of wealth.

A still more cogent argument in favor of the strictly speculative treatment of the problem is this. The problem of perception may be said to be a *reversed* problem. What are the means in every other problem are in *this* problem the end; and what is the end in every other problem is in this problem the means. In every other problem the solution of the problem is the end desiderated: the means are the thinking requisite for its solution. But here the case is inverted. In *our* problem the desiderated solution is the means; the end is the development, or, we should rather say, the creation of speculative thought, a kind of thought different altogether from ordinary popular thinking. "Oh! then," someone will perhaps exclaim, "after all, the whole question about perception resolves it into a *mere gymnastic* of the mind." Good sir, do you know what you are saying? Do *you* think that the mind itself is anything except a mere gymnastic of the mind? If you do, you are most deplorably mistaken. Most assuredly the mind only *is* what the mind *does*. The existence of thought is the exercise of thought. Now if this be true, there is the strongest possible reason for treating the problem after a purely speculative fashion. The problem and its desired solution, these are only the means which enable a new species of thinking (and that the very highest), viz., speculative thinking, to deploy into existence. This deployment is the end. But how can this end be attained if we check the speculative evolution in its first movements, by throwing ourselves into the arms of the *apparently* Common Sense convictions of Dr. Reid? We use the word "apparently," because, in reference to this problem, the apparently Commons Sense convictions of Dr. Reid are not the *really* Common Sense convictions of mankind. These latter can only be got at through the severest discipline of speculation.

Our final answer, then, to the question which led us into this digression is this: It is quite true that the material world exists; it is quite true that we believe in this existence, and always act in conformity with our faith. Whole books may be written in confirmation of these truths. They may be published and paraded in a manner which apparently settles the entire problem of perception. And yet this is not the right way to go to work. It settles nothing but what all men, women, and children have already settled. The truths thus formally substantiated were produced without an effort; everyone has already got from Nature at least as much of them as he cares to have; and therefore, whatever their importance may be, they cannot, with any sort of propriety, be made the subjects of conveyance from man to man. We must either leave the problem altogether alone (a thing, however, which we should have thought of sooner), or we must adopt the speculative treatment. The argument, moreover, contained in the preceding paragraph, appears to render this treatment imperative; and accordingly we now return to it, after our somewhat lengthened digression.

We must take up the thread of our discourse at the point where we dropped it. The crisis to which the discussion had conducted us was this: that the existence of matter could not be believed in *at all*. The psychological analysis necessarily lands us in this conclusion: for the psychological analysis gives us, for matter, nothing but matter *per se*. But matter *per se* is what no man does or can believe in. We are reluctant to reiterate the proof; but it is this: to believe in the existence of matter *per se* is to believe in the existence of matter liberated from perception; but we cannot believe in the existence of matter liberated from perception, for no power of thinking will liberate matter from perception; therefore we cannot believe in the existence of matter *per se*. This argument admits of being exhibited in a still more forcible form. We commence with an illustration. If a man believes that a thing exists as one thing, he cannot believe that this same thing exists as another thing. For instance, if a man believes that a tree exists as a tree, he cannot believe that it exists as a house. Apply this to the subject in hand. If a man believes that matter exists as a thing *not* disengaged from perception, he cannot believe that it exists as a thing *disengaged* from perception. Now, there cannot be a doubt that the *only* kind of matter in which man believes is matter *not* disengaged from perception. He therefore cannot believe in matter *disengaged* from perception. His mind is already preoccupied by the belief that matter is *this one thing*, and, therefore, he cannot believe that it is *that other thing*. His faith is, in this instance, forestalled, just as much as his faith is forestalled from believing that a tree is a house, when he already believes that it is a tree.

There are two very good reasons, then, why we cannot believe in the existence of matter at all, if we accept as our starting-point the psychological analysis. This analysis gives us, for matter, matter *per se*. But matter *per se* cannot be believed in: 1st, because the condition on which the belief depends cannot be complied with; and 2ndly, because the matter which we *already* believe in is something quite different from matter *per se*. In trying to believe in the existence of matter *per se* we always find that we are believing in the existence of *something else*, namely, in the existence of matter *cum perceptione*. But it is not to the psychological analysis that we are indebted for this matter, which is something else than matter *per se*. The psychological analysis does its best to annihilate it. It gives us nothing but matter *per se*, a thing which neither is nor can be believed in. We are thus prevented from believing in the existence of *any* kind of matter. In a word, the psychological analysis of the perception of matter necessarily converts all those who embrace it into skeptics or idealists.

In this predicament what shall we do? Shall we abandon the analysis as a treacherous principle, or shall we, with Dr. Reid, make one more stand in its defense? In order that the analysis may have fair play we shall give it another chance, by quoting Mr. Stewart's exposition of Reid's doctrine, which must be regarded as a perfectly faithful representation. "Dr. Reid," says Mr. Stewart, "was the first person who had courage to lay completely aside all the common *hypothetical* language concerning perception, and to exhibit *the difficulty*, in all its magnitude, by a plain *statement of the fact*. To what, then, it may be asked, does this statement amount? Merely to this: that the mind is so formed that certain impressions produced on our organs of sense, by external objects, are *followed* by corresponding sensations, and that these sensations (which have no more resemblance to the qualities of matter, than the words of a language have to the things they denote) are *followed* by a perception of the existence and qualities of the bodies by which the impressions are made; that all the steps of this process are equally incomprehensible.[3] There are at least two points which are well worthy of being attended to in this quotation. *First*, Mr. Stewart says that Reid "exhibited the difficulty of the problem of perception, in all its magnitude, by a plain statement of fact." What does that mean? It means this: that Reid stated, indeed, the fact correctly, namely, *that* external objects give rise to sensations and perceptions, but that still his statement did not penetrate to the heart of the business, but, by his own admission, left the difficulty, undiminished. What difficulty? The difficulty as to *how* external objects give rise to sensations and perceptions. Reid did not undertake to settle that point—a wise declinature, in the estimation of Mr. Stewart. Now Mr. Stewart, understanding, as he did, the philosophy of causation, ought to have known that every difficulty as to *how* one thing gives rise to another, is purely a difficulty of the mind's creation, and not of nature's making, and is, therefore, no difficulty at all. Let us explain this. A man says he knows *that* fire explodes gunpowder; but he does not know *how* or by what means it does this. Suppose, then, he finds out the means, he is still just where

---

[3] 'Elements of the Philosophy of the Human Mind,' part I. ch. i.

he was; he must again ask how or by what means these discovered means explode the gunpowder; and so on *ad infinitum*. Now the mind may quibble with itself forever, and *make* what difficulties it pleases in this way; but there is no *real* difficulty in the case. In considering any sequence, we always know the *how* or the means as soon as we know the *that* or the fact. These means may be more proximate or more remote means, but they are invariably given either proximately or remotely along with and in the fact. As soon as we know *that* fires explodes gunpowder, we know *how* fire explodes gunpowder; for fire is itself the means which explodes gunpowder, the *how* by which it is ignited. In the same way, *if* we knew that matter gave rise to perception, there would be no difficulty as to *how* it did so. Matter would be itself the means which gave rise to perception. We conceive, therefore, that Mr. Stewart did not consider what he was saying when he affirmed that Reid's plain statement of facts exhibited *the difficulty* in all its magnitude. If Reid's statement, *be* a statement of fact, all difficulty vanishes, the question of perception is relieved from very species of perplexity. If it *be* the fact that perception is consequent on the presence of matter, Reid must be admitted to have explained, to the satisfaction of all mankind, *how* perception is brought about. Matter is itself the means by which it is brought about.

Secondly, then, Is it the fact that matter gives rise to perception? That is the question. Is it the fact that these two things stand to each other in the relation of antecedent and consequent? Reid's "plain statement of fact," as reported by Mr. Stewart, maintains that they do. Reid lays it down as a fact, that perceptions *follow* sensations, that sensations *follow* certain impressions made on our organs of sense by external objects, which stand first in the series. The sequence, then, is this: 1*st*, Real external objects; 2*d*, Impressions made on our organs of sense; 3*d*, Sensations; 4*th*, Perceptions. It will simplify the discussion if we leave out of account Nos. 2 and 3, limiting ourselves to the statement that real objects precede perceptions. This is declared to be a fact, of course an *observed* fact; for a fact can with no sort of propriety be called a fact, unless some person or other has *observed* it. Reid "laid completely aside all the common *hypothetical* language concerning perception." His plain statement (so says Mr. Stewart) contains nothing but facts, facts established, of course, by observation. It is a fact of observation, then, according to Reid, that real objects precede perceptions; that perceptions follow when real objects are present. Now, when a man proclaims as fact such a sequence as this, what must he first of all have done? He must have observed the antecedent *before* it was followed by the consequent; he must have observed the cause out of combination with effect; otherwise his statement is a pure hypothesis or fiction. For instance, when a man says that a shower of rain (No. 1) is followed by a refreshed vegetation (No. 2), he must have observed both No. 1 and No. 2, and he must have observed them as two separate things. Had he never observed anything but No. 2 (the refreshed vegetation), he might form what conjectures he pleased in regard to its antecedent, but he never could lay it down *as an observed fact*, that this antecedent was a shower of rain. In the same way, when a man affirms it to be a fact of observation (as Dr. Reid does, according to Stewart), that material objects are *followed* by perceptions, it is absolutely necessary for the credit of his statement that he should have observed this to be the case; that he should have observed material objects before they were followed by perceptions; that he should have observed the antecedent separate from the consequent: otherwise his statement, instead of being complimented as a plain statement of fact, must be condemned as a tortuous statement of hypothesis. Unless he has observed No. 1 and No. 2 in sequence, he is not entitled to declare that this is an observed sequence. Now, did Reid, or did any man, ever observe matter anterior to his perception of it? Had Reid a faculty which enabled him to catch matter before it had passed into perception? Did he ever observe it, as Hudibras says, "undressed"? Mr. Stewart implies that he had such a faculty. But the notion is preposterous. No man can observe matter prior to his perception of it; for his observation of it presupposes his perception of it. Our observation of matter *begins* absolutely with the perception of it. Observation always gives the perception of matter as the *first* term in the series, and not matter itself. To pretend (as Reid and Stewart do) that observation can go behind perception, and lay hold of matter before it has given rise to perception, this is too ludicrous a doctrine to be even mentioned; and we should not have alluded to it, but for the countenance which it has received from the two great apostles of common sense.

This last bold attempt, then, on the part of Reid and Stewart (for Stewart adopts the doctrine which he reports) to prop their tottering analysis on direct observation and experience, must be pronounced a failure. Reid's "plain statement of fact" is not a *true* statement of *observed* fact; it is a vicious statement of *conjectured* fact. Observation depones to the existence of the perception of matter as the first *datum* with which it has to deal, but it depones to the existence of nothing anterior to this.

But will not abstract thinking bear out the analysis by yielding to us matter *per se* as a legitimate inference of reason? No; it will do nothing of the kind. To make good this inference, observe what abstract thinking must do. It must bring under the notice of the mind matter *per se* (No. 1) as something which is *not* the perception of it (No. 2); but whenever thought tries to bring No. 1 under the notice of the mind, it is No. 2 (or the perception of matter) which invariably comes. We may ring for No. 1, but No. 2 always answers the bell. We may labor to construe a tree *per se* to the mind, but what we always *do* construe to the mind is the perception of a tree. What we want is No. 1, but what we always get is No. 2. To unravel the thing explicitly, the manner in which we impose upon ourselves is this as explanatory of the perceptive process, we construe to our minds *two number two's*, and one of these we *call* No. 1. For example, we have the perception of a tree (No. 2); we wish to think the tree itself (No. 1) as that which gives rise to the perception. But this No. 1 is merely No. 2 over again. *It* is thought of as the perception of a tree, *i.e.*, as No. 2. We *call* it the tree itself, or No. 1; but we *think* it as the perception of the tree, or as No. 2. The first or explanatory term (the matter *per se*) is merely a repetition in thought (though called by a different name) of the second term, the term to be explained, viz., the perception of matter. Abstract thinking, then, equally with direct observation, refuses to lend any support to the analysis; for a thing cannot be said to be analyzed when it is merely multiplied or repeated, which is all that abstract thinking does in regard to the perception of matter. The matter *per se*, which abstract thinking supposes that it separates from the perception of matter, is merely an iteration of the perception of matter.

Our conclusion therefore is, that the analysis of the perception of matter into the two things, perception and matter (the ordinary psychological principle), must, on all accounts, be abandoned. It is both treacherous and impracticable.

Before proceeding to consider the metaphysical solution of the problem, we shall gather up into a few sentences the reasonings which in the preceding discussion is diffused over a considerable surface. The ordinary, or psychological doctrine of perception, reposes upon an analysis of the perception of matter into two separate things, a modification of our minds (the one thing) consequent on the presence of matter *per se*, which is the other thing. This analysis inevitably leads to a theory of representative perception, because it yields as its result a proximate and a remote object. It is the essence of representationism to recognize both of these as instrumental in perception. But representationism leads to skepticism, for it is possible that the remote or real object (matter *per se*), not being an object of consciousness, may not be instrumental in the process. Skepticism doubts its instrumentality, and doubting its instrumentality, it of course doubts its existence; for not being an object of consciousness, its existence is only postulated in order to account for something which *is* an object of consciousness, viz., perception. If, therefore, we doubt that matter has any hand in bringing about perception, we, of course, doubt the existence of matter. This skepticism does. Idealism denies its instrumentality and existence. In these circumstances what does Dr. Reid do? He admits that matter *per se* is not an object of consciousness; but he endeavors to save its existence by an appeal to our natural and irresistible belief in its existence. But skepticism and idealism doubt and deny its existence of matter *per se*, not merely because it is no object of consciousness, but, moreover, because it is no object of belief. And in this they are perfectly right. It *is* no object of belief. Dr. Reid's appeal, therefore, goes for nothing. He has put into the witness box a nonentity. And skepticism and idealism are at any rate for the present reprieved. But do not skepticism and idealism go still further in their denial? Do they not extend it from a denial in the existence of matter *per se*, to a denial in the existence of matter altogether? Yes, and they must do this. They can only deal with the matter which the psychological analysis affords. The only kind of matter which the psychological analysis affords is matter *per se*, and it affords this as all matter whatsoever. Therefore, in denying the existence of matter *per se*, skepticism and idealism must deny the existence of matter out and out. This, then, is the legitimate *terminus* to which the accepted analysis conducts us. We are all, as we at present stand, either skeptics or idealists, every man of us. Shall the analysis, then, be given up? Not if it can be substantiated by any good plea; for *truth* must be accepted, be the consequences what they may. Can the analysis, then, be made good either by observation or by reasoning, the only competent authorities, now that belief has been declared *hors de combat*? Stewart says that Reid made it good by means of direct observation; but the claim is too ridiculous to be listened to for a single instant. We have also shown that reasoning is incompetent to make out and support the analysis; and therefore our conclusion is, that it falls to the ground as a thing altogether impracticable as well as false, and that the attempt to re-establish it ought never, on any account, to be renewed.

We have dwelt so long on the exposition of the psychological or analytic solution of the problem of perception that we have but little space to spare for the discussion of the metaphysical doctrine. We shall unfold it as briefly as we can.

The principle of the metaphysical doctrine is precisely the opposite of the principle of the psychological doctrine. The one attempts an analysis; the other forbears from all analysis of the given fact, the perception of matter. And why does metaphysic make no attempt to dissect this fact? Simply because the thing cannot be done. The fact yields not to the solvent of thought: it yields not to the solvent of observation: it yields not to the solvent of belief, for man has no belief in the existence of matter from which perception (present and remembered) has been withdrawn. An impotence of the mind does indeed apparently resolve the supposed synthesis; but essential thinking exposes the imposition, restores the divided elements to their pristine integrity, and extinguishes the theory which would explain the *datum* by means of the concurrence of a subjective or mental, and an objective or material factor. The convicted weakness of psychology is thus the root which gives strength to metaphysic. The failure of psychology affords to metaphysic a foundation of adamant. And perhaps no better or more comprehensive description of the object of metaphysical or speculative philosophy could be given than this: that it is a science which exists, and has at all times existed, chiefly for the purpose of exposing the vanity and confounding the pretensions of what is called the "science of the human mind." The turning-round of thought from psychology to metaphysic is the true interpretation of the Platonic conversion of the soul from ignorance to knowledge, from mere opinion to certainty and satisfaction: in other words, from a discipline in which the thinking is only *apparent*, to a discipline in which the thinking is *real*. Ordinary observation does not reveal to us the real but only the apparent revolutions of the celestial orbs. We must call astronomy to our aid if we would reach the truth. In the same way ordinary or psychological thinking may show us the apparent movements of thought, but it is powerless to decipher the real figures described in that mightier than planetary scheme. Metaphysic alone can teach us to read aright the intellectual skies. Psychology regards the universe of thought from the Ptolemaic point of view, making man, as this system made the earth, the center of the whole: metaphysic regards it from the Copernican point of view, making God, as this scheme makes the sun, the regulating principle of all. The difference is as great between "the science of the human mind" and metaphysic as it is between the Ptolemaic and the Copernican astronomy, and it is very much of the same kind.

But the opposition between psychology and metaphysic, which we would at present confine ourselves to the consideration of, is this: the psychological blindness consists in supposing that the analysis so often referred to is practicable, and has been made out: the metaphysical insight consists in seeing that the analysis is null and impracticable. The superiority of metaphysic, then, does not consist in doing or in attempting more than psychology. It consists in seeing that psychology proposes to execute the impossible (a thing which psychology does not herself see, but persists in attempting); and it consists, moreover, in refraining from this audacious attempt, and in adopting a humbler, a less adventurous, and a more circumspect method. Metaphysic (viewed in its ideal character) aims at nothing but what it can fully overtake. It is quite a mistake to imagine that this science proposes to carry a man beyond the length of his tether. The psychologist, indeed, launches the mind into imaginary spheres; but metaphysic binds it down to the fact, and there sternly bids it to abide. *That* is the profession of the metaphysician considered in his beau-ideal. That, too, is the practice (making allowance for the infirmities incident to humanity, and which prevent the ideal from ever being perfectly realized), the practice of all the true astronomers of thought, from Plato down to Schelling and Hegel. If these philosophers accomplish more than the psychologist, it is only because they attempt much less.

In taking up the problem of perception, all that metaphysic demands is the *whole* given fact. That is her only postulate, and it is undoubtedly a stipulation which she is justly entitled to make. Now, what is in this case the *whole* given fact? When we perceive an object, what is the whole given fact before us? In stating it we must not consult elegance of expression; the whole given fact is this: "We apprehend the perception of an object." The fact before us is comprehended wholly in that statement, but in nothing short of it.

Now, does metaphysic give no countenance to an analysis of this fact? That is a new question, a question on which we have not yet touched. Observe, the fact which metaphysic declares to be absolutely unsusceptible of analysis is "the perception of matter." But the fact which we are now considering is a totally different fact; it is *our apprehension of* the perception of matter, and it does not follow that metaphysic will also declare this fact to be ultimate and indecompoundable. Were metaphysic to do this it would reduce us to the condition of subjective or egoistic idealism; but metaphysic is not so absurd. It denies the divisibility of the one fact, but it does itself divide the other. And it is perfectly competent for metaphysic to do this, inasmuch as "our apprehension of the perception of matter" is a different fact from "the perception of matter itself." The former is, in the estimation of metaphysic, susceptible of analysis, the latter is not. Metaphysic thus escapes the imputation of leading us into subjective idealism. This will become more apparent as we proceed.

"Our apprehension of the perception of matter;" this, then, is the whole given fact with which metaphysic has to deal. And this fact metaphysic proceeds to analyze into a subjective and an objective factor, giving to the human mind that part of the *datum* which belongs to the human mind, and withholding from the human mind that part of the *datum* to which it has no proper or exclusive claim. But at what point in the *datum* does metaphysic insert the dissecting-knife, or introduce the solvent which is to effect the proposed dualization at a very different point from that at which psychology insinuates her "ineffectual fire." Psychology cuts down between perception and matter, making the former subjective and the latter objective. Metaphysic cuts down between "our apprehension" and "the perception of matter;" making the latter, "the perception of matter," totally objective, and the former, "our apprehension," alone subjective. Admitting, then, that the total fact we have to deal with is this, "our apprehension of the perception of matter," the difference of treatment which this fact experiences at the hand of psychology and metaphysic is this: they both divide the fact; but psychology divides it as follows: "Our apprehension of the perception of," that is the subjective part of the *datum*, the part that belongs to the human mind; "Matter *per se*" is the objective part of the *datum*, the part of the *datum* which exists independently of the human mind. Metaphysic divides it at a different point, "our apprehension of": this, according to metaphysic, is the subjective part of the process, it is all which can with any propriety be attributed to the human mind: "the perception of matter," this is the objective part of the *datum*, the part of it which exists independently of the human mind, and to the possession of which the human mind has no proper claim, no title at all.

Before explaining what the grounds are which authorize metaphysic in making a division so different from the psychological division of the fact which they both discuss, we shall make a few remarks for the purpose of extirpating, if possible, any lingering prejudice which may still lurk in the reader's mind in favor of the psychological partition.

According to metaphysic, the perception of matter is not the whole given fact with which we have to deal in working out this problem (it is not the whole given fact; for, as we have said, our apprehension of, or participation in, the perception of matter, this is the whole given fact); but the perception of matter is the *whole objective* part of the given fact. But it will perhaps be asked, Are there not here two given facts? Does not the perception of matter imply two *data*? Is not the perception one given fact, and is not the matter itself another given fact, and are not these two facts perfectly distinct from one another? No; it is the false analysis of psychologists which we have already exposed that deceives us. But there is another circumstance which perhaps contributes more than anything else to assist and perpetrate our delusion. This is the construction of language. We shall take this opportunity to put the student of philosophy upon his guard against its misleading tendency.

People imagine that because two (or rather three), words are employed to denote the fact (the perception of matter), that therefore there are two separate facts and thoughts corresponding to these separate words. But it is a great mistake to suppose that the analysis of facts and thoughts necessarily runs parallel with the analysis of sounds. Man, as Homer says, is μέροψ, or a word-divider; and he often carries this propensity so far as to divide words where there is no corresponding division of thoughts or of things. This is a very convenient practice in so far as the ordinary business of life is concerned, for it saves much circumlocution, much expenditure of sound. But it runs the risk of making great havoc with scientific thinking; and there cannot be a doubt that it has helped to confirm psychology in its worst errors, by leading the unwary thinker to suppose that he has got before him a complete fact or thought, when he has merely got before him a complete word. There are whole words which, taken by themselves, have no thoughts or things corresponding to them, anymore than there are thoughts and things corresponding to each of the separate syllables of which these words are composed. The words "perception" and "matter" are cases in point. These words have no meaning, they have neither facts nor thoughts corresponding to them when taken out of correlation to each other. The word, "perception" must be supplemented (mentally at least) by the words "of matter," before it has any kind of sense, before it denotes anything that exists; and in like manner the word "matter" must be mentally supplemented by the words "perception of," before it has any kind of sense, or denotes any real existence. The psychologist would think it absurd if anyone were to maintain that there is one separate existence in nature corresponding to the syllable *mat-*, and another separate existence corresponding to the syllable *ter*, the component syllables of the word "matter." In the estimation of the metaphysician it is just as ridiculous to suppose that there is an existing fact or modification in us corresponding to the three syllables *perception*, and a fact or existence in nature corresponding to the two syllables *matter*. The word "perception" is merely part of a word which, for convenience sake, is allowed to represent the whole word; and so is the word "matter." The word "perception-of-matter" is always the one total word, the word to the mind, and the existence which this word denotes is a totally objective existence.

But in these remarks we are reiterating (we hope, however, that we are also enforcing) our previous arguments. No power of the mind can divide into two facts, or two existences, or two thoughts, that one prominent fact which stands forth in its integrity as the perception-of-matter. Despite, then, the misleading construction of language, despite the plausible artifices of psychology, we must just accept this fact as we find it; that is, we must accept it indissoluble and entire, and we must keep it indissoluble and entire. We have seen what psychology brought us to by tampering with it, under the pretense of a spurious, because impracticable analysis.

We proceed to exhibit the grounds upon which the metaphysician claims for the perception of matter a totally objective existence. The question may be stated thus: Where are we to place this *datum*? *in* our minds or *out* of our minds? We cannot place part of it in our own minds and part of it out of our minds, for it has been proved to be not subject to partition. Wherever we place it, then, there must we place it whole and undivided. Has the perception of matter, then, its proper location in the human mind, or has it not? Does its existence depend upon our existence, or has it a being altogether independent of us?

Now that, and that alone, is the point to decide which our natural belief should be appealed to; but Dr. Reid did not see this. His appeal to the conviction of common sense was premature. He appealed to this belief without allowing skepticism and idealism to run their full course; without allowing them to confound the psychological analysis, and thus bring us back to a better condition by compelling us to accept the fact, not as given in the spurious analysis of man, but as given in the eternal synthesis of God. The consequence was, that Reid's appeal came to naught. Instead of interrogating our belief as to the objective existence of the perception of matter (the proper question), the question which he brought under its notice was the objective existence of matter *per se*, matter *minus* perception. Now, matter *per se*, or *minus* perception, is a thing which no belief will countenance. Reid, however, could not admit this. Having appealed to the belief, he was compelled to distort its evidence in his own favor, and to force it, in spite of itself, to bear testimony to the fact which he wished it to establish. Thus Dr. Reid's appeal not only came to naught, but, being premature, it drove him, as has been said and shown, to falsify the primitive convictions of our nature. Skepticism must indeed be terrible when it could thus hurry an honest man into a philosophical falsehood.

The question, then, which we have to refer to our natural belief, and abide the answer whatever it may be, is this: Is the perception of matter (taken in its integrity, as it must be taken), is it a modification of the human mind, or is it not? We answer unhesitatingly for ourselves, that *our* belief is that it is not. This "confession of faith" saves us from the imputation of subjective idealism, and we care not what other kind of idealism we are charged with. We can think of no sort of evidence to prove that the perception of matter is a modification of the human mind, or that the human mind is its proper and exclusive abode; and all our belief sets in towards the opposite conclusion. Our primitive conviction, when we do nothing to pervert it, is, that the perception of matter is not, either wholly or in part, a condition of the human soul; is not bounded in any direction by the narrow limits of our intellectual span; but that it "dwells apart," a mighty and independent system, a city fitted up and upheld by the everlasting God. Who told us that we were placed in a world composed of matter, which gives rise to our subsequent internal perceptions of it, and not that we were let down at once into a universe composed of external perceptions of matter, that were there beforehand and from all eternity, and in which we, the creatures of a day, are merely allowed to participate by the gracious Power to whom they really appertain? We, perversely philosophizing, told ourselves the former of these alternatives; but our better nature, the convictions that we have received from God Himself, assure us that the latter of them is the truth. The latter is by far the simpler, as well as by far the sublimer doctrine. But it is not on the authority either of its simplicity or its sublimity that we venture to propound it; it is on account of its perfect consonance, both with the primitive convictions of our unsophisticated common sense, and with the more delicate and complex evidence of our speculative reason.

When a man consults his own nature in an impartial spirit, he inevitably finds that his genuine belief in the existence of matter is not a belief in the independent existence of matter *per se*, but it is a belief in the independent existence of the perception of matter which he is for the time participating in. The very last thing which he naturally believes in is, that the perception is a state of his own mind, and that the matter is something different from it, and exists apart *in naturâ rerum*. He may *say* that he believes this, but he never does really believe it. At any rate he believes, in the *first* place, that they exist *together*, wherever they exist. The perception which a man has of a sheet of paper does not come before him as something distinct from the sheet of paper itself. The two are identical, they are indivisible; they are not two, but one. The only question then is, Whether the perception of a sheet of paper (taken as it must be in its indissoluble totality) is a state of the man's own mind, or is no such state. And, in settlement of this question, there cannot be a doubt that he believes, in the *second* place, that the perception of a sheet of paper is not a modification of his own mind, but is an objective thing which exists altogether independent of him and one which would still exist, although he and all other created beings were annihilated. All that he believes to be his (or subjective) is *his participation in* the perception of this object. In a word, it is the perception of matter, and not matter *per se*, which is the *kind* of matter in the independent and permanent existence of which man rests and reposes his belief. There is no truth or satisfaction to be found in any other doctrine.

This metaphysical theory of perception is a doctrine of pure intuitionism: it steers clear of all the perplexities of representationism; for it gives us in perception only one, that is, only a proximate object, this object is the perception of matter, and this is one indivisible object. It is not, and cannot be split into a proximate and a remote object. The doctrine, therefore, is proof against all the cavils of skepticism. We may add, that the entire objectivity of this *datum* (which the metaphysical doctrine proclaims) makes it proof against the imputation of idealism, at least of every species of absurd or objectionable idealism.

But what are these objective perceptions of matter, and to whom do they belong? This question leads us to speak of the circumstance which renders the metaphysical doctrine of perception so truly valuable. This doctrine is valuable chiefly on account of the indestructible foundation which it affords to the *a priori* argument in favor of the existence of God. The substance of the argument is this: Matter is the perception of matter. The perception of matter does not belong to man; it is no state of the human mind, man merely participates in it. But it must belong to some mind, for perceptions without an intelligence in which they inhere are inconceivable and contradictory. They must therefore be the property of the Divine mind; states of the everlasting intellect; *ideas* of the Lord and Ruler of all things, and which come before us as *realities*, so forcibly do they contrast themselves with the evanescent and irregular ideas of our feeble understandings. We must, however, beware, above all things, of regarding these Divine ideas as *mere* ideas. An idea, as usually understood, is that from which all reality has been abstracted; but the perception of matter is a Divine idea, from which the reality has not been abstracted, and from which it cannot be abstracted.

But what, it will be asked, what becomes of the senses if this doctrine be admitted? What is their use and office? Just the same as before, only with this difference, that whereas the psychological doctrine teaches that the exercise of the senses is the condition upon which we are permitted to apprehend objective material things, the metaphysical doctrine teaches that the exercise of the senses is the condition upon which we are permitted to apprehend or participate in the objective perception of material things. There is no real difficulty in the question just raised; and therefore, with this explanatory hint, we leave it, our space being exhausted.

Anticipations of this doctrine are to be found in the writings of every great metaphysician, of every man that ever speculated. It is announced in the speculations of Malebranche, still more explicitly in those of Berkeley; but though it forms the substance of their systems, from foundation-stone to pinnacle, it is not proclaimed with sufficiently unequivocal distinctness by either of these two great philosophers. Malebranche made the perception of matter totally objective, and vested the perception in the Divine mind, as we do. But he erred in this respect: having made the perception of matter altogether objective, he analyzed it in its objectivity into perception (*idée*) and matter *per se*. We should rather say that he attempted to do this; and of course he failed, for the thing, as we have shown, is absolutely impossible. Berkeley made no such attempt. He regarded the perception of matter as not only totally objective, but as absolutely indivisible; and therefore we are disposed to regard him as the greatest metaphysician of his own country (we do not mean Ireland; but England, Scotland, and Ireland), at the very least.

V

Institutes of Metaphysic

SELECTION 6
INTRODUCTION

§1. THROUGHOUT the following work the word "Philosophy," when used by itself, is to be taken as synonymous with *speculative science*, or "metaphysics," as they are usually termed. What philosophy or metaphysic *is*, will unfold itself it is to be hoped, in the sequel. At the outset it is merely necessary to state that, as employed in these pages, the term does not include either natural philosophy or mathematical science, but excludes them expressly from its signification. (The word "Philosophy" as here employed)

§2. A system of philosophy is bound by two main requisitions, — it ought to be true, and it ought to be reasoned. If a system of philosophy is not true it will scarcely be convincing; and if it is not reasoned, a man will be as little satisfied with it as a hungry person would be by having his meat served up to him raw. Truth is the ultimate end of philosophy: hence a system of philosophy ought to be true. The formation of reason (as affected by the discharge of its proper function, which is the ascertainment and concatenation of necessary principles and conclusions) is the proximate end of philosophy; hence a system of philosophy ought to be reasoned. Philosophy, therefore, in its ideal perfection, is a body of reasoned truth. (The two main requisitions of philosophy)

§33. Truth will generally take care of itself, if a man looks vigilantly and conscientiously after the interests of the scientific reason. Although the mere semblance of truth — that is, the plausibilities of ordinary thinking — are altogether repugnant to reason, there is a natural affinity between truth and reason which can never fail to bring them into contact when the inquirer knows exactly what he is aiming at, and is determined to reach it. Real truth, therefore, is attainable, on account of its affinity to right reason; and if a man has reason, he surely can use it rightly. Therefore no plea is available against philosophy on the ground that it is an absolute impracticability, or that it is impossible to bring reason into harmony and coincidence with truth. (A remedial system uniting truth and reason not impossible)

§36. The general character of this system is, that it is a body of necessary truth. It starts from a single proposition which, it is conceived, is an essential axiom of all reason, and one which cannot be denied without running against a contradiction. The axiom may not be self-evident in an instant; but that, as has been remarked, is no criterion. A moderate degree of reflection, coupled with the observations by which the proposition is enforced, may satisfy anyone that its nature is such as has been stated. From this single proposition the whole system is deduced in a series of demonstrations, each of which professes to be as strict as any demonstration in Euclid, while the whole of them taken together constitute one great demonstration. If this rigorous necessity is not their character to the very letter — if there is a single weak point in the system, — if there be any one premise or any one conclusion which is not as certain as that two and two make four, the whole scheme falls to pieces, and must be given up, root and branch. Everything is periled on the pretension that the scheme is rigidly demonstrated throughout; for a philosophy is not entitled to exist, unless it can make good this claim. (It is a body of necessary truth. Its pretensions stated.)

§39. This system is in the highest degree polemical; and why? Because philosophy exists only to correct the inadvertencies of man's ordinary thinking. She has no other mission to fulfill; no other object to overtake; no other business to do. If man naturally thinks aright, he need not be taught to think aright. If he is already, and without an effort, in possession of the truth, he does not require to be put in possession of it. The occupation of philosophy is gone: her office is superfluous: there is nothing for her to put hand to. Therefore philosophy assumes, and must assume, that man does not naturally think aright, but must be taught to do so; that truth does not come to him spontaneously, but must be brought to him by his own exertions. But if a man does not naturally think aright, he must think, we shall not say wrongly — (for that implies malice prepense) — but inadvertently; and if truth be not his inheritance by nature — if he has to work for it, as he must for all his other bread — then the native occupant of his mind, his birthright succession, must be, we shall not say falsehood — (for that, too, implies malice prepense) — but it must be error. The original dowry, then, of universal man, is inadvertency and error. This assumption is the ground and only justification of the existence of philosophy. (Why philosophy must be polemical. She exists only to correct the inadvertencies of ordinary thinking.)

§56. These, then are the two main branches of our science. It is clear that we cannot declare *what is* — in other words, cannot get a footing on ontology until we have ascertained *what is known* — in other words, until we have exhausted all the details of a thorough and systematic epistemology. It may be doubtful whether we can get a footing on ontology even then. But at any rate, we cannot pass to the problem of absolute existence, except through the portals of the solution to the problem of knowledge. Because we are scarcely in a position to *say* what is, unless we have at least attempted to *know* what is; and we are certainly not in a position to know what is, until we have thoroughly examined and resolved the question — what is the meaning of *to know*? What is knowledge? What is knowing, and the known? Until these questions be answered, it is vain and futile to say that absolute existence is that which is *known*. (Epistemology and ontology the two main divisions of philosophy)

§58. Absolute Being may be, very possibly, that which we are ignorant of. Our ignorance is excessive — it is far more extensive than our knowledge. This is unquestionable. After we have fixed, then, the meaning, the conditions, the limits, the object, and the capacities of knowledge, it still seems quite possible, indeed highly probable, that absolute existence may escape us, by throwing itself under the cover, or within the pale, of our ignorance. We may be altogether ignorant of *what is*, and may thus be unable to predicate anything at all about it. This is a most confounding obstacle to our advance. It has indeed, as yet, brought every inquirer to the dust, and thrown back every foot that has attempted to scale the hitherto un-breached and apparently impregnable fastnesses of ontology. Before commencing our operations, therefore, it will be prudent and necessary to hold a council of war. (Because "Absolute Existence" may be that which we are ignorant of)

§60. *Now* our course is pretty clear, and our way made straight before us. The epistemology has fixed what alone any intelligence can know. The agnoiology has fixed what alone any intelligence can be ignorant of—consequently absolute existence being either that which we know, or that which we are ignorant of (and it shall be demonstrated that there is no other alternative), it must respond either to the result of the epistemology, or to the result of the agnoiology. But if the result of the epistemology and the results of the agnoiology are coincident (and their coincidence shall be demonstrated), then it matters not whether absolute being be that which we know, or that which we are ignorant of; we can demonstratively fix its character all the same; we can screw it down, whichever of them it be; we can attach to it a predicate, which is all that is wanted, and which is all that philosophy promises as her ultimate bestowal on mankind. All this shall be clearly shown in the ontology—the conclusion of which need not now be forestalled. This only may be added, that in solving the problem—*What is*? we shall have resolved definitively the ultimate or last question of all philosophy—that query which is always the first to make its appearance, but which requires to be staved off and off, until we have got in hand all the elements of its solution—What is Truth? (Now we can settle the problem of ontology—and how).

SELECTION 7

SECTION I.
THE EPISTEMOLOGY OR THEORY OF KNOWING

PROPOSITION I

THE PRIMARY LAW OR CONDITION OF ALL KNOWLEDGE

Along with whatever any intelligence knows, it must, as the ground or condition of its knowledge have some cognizance of *itself*.

OBSERVATIONS AND EXPLANATIONS

1. *Self* or the "me" is the common center, the continually known rallying-point, in which all our cognitions meet and agree. It is the *ens unum, et simper cognitum, in omnibus notitiis*. Its apprehension is essential to the existence of our, and of all, knowledge. And thus Proposition I forms an explicit answer to the question laid down in the Introduction (§85) as the first question of philosophy: What is the one feature present in all our knowledge,—the common point in which all our cognitions unite and agree,—the element in which they are identical? The *ego* in this feature, point, or element: it is the

common center which is at all times known, and in which all our cognitions, however diverse they may be in other respects, are known as uniting and agreeing; and besides the *ego*, or oneself, there is no other identical quality in our cognitions — as any one may convince himself upon reflection. He will find that he cannot lay his finger upon anything except *himself*, and say — This article of cognition I *must* know along with whatever I know. (Prop I, answers the first question of philosophy)

2. The apprehension of oneself by oneself is the most general and essential circumstance on which knowledge depends, because, unless this law be complied with, no intellectual apprehension of any kind is possible; and wherever it is complied with, some kind of knowledge is necessary. Each of the subsequent propositions (with the exception of the last of the epistemology) gives expression to a necessary law of knowledge; but this first proposition lays down the fundamental necessity to which all intelligence is subject in the acquisition of knowledge. It states the primary canon in the code of reason from which all the other necessary laws are derivations. (It expresses the most general and essential law of all knowledge)

3. The condition of knowledge here set forth is not an operation which is performed once for all, and then dispensed with, while we proceed to the cognition of other things. Neither is it an operation which is ever entirely intermitted, even when our attention appears to be exclusively occupied with matters quite distinct from ourselves. The knowledge of self is the running accompaniment to all our knowledge. It is through and along with *this* knowledge that all *other* knowledge is taken in. (It declares that self-consciousness is never entirely suspended when the mind knows anything)

4. An objection may be raised to this proposition on the ground that it is contradicted by experience. It may be said that when we are plunged in the active pursuits of life, or engaged in the contemplation of natural objects, we frequently pass hours, it may be days, without ever thinking of ourselves. This objection seems to militate against the truth of our first proposition. How is it to be obviated? (Objection that self-consciousness seems at times to be extinct)

5. If the proposition maintained that our attention was at all times clearly and forcibly directed upon ourselves, or that the *me* was constantly a prominent object of our regard, the objection would be fatal to its pretensions. The proposition would be at once disproved by an appeal to experience; for it is certain that during the greater part of

our time we take but little heed of ourselves. But a man may take very little note, without taking absolutely no note of himself. The proposition merely asserts, that a man (or any other intelligence) is never altogether incognizant, is never totally oblivious, of himself, even when his attention is most engaged with other matters. However far it may be carried, the forgetfulness of self is only partial and apparent; it is never real and total. There is always a latent reference of one's perceptions and thoughts to oneself as the person who experiences them, which proves that, however deeply we may be engrossed with the objects before us, we are never stripped entirely of the consciousness of ourselves. And this is all that our proposition contends for. There is a calm unobtrusive current of self-consciousness flowing on in company with all our knowledge, and during every moment of our waking existence; and this self-consciousness is the ground or condition of all our other consciousness. Nine hundred and ninety-nine parts of our attention may be always devoted to the thing or business we have in hand: it is sufficient for our argument if it be admitted that the thousandth part, or even a smaller fraction, of it is perpetually directed upon ourselves. (Objection obviated. Proposition explained)

6. But how is our apparent self-oblivion to be explained? If it is not to be accounted for on the supposition that we ever drop entirely out of our own observation, we must be prepared to explain it on some other principle. And so we are. This oversight, which in many cases is all but complete, may be accounted for in the most satisfactory manner by means of a principle of our nature which may be termed the law of familiarity, the effect of which law is well expressed in the old adage, "Familiarity breeds neglect." Whatever we are extremely intimate with, we are very apt to overlook; and precisely in proportion to the novelty or triteness of any event are the degrees of our attention called forth and exercised. We are enchained by the comparatively rare,—we indifferent towards the comparatively frequent. That which is strange rivets our intellectual gaze,—that to which we are accustomed passes by almost unheeded. No influence has a greater effect than use and wont in dimming the eye of attention, and in blunting the edge of curiosity. This truth might be illustrated to an unlimited extent. It is sufficient for the present purpose to remark that each of us is *more* familiar, and is therefore *less* occupied with himself than he is with any other object that can be brought under his consideration. We are constantly present to our-

selves, — hence we scarcely notice ourselves. We scarcely remark the condition of our knowledge, so unremittingly do we obey it. Indeed, in our ordinary moods we seem to slip entirely out of our own thoughts. This is the inevitable consequence of our close familiarity, our continual intimacy, our unbroken acquaintance with ourselves. But we never do slip entirely out of our own thoughts. However slender the threads may be which hold a man before his own consciousness, they are never completely broken through. (Our apparent inattention to self accounted for by the principle of familiarity)

8. A theory of self-consciousness, opposed to the doctrine advanced in our first proposition, has been sometimes advocated. It reduces this operation to a species of reminiscence: it affirms that we are *first* cognizant of various sensible impressions, and are not conscious of ourselves until we reflect upon them *afterwards*. But this doctrine involves a contradiction; for it supposes us to recollect certain impressions to have been ours, *after* they have been experienced, which we did not know to be ours *when* they were experienced. A man cannot remember what never happened. If the impressions were not known to be ours at the time, they could not subsequently be remembered to have been ours, because their recollection would imply that we remembered an antecedent connection between ourselves and them; which connection, however, had no place in our former experience, inasmuch as this theory declares that no self was in the first instance apprehended; — therefore, if the impressions are recognized on reflection to have been ours, they must originally have been known to be ours. In other words, we must have been conscious of self at the time when the impressions were made. (A theory of self-consciousness at variance with Prop., I refuted)

9. Looked at in itself, or as an isolated truth, our first proposition is of no importance; but viewed as the foundation of the whole system, and as the single staple on which all the truths subsequently to be advanced depend, it cannot be too strongly insisted on, or too fully elucidated. Everything hinges on the stability which can be given to this proposition — on the acceptance it may meet with. If it falls, the system entirely fails; if it stands, the system entirely succeeds. It is to be hoped that the reader will not be stopped or discouraged by the apparent truism which it involves. He may think that, if the main truth which this philosophy has to tell him is, that all his cognitions and perceptions are known by him to be his own, he will have very little to thank it for. Let him go on, and see what follows. Meanwhile,

considering the great weight which this proposition has to bear, we may be excused for bestowing a few more words on its enforcement. (Importance of Prop. I as foundation of the whole system)

11. But it is Reason alone which can give to this proposition, the certainty and extension which are required to render it a sure foundation for all that is to follow. Experience can only establish it as a limited matter of fact; and this is not sufficient for the purposes of our subsequent demonstrations. It must be established as a necessary truth of reason—as a law binding on intelligence universally—as a conception, the opposite of which is a contradiction and an absurdity. Strictly speaking, the proposition cannot be demonstrated, because, being itself the absolute starting-point, it cannot be deduced from any antecedent data; but it may be explained in such a way as to leave no doubt as to its axiomatic character. It claims all the stringency of a geometrical axiom, and its claims, it is conceived, are irresistible. If it were possible for an intelligence to receive knowledge at *any one* time without knowing that it was *his* knowledge, it would be possible for him to do this at *all* times. So that an intelligent being might be endowed with knowledge without once, during the whole term of his existence, knowing that he possessed it. Is there not a contradiction involved in that supposition? But if that supposition be a contradiction, it is equally contradictory to suppose that an intelligence can be conscious of his knowledge, at any single moment, without being conscious of it as his. A man has knowledge, and is cognizant of perceptions only when he brings them home to himself. If he were not aware that they were his, he could not be aware of them at all. Can *I* know without knowing that it is *I* who know? No, truly. But if a man, in knowing anything, must always know that he knows it, he must always be self-conscious. And therefore reason establishes our first proposition as a necessary truth—as an axiom, the denial of which involves a contradiction, or is, in plain words, nonsense. (Its best evidence is reason, which fixes it as a necessary truth or axiom)

12. Every metaphysical truth is faced by an opposite error which has its origin in ordinary thinking, and which it is the business of speculation to supplant. It will conduce, therefore, to the elucidation of our first proposition, if, following the plan laid down in the Introduction (§47), we place alongside of it the counter-proposition which it is designed to overthrow. *First counter-proposition*: "To constitute knowledge, all that is required is that there should be some-

thing to be known, and an intelligence to know it, and that the two should be present to each other. It is not necessary that this intelligence should be cognizant of itself at the same time." (First counter-proposition)

13. This counter-proposition gives expression to the condition of knowledge, as laid down by ordinary thinking; and, it may be added, as laid down by our whole popular psychology. To constitute knowledge, there must be a subject or mind to know, and an object or thing to be known: let the two, subject and object (as they are frequently called, and as we shall frequently call them), be brought together, and knowledge is the result. This is the whole amount both of the common opinion and of the psychological doctrine as to the origin of knowledge. The statement does not expressly deny that the subject must always know itself, in order to be cognizant of the object. It neither denies nor admits this in express terms; and, therefore, it is not easy to grapple with the ambiguity which it involves. But it certainly leans more to the side of denial than to the side of affirmation. The ordinary psychological doctrine seems to be, that the subject, or mind, is at times cognizant of itself to the exclusion of the object, and is at time cognizant of the object to the exclusion of itself, and again is at times cognizant both of itself and the object at once. Its general position is, beyond a doubt, merely this, that to constitute knowledge there must *be* an intelligent subject, and something for this intelligent subject to know — not that this intelligence must in every act of knowledge be cognizant of itself. But this doctrine is equivalent to the counter-proposition just advanced, because it declares that the cognizance of self is *not necessarily* the condition and concomitant of all knowledge. (It embodies the result of ordinary thinking and of popular psychology)

15. To mark strongly the opposition between the propositions and the counter-propositions, it may be stated that the propositions declare what we *do* think, the counter-propositions declare what we *think* we think, but do *not* think: in other words, the propositions represent our *real* thinking, the counter-propositions our *apparent* thinking. For example, the first counter-proposition affirms that we can know things without knowing ourselves; but we only apparently do this — we only think that we know them without obeying the condition specified: in other words, we think, or rather think that we think, a contradiction; for it is impossible *really* to think, a contradiction. The proposition states what we really think and know as the

condition of all our knowledge. (A mark of distinction between the propositions and the counter-propositions)

16. This first proposition expresses the principal law by which the unintelligible is converted into the intelligible. Let self be apprehended, and everything becomes (potentially) apprehensible or intelligible: let self be un-apprehended, and everything remains necessarily in-apprehensible or unintelligible. Considered under this point of view, the nearest approach made to this proposition in ancient times was probably the Pythagorean speculation respecting number as the ground of all conceivability. In nature, *per se*, there is neither unity nor plurality—nothing is one thing, and nothing is many things; because there cannot be one thing unless by a mental synthesis of many things or parts; and there cannot be many things or parts unless each of them is one thing: in other words, in nature, *per se*, there is nothing but absolute inconceivability. If she can place before us "thing," she cannot place before us *a*, or *one* thing. So said Pythagoras. According to him, it is intelligence alone which contributes *a* to "thing"—gives unity, not certainly to plurality (for to suppose plurality is to suppose unity already given), but to that which is neither one nor many; and thus converts the unintelligible into the intelligible—the world of nonsense into the world of intellect. (Prop. I. has some affinity to Pythagorean doctrine of numbers)

17. This doctrine has been strangely misunderstood. Its expositors have usually thought that things are already numbered by nature either as one or many, and that all that Pythagoras taught was that we *re*-number them when they come before us; as if such a truism as that could ever have fallen from the lips of a great thinker; as if such a common-place was even entitled to the name of an opinion. A theory which professes to explain how things become intelligible must surely not suppose that they are intelligible before they become so. If a man undertakes to explain how water *becomes* ice, he must surely not suppose that it already *is* ice. He must date from some anterior condition of the water—its fluidity, for instance. Yet the Pythagorean theory of number, as the ground of all intelligibility, is usually represented in this absurd light. Number, by which "thing" becomes intelligible, either as one or many, is believed to be admitted by this theory to be cleaving to "thing" even in its unintelligible state. Were this so, the thing would not be unintelligible, and there would be no explanation of the conversion of the incogitable (the anoetic) into the cogitable (the noetic), the very point which the theory professes to

explicate. The theory may be imperfect; but it is one of the profoundest speculations of antiquity. The modern interpretation has emptied it of all significance. (Misunderstanding as to Pythagorean doctrine)

18. The law laid down in Proposition I. is merely a higher generalization and clearer expression of the Pythagorean law of number. Whatever is to be known *must* be known as one, or as many, or as both; but whatever is to be known can be made *one* only by being referred to *one* self; and whatever is to be known can be made many only when each of the plurals has been made one by being referred to one self; and whatever is to be known can be made both one and many only by the same process being gone through, — that is to say, its unity and its plurality can only be effected by its reduction to the unity of self. (Prop. I. a higher generalization of the Pythagorean law)

19. Passing over at present all intermediate approximations, we find anticipations of this first proposition in the writings of the philosophers of Germany. It puts in no claim to novelty, however novel may be the uses to which these Institutes apply it. Kant had glimpses of the truth; but his remarks are confused in the extreme in regard to what he calls the unity (analytic and synthetic) of consciousness. This is one of the few places in his works from which no meaning can be extracted. In his hands the principle answered no purpose at all. It died in the act of being born, and was buried under a mass of subordinate considerations before it can be said to have even breathed. Fichte got hold of it, and lost it — got hold of it, and lost it again, through a series of eight or ten different publications, in which the truth slips through his fingers when it seems just on the point of being turned to some account. Schelling promised magnificent operations in the heyday of his youth, on a basis very similar to that laid down in this first proposition. But the world has been waiting for the fulfillment of these promises, — for the fruits of that exuberant blossom, — during a period of more than fifty years. May its hopes be one day realized! No man is fitter, if he would but take the pains, than this octogenarian seer, to show that Speculation is not all one "barren heath."*[1] Hegel, — but who has ever yet uttered one intelligible word about Hegel? Not any of his countrymen, — not any foreigner, — seldom even himself. With peaks, here and there, more lucent than the

---

[1] * Schelling is now dead; he died in 1855.

sun, his intervals are filled with a sea of darkness, un-navigable by the aid of any compass, and an atmosphere, or rather vacuum, in which no human intellect can breathe. Hegel had better not be meddled with just at present. It is impossible to say to what extent this proposition coincides, or does not coincide, with his opinions; for whatever truth there may be in Hegel, it is certain that his meaning cannot be wrung from him by any amount of mere reading, any more than the whisky which is in bread—so at least we have been informed—can be extracted by squeezing the loaf into a tumbler. He requires to be *distilled*, as all philosophers do, more or less—but Hegel to an extent which is unparalleled. A much less intellectual effort would be required to find out the truth for oneself than to understand *his* exposition of it. Hegel's faults, however, and those of his predecessors subsequent to Kant, lie, certainly, not in the matter, but only in the manner of their compositions. Admirable in the substance and spirit and direction of their speculations, they are painfully deficient in the accomplishment of intelligible speech, and inhumanly negligent of all the arts by which alone the processes and results of philosophical research can be recommended to the attention of mankind. (Anticipations of Prop I. by the philosophers of Germany)

PROPOSITION II

THE OBJECT OF ALL KNOWLEDGE

The object of knowledge, whatever it may be, is always something more than what is naturally or usually regarded as the object. It is always is, and must be, the object with the addition of oneself,—object *plus* subject,—thing, or thought, *mecum*. Self is an integral and essential part of every object of cognition.

DEMONSTRATION

It has been already established as the condition of all knowledge, that a thing can be known only provided the intelligence which apprehends it knows itself at the same time. But if a thing can be known only provided oneself be known along with it, it follows that the thing (or thought) and oneself *together* must, in every case, be the object, the true and complete object, of knowledge; in other words, it follows that that which we know always is and must be object *plus* subject, object *cum alio*,—thing or thought with an addition to it,—

which addition is the *me*. Self, therefore, is an integral and essential part of every object of cognition.

Or again. Suppose a case in which a thing or a thought is apprehended without the *me* being apprehended along with it. This would contradict Proposition I., which has fixed the knowledge of self as the condition of all knowledge. But Proposition I. is established; and therefore the *me* must in all cases form part of that which we know; and the only object which any intelligence ever has, or ever can have any cognizance of is, itself-in-union-with-whatever-it-apprehends.

PROPOSITION III

THE INSEPARABILITY OF THE OBJECTIVE AND THE SUBJECTIVE

The objective part of the object of knowledge, though distinguishable, is not separable in cognition from the subjective part, or the ego; but the objective part and the subjective part do together constitute the unit or *minimum* of knowledge.

DEMONSTRATION

If the objective part of knowledge were separable in cognition from the ego or subjective part, it could be apprehended without the ego being apprehended along with it. But this has been proved by Proposition II, to be impossible. Therefore the objective part of the object of knowledge is not separable in cognition from the subjective part, or the ego.

Again, The unit or *minimum* of cognition is such an amount of knowledge that if any constituent part of it be left out of account, the whole cognition of necessity disappears. But the objective *plus* the subjective constitutes such a unit or *minimum*: because if the objective part be entirely removed from the object of our knowledge, and if the mind be left with no thing or thought before it, it can have no cognition—so if the subjective part, or itself, be entirely removed from the mind's observation, the cognition equally disappears, to whatever extent we may suppose the mere objective part of the presentation to be still before us. All cognizance of it is impossible by Proposition I. Therefore the objective and the subjective do together constitute the unit or *minimum* of cognition.

4. Inseparability in cognition does not mean inseparability in space. The necessary laws of knowledge admit of our apprehending things as separable, and as separate, in space from ourselves to any

extent we please; but they do not admit of our apprehending things as separate or as separable in cognition from ourselves in any sense whatever. It is to be suspected that some misconception on this point has been pretty general among the cultivators of philosophy, and that some who may have had a glimpse of the truth have shrunk from advocating, and even from contemplating, the inseparability in cognition of subject and object, from confounding this idea with the idea of their inseparability in space. Subject and object may be separated from each other in space more widely than the poles; it is only in cognition that they are absolutely inseparable. They may very well be separated in space; but space itself cannot be separated in cognition from the subject—space is always known and thought of as *my* cognizance of space—therefore a separation in space has no effect whatever in bringing about a separation in cognition, of object from subject. The cultivators of philosophy just referred to seem to have been apprehensive lest, in denying the separability in cognition of subject and object, they might appear to be calling in question the existence of *external* things, and thereby falling into idealism. As if any genuine idealism ever denied the existence of external things, ever denied that these things were actually and *bonâ fide* external to us. Idealism never denied this: it only asks what is the meaning of "external" considered out of all relation to "internal," and it shows that, out of this relation, the word "external" has, and can have, no meaning. (Inseparability in cognition not to be confounded with inseparability in space: the external and the internal)

5. The unit or *minimum* of cognition is such an amount (and no more) of cognition as can be known. The knowable must mount up to a certain point before it can become the knowable least. In this respect the magnitude of the knowable is quite different from visible or ponderable magnitude. The visible or ponderable least cannot be determined absolutely, because there is no necessary law of reason fixing it. It is a varying quantity contingent on the capacities of the seer or the weigher. But the knowable least is determined absolutely by an essential law of all intelligence; it cannot be less than some thing or thought, with the addition of oneself. It cannot be less than object + subject; because anything less than this is absolutely unknowable by a necessary law of reason. No necessary law of knowledge fixes that the capacity of seeing or hearing or weighing shall not go below a certain limit: because with finer organs or with finer instruments a new *minimum* of sight or of sound or of weight

might, forever and ever, be revealed. But the capacity of knowing is sternly and everlastingly, and universally prohibited from going below a certain limit: it cannot descend to the apprehension of less than object + subject. This, therefore, is the least, the ultimate that can be known *by itself*. Object (whatever the object may be, for this of course is not fixed by any necessary law of reason) *plus* subject is the *minimum scibile per se*. (The unit of cognition explained. How it is determined)

10. Every man in his ordinary moments conceives that he can and does separate in cognition the thing which he knows from himself the knower of it. He looks upon it as something which he can and does apprehend without apprehending himself. Hence he sees no difficulty whatever in separating it intelligently from himself. Hence, too, he fancies that *it* is a unit of knowledge, and that *he* is another unit of knowledge. This supposition, which contradicts the necessary laws of all reason, is no worse than an inadvertency on the part of common opinion, although it is one of the most inveterate of those natural oversights which metaphysic exists for the sole purpose of correcting. (It embodies an inadvertency of natural thinking).

12. The psychologist finds himself in a dilemma. He sees that if he expressly denies the inseparability in cognition of the objective and the subjective elements of knowledge, he mistakes and misstates the laws of cognition; and he sees that if he admits that object and subject form the unit or *minimum* of cognition, he deprives himself of the best or only argument by which he may prove that each of them is a separate unit of *existence*. This consideration shocks him; and he endeavors to salve the point by admitting that subject and object are inseparable in cognition (this saves the phenomena in so far as the laws of knowledge are concerned), and by denying that they constitute only a single unit of cognition (this enables him to keep in his hands a valid argument for their duality of existence). But he retains it at a considerable expense—by swallowing a contradiction of his own brewing, which no palliatives will ever enable him, or anyone else, to digest. Such, we may be assured, is the secret history of the psychological deliverance on this point. The psychologist has not the firmness to stand to the truth, be the consequences what they may. (The psychological error accounted for)

13. The common division of the sciences into the two leading categories,—the science of mind and the science of matter,—when

regarded as more than a mere verbal, and to a certain extent convenient distinction, is founded on the fallacy contained in this psychological deliverance, and partakes of its fallaciousness. Indeed, to lay down the dualism of subject and object as complete and absolute, (that is, as an out-and-out duality which is not also a unity), which psychology not un-frequently does, is to extinguish every glimmering of the scientific reason; for this implies that the dualism is laid down in cognition, as complete and absolute, which it can only be when intelligence can act in opposition to its own necessary and insuperable laws. In case it should be thought that psychology is rather unsparingly dealt with throughout this work, it may be here observed that it is only in so far as psychology ventures to treat of the fundamental question in regard to knowledge, and to intrude into the region of the *prima philosophia*, that her procedure is reprehended, and her insufficiency exposed. Within her own proper sphere—the investigation, namely, of such mental operations as memory, association of ideas etc.—the performances of psychology are by no means to be slighted. (Distinction of science of mind and science of matter characterized)

15. The circumstances that the object and subject of knowledge, the thing and the *me*, can be distinguished in cognition, seems to have led to the mistake embodied in this counter-proposition. People seem to have supposed that because these were distinguishable, they were also separable in the mind. They, perhaps, fancy that the assertion that the ego and non-ego are inseparable in cognition, is equivalent to the assertion that thought confounds and identifies them with each other. Such a supposition, if ever entertained, indicates merely a confusion of ideas. Many things are distinguishable in cognition, which it is yet impossible to know in separation from each other; and many things are inseparable in cognition, which it is yet impossible to confound or identify with each other. A stick has two ends. Its one end is quite distinguishable in cognition from the other end; but it is absolutely inseparable in cognition from the other end. A stick with only one end is altogether incogitable. Again,—a stick has two ends. These are absolutely inseparable in cognition. But the one end is not the same as the other end. It is impossible for the mind to separate them; it is equally impossible for the mind to confound them. Of course, any given end of a stick can be cut away; but not in such a manner as to leave it with only one end, either for itself or for cognition. The end removed always is, and must be, replaced by a

new end. (Many things are distinguishable, which are not separable, in cognition)

16. So in regard to subject and object. Any given subject may be removed from any given object, and any given object may be removed from any given subject. But the necessary law of every apprehended object is, that an ego or subject must be apprehended along with it; and the necessary law of every apprehended subject is, that an object or thought, of one kind or other, must be apprehended along with it. This is what the law of all intelligence necessitates; in other words, both subject and object are required to make up the unit or *minimum* of cognition. The object, by itself, is less than this unit or *minimum*, and the subject, by itself, is less than this unit or *minimum*; and therefore, each of them, by itself, is absolutely inapprehensible. Yet no one is ever so insane as to confound the objective part of his knowledge with the subjective part of it, or to mistake a thing for himself. (Illustrations applied to subject and object)

17. The circumference of a circle and its center furnish another example of two elements of cognition, which, though perfectly distinguishable, are altogether inseparable in the mind. The circumference of a circle cannot be known without the center being known, and the center of a circle cannot be known without the circumference being known; yet who ever supposes that the circumference *is* the center, or the center the circumference? In the same way, why should our proposition lead people to infer that that part of the total object of knowledge which is called the subject *is* that other part of it which is usually called the object, or that that part of it which is usually called the object *is* that other part of it which is called the subject? One would think that the distinction might be understood and kept clearly in view without running even into the smallest degree of confusion. At any rate, these remarks, taken along with the explanation given in the third paragraph of this article, may be sufficient to obviate the main misconceptions which have prevented our third proposition from occupying its rightful place in speculative science, and have led generally to the adoption of the third counter-proposition. (Further illustration)

18. All that this proposition contends for may be expressed very shortly and simply by saying—that it is impossible for a man to consider any of the objects of his consciousness, whatever these may be, as at any time the objects of *no* consciousness—

"Quo semel est imbuta recens, servabit odorem Testa diu."

Everything which I, or any intelligence, can apprehend, is steeped primordially in *me*; and it ever retains, and every must retain, the flavor of that original impregnation. Whether the object be what we call a thing or what we call a thought, it is equally impossible for any effort of thinking to grasp it as an intelligible thing or as an intelligible thought, when placed out of all connection with the ego. This is a necessary truth of all reason—an inviolable law of all knowledge—and we must just take it as we find it. (Short statement of what this proposition contends for)

PROPOSITION IV

MATTER PER SE

Matter *per se*, the whole material universe by itself, is of necessity absolutely unknowable.

DEMONSTRATION

The whole material universe by itself, or *per se*, is a mere collection of objects without a subject or self. But it was proved in Proposition II, that the only objects which can possibly be known are objects *plus* a subject or self. Therefore the whole material universe by itself, or *per se*, is of necessity absolutely unknowable.

8. Both the materialist and the idealist have tacitly prejudged an important preliminary question in their discussion respecting the existence of matter. The question is this—Is there, or is there not, any necessary and invincible law of knowledge and of reason which prevents matter *per se* from being known? The materialist, prejudging this question in the negative, silently decides that there is nothing in the nature of intelligence, or in the constitution and essence of knowledge, to prevent matter *per se* from being known. Holding, therefore, the knowledge of matter *per se* to be possible, and surrounded by the glories of a wonderful creation, he very naturally concludes that this knowledge is actual; and holding this knowledge to be actual, he cannot but conclude that matter *per se* exists. The inference from knowledge to existence is always legitimate. It is not surprising, therefore, that he should be bewildered and irritated by the speculations of those who have called in question the existence of matter *per se*. But the idealist also has his grounds of justification. He has silently decided this preliminary question in the affirmative. He has seen that in the very nature of reason, in the very constitution of knowledge, there is a necessary and insuperable law which renders

any apprehension of matter *per se* a contradiction and an impossibility. Hence his doubts, and even his denial, of the existence of matter *per se* are not altogether so unreasonable as they are liable to appear to those who are ignorant of the answer which he has tacitly and only half-consciously returned to the preliminary question referred to. (A preliminary question prejudged by materialist and by idealists)

9. This preliminary question has been prejudged—that is, has been settled in opposite ways without examination—by the materialist and by the idealist, owing to their having proceeded to ontology (the science of Being) before they had proposed and exhausted the problems of a rigorous and demonstrative epistemology (the science of Knowing). Owing to this reversal of the right method of philosophy, while the materialist has tacitly returned a wrong answer to this preliminary question, the idealist has obtained only a glimpse of the truth. The materialist rejects the law with an emphasis all the more strong, because the question which inquires about it can scarcely be said to have occurred to him. He never even dreams that there is an invincible law of reason which prevents all intelligence from knowing matter *per se*. He has silently decided in his own mind that there is no such law; and hence he has no difficulty in coming to a decision in favor of independent material existence. On the other hand, the idealist has certainly got some perception of this law; but having passed on to the question of existence before he had thoroughly ascertained the laws of knowledge, and in particular before he had mastered the condition of all knowledge, as laid down in Proposition I., he has reached an ontological conclusion affirming the non-absolute existence of matter, which, however true it may be, is ambiguous, precipitate, and ill-matured,—and indeed not intelligible; for nothing which is ambiguous in intelligent. (Cause of this precipitate judgment. Its evil consequences.)

PROPOSITION V

MATTER AND ITS QUALITIES PER SE

All the qualities of matter *by themselves* are, of necessity, absolutely unknowable.

DEMONSTRATION

The qualities of matter by themselves are, equally with matter itself, an objective presentment without a subject. But it has been proved by Proposition II. that no objective can be known without a subjective or self being known along with it. Therefore, all the qualities of matter, by themselves, are absolutely unknowable.

PROPOSITION VII

WHAT THE UNIVERSAL AND THE PARTICULAR IN COGNITION ARE

The ego (or mind) is known as the element common to all cognitions, — matter is known as the element peculiar to some cognitions: in other words, we know *ourselves* as the unchangeable, necessary, and universal part of our cognitions, while we know matter, in all its varieties, as a portion of the changeable, contingent, and particular part of our cognitions — or, expressed in the technical language of logic, the ego is the known *summum genus*, the known generic part, of all cognitions — matter is the known differential part of some cognitions.

DEMONSTRATION

It is a necessary truth of reason that the ego must be known (that is, must be known to itself) whenever it knows anything at all (by Prop. I): in other words, no cognition, in which one does not apprehend oneself, is possible. Therefore the ego or oneself is known as the element common to all cognition, — that is, as the *summum genus* of cognition. Again, it is not a necessary truth of reason that matter must be known whenever anything at all is known: in other words, cognitions in which no material element is apprehended are, if not actual, at any rate possible and conceivable. No contradiction is involved in that supposition; and therefore, matter is not known as the element common to all cognition, but only as the element peculiar to some cognitions — that is, as the differential part of some cognitions. And hence the ego is the unchangeable, necessary, and universal part of cognition, while matter, in all its varieties, is only a portion (not the whole) of the changeable contingent, and particular part of cognition.

PROPOSITION VIII

THE EGO IN COGNITION

The ego cannot be known to be material — that is to say, there is a necessary law of reason which prevents it from being apprehended by the senses.

DEMONSTRATION

The ego is known as that which is common to all cognitions, and matter is known as that which is peculiar to some cognitions (Prop. VII.) But that which is known as common to all cognitions cannot be known as that which is peculiar to some cognitions, without supposing that a thing can be known to be different from what it is known to be, — which supposition is a violation of the law of contradiction (*see* Introduction §28). Therefore the ego cannot be known to be material, etc.

10. Whether all existence is particular, and whether the ego *is* something particular (be it material, or be it immaterial), is a question with which the epistemology has no concern. This section of the science decides only what the ego is known, and not known, as; and it declares (as it has already declared in Prop. VII) in emphatic terms, that the ego or mind is not known as any *particular* thing, either material or immaterial, but is known only as a *universal*, that is, as the element common to all cognition, and not peculiar to any. The element which every cognition presents, and must present, can have no particularity attaching to it, except the characteristic of absolute universality. To attempt to conceive it as some particular thing, by affixing to it some peculiar or distinctive mark, would be to reduce it from universality to particularity — in other words, would be to destroy the conception of mind in the very act of forming it. (It is known only as the universal)

PROPOSITION IX

THE EGO PER SE

The ego, or self, or mind, *per se*, is, of necessity, absolutely unknowable. *By itself* — that is, in a purely un-determinate state, or separated from all things, and divested of all thoughts — it is no possible object of cognition. It can know itself only in some particular state, or in union with some non-ego; that is, with some element contradistinguished from itself.

DEMONSTRATION

The ego is the element common to all cognition — the universal constituent of knowledge (Proposition VII). But every cognition must contain a particular or peculiar, as well as a common or universal, part, and there can be no knowledge of either of these parts by itself, or prescinded from the other part (Proposition VI). Therefore there can be no knowledge of the ego, or self, or mind, *per se*, or in a purely indeterminate state, or separated from all things, and divested of all thoughts. It can know itself only in some particular state, or in union with some non-ego; that is, with some element contra-distinguished from itself.

PROPOSITION XI

PRESENTATION AND REPRESENTATION

That alone can be represented in thought which can be presented in knowledge: in other words, it is impossible to think what it is impossible to know; or, more explicitly, it is impossible to think that of which knowledge has supplied, and can supply, no sort of type.

DEMONSTRATION

Representation is the iteration in thought of what was formerly presented in knowledge. It is therefore a contradiction to suppose that what never was, and never can be, known, can be iterated or represented in thought. Repetition necessarily implies a foregone lesson. Therefore that alone can be represented in thought which can be presented in knowledge; in other words, it is impossible to think what it is impossible to know;—it is impossible to think that of which knowledge has supplied, and can supply, no sort of type.

PROPOSITION XII

MATTER PER SE AGAIN

The material universe *per se*, and all its qualities *per se*, are not only absolutely unknowable, they are also of necessity absolutely unthinkable.

DEMONSTRATION

The material universe and its qualities *per se* cannot be known or presented to the mind—(Props. IV. and V.) But what cannot be known or presented to the mind, cannot be thought of, or represented by the mind—(Prop. XI.) Therefore the material universe, and all its qualities *per se*, are absolutely unthinkable as well as absolutely unknowable.

PROPOSITION XIII

THE INDEPENDENT UNIVERSE IN THOUGHT

The only *independent* universe which any mind or ego can think of is the universe in synthesis with some *other* mind or ego.

DEMONSTRATION

Objects *plus* a subject, or self, is the only universe which can be known (Props. I. and II.) The only universe which can be thought of is the universe which can be known (Prop. XI.) Therefore, objects *plus* a subject, or self, is the only universe which can be thought of. Consequently, whenever any mind or ego thinks of the universe as independent of itself, it must still think of it as made up of objects *plus* a subject. Therefore, the only *independent* universe which any mind or ego can think of is the universe in synthesis with some *other* mind or ego.

PROPOSITION XIV

THE PHENOMENAL IN COGNITION

There is no mere phenomenal in cognition; in other words, the phenomenal by itself is absolutely unknowable and inconceivable.

DEMONSTRATION

The first premise fixes *the definition of phenomenon*. "Whatever can be known or conceived only when something else is known or conceived along with it, is a phenomenon, or the phenomenal." But whatever can only be so known, or conceived, cannot be known or conceived by itself. Therefore there is no mere phenomenal in cognition; in other words, the phenomenal by itself is absolutely unknowable and inconceivable.

PROPOSITION XV

WHAT THE PHENOMENAL IN COGNITION IS

Objects, whatever they may be, are the phenomenal in cognition; matter in all its varieties is the phenomenal in cognition; thoughts or mental states whatsoever are the phenomenal in cognition; the universal is the phenomenal in cognition; the particular is the phenomenal in cognition; the ego, or mind, or subject, is the phenomenal in cognition.

DEMONSTRATION

Objects, whatever they may be, can be known only along with self or the subject (by Prop. I.); matter in all its varieties can be known only along with self or the subject (by Prop. I.); thoughts or mental states whatsoever can be known only along with self or the subject (by Prop. I.); the universal can be known only along with the particular (by Prop. VI.); the particular can be known only along with the universal (by Prop. VI.) The ego, or mind, or subject, or oneself, can be known only along with some thing or thought or determinate condition of one kind or another (by Prop. IX.) Therefore all these, conformably to the definition of phenomenon, are the phenomenal in cognition.

PROPOSITION XVI

THE SUBSTANTIAL IN COGNITION

There is a substantial in cognition; in other words, substance, or the substantial, is knowable, and is known by us.

DEMONSTRATION

The first premise fixes the *definition of known substance*: "Whatever can be known without anything else being, of necessity, known along with it, is a known substance." But some such thing must be known, otherwise all knowledge would be impossible; because it is obvious that no knowledge could ever take place, if, in order to know a thing, we always required to know something else, and if, in order to know the thing and the something else, we again required to know something else, and so on *in infinitum*. Under such an interminable process knowledge could never arise. But knowledge does arise. Therefore a point must be reached at which something is known without anything else being, of necessity, known along with it. And this is something, whatever it may turn out to be, is known substance, according to the definition. Therefore there is a substantial in cognition; in other words, substance is knowable, and is known by us.

PROPOSITION XVII

WHAT THE SUBSTANTIAL IN COGNITON IS

Object *plus* subject is the substantial in cognition; matter *mecum* is the substantial in cognition; thoughts or mental states whatsoever, *together* with the self or subject, are the substantial in cognition; the universal, in union with the particular, is the substantial in cognition; the ego or mind in any determinate condition, or with anything or thought present to it, is the substantial in cognition. This synthesis, thus variously expressed, is the substantial, and the only substantial, in cognition.

DEMONSTRATION

Object *plus* subject — matter *mecum* — thoughts or mental states whatsoever, together with the self or subject — the ego or mind in any determinate condition, or with anything or thought present to it — the universal in union with the particular — these varieties of expression declare what constitutes the only synthesis which can be known or conceived without anything else being known or conceived along with it (see in particular Props. II. III. VI. IX. XIII.) Therefore this synthesis (thus variously expressed) is the substantial, and the only substantial, in cognition, conformably to the definition of substance given in Prop. XVI.

OBSERVATIONS AND EXPLANATIONS

1. *Seventeenth Counter-proposition* — "Object *plus* subject — matter *mecum* — thoughts or mental states whatsoever, together with the self or subject — the universal in union with the particular — this synthesis, thus variously expressed, is merely the phenomenal in cognition. The substantial is rather the separate members of the synthesis, than the total synthesis itself. Thus object apart from subject — matter apart from mind — the ego apart from the non-ego, and separated from all thoughts and determinations — the non-ego divorced from the ego, and existing as it best can — these are the substantial, not indeed in human knowledge, for human knowledge cannot lay hold of the substantial, but in reality, *in rerum natura*. They are the occult bases of all the phenomena, intellectual and material, which alone come before us; and among these, and equally phenomenal in its character, falls to be ranked what is called the synthesis in cognition of object and subject — matter and me — mind with thoughts or things present to it — the universal and the particular — the ego and the non-ego." (Seventeenth counter-proposition)

2. This counter-proposition is a conglomeration of epistemology and the ontology, with a slight tincture of common opinion, and a large menstruum of psychological doctrine. To disentangle its contents, therefore, it must be put through a refining process — first, in order to clear it from all ontological admixture, and to disengage and

exhibit that part of it which psychology opposes to the proposition; and, secondly, in order to disengage and exhibit that part of it which ordinary thinking opposes to the proposition. (Conglomerate character of the counter-proposition)

3. *First*, part of this counter-proposition is obviously ontological. Although psychology professes to have no faith in ontology, and disclaims all connection with so unapproachable a department of metaphysics, she nevertheless retains such a hold over this un-reclaimed province as enables her, unless vigorously withstood, to disconcert the operations of the exact reason, and to impede the progress of genuine speculation. Thus, when the question is put, What is the substantial in cognition? psychology is not content with answering that there is no substantial in cognition, and that what is supposed to be such is merely the phenomenal: she goes on to declare what the substantial *in existence* is; and thus people's attention is called off from the proper and only point under consideration, while the truth, which is not over-willing to be caught at anytime, slips quietly away during the confusion. "We first raise a dust," says Berkeley, "and then complain that we cannot see"—a very true remark. The speculative thinker asks a question about knowledge, whereupon the psychologist instantly kicks up a turmoil about existence, so that neither of them can see what they are looking for. The question, What is the substantial *in cognition*? is no more answered by saying that some occult substratum of qualities is the substantial *in existence*, than the question. Who is the Great Mogul? is answered by the reply that Her Majesty Queen Victoria is the Sovereign of England. We therefore throw overboard, in the meantime, the ontological surplusage contained in the counter-proposition, and limit it to the relevant averment "that object *plus* a subject is not the substantial, but is the mere phenomenal, in cognition. (Elimination of its ontological surplusage)

4. The contradiction involved in the counter-proposition thus restricted is instantly brought to light by an appeal to the definitions of substance and phenomenon (Prop. XVI. Dem., Prop. XIV. Dem) The known substantial is whatever, and only whatever, can be known or thought of without anything else being known or thought of along with it. Does anything else require to be known or thought of along with objects *plus* a subject, or along with matter *mecum*, or along with the universe + the particular? It is obvious that nothing else does (see Props. II, III, VI.) Does anything more require to be

apprehended than the ego or oneself in some determinate condition? Nothing more requires to be apprehended (Prop. IX.) Therefore this synthesis, however it may be expressed, is the substantial in cognition, and is established as such on necessary ground of reason; and consequently the counter-proposition is the denial of a necessary truth of reason.

Again: The phenomenal is whatever, and only whatever, can be known or thought of only when something else is known or thought of along with it. Can objects *plus* a subject—or can matter *mecum*—or can the universal + the particular—or can the ego or oneself in some determinate condition,—can the synthesis of these be known only when something else is known along with it? No indeed. The synthesis can be known by itself, and un-supplemented by anything further. Therefore this synthesis is not the phenomenal in cognition, and is proved not to be this on necessary principles of reason; and, consequently the counter-proposition is an affirmation which contradicts a necessary truth of reason. Thus it involves a mental contradiction, whether looked at in its negative or in its affirmative aspect. (It's contradictory character exposed in so far as it is psychological)

11. Lest it should be supposed that these Institutes are obnoxious to the same sentence of reprehension which has just been pronounced upon psychology, inasmuch as it may be said that they too represent substance as constituted by a synthesis of phenomena (object + subject), the following difference must be pointed out, and carefully borne in mind. The charge against psychology is, that the substance for which she contends is no substance at all, but is the mere phenomenal, because it requires to be supplemented in thought by something more—namely, by the "me;" whereas the substantial, for which strict speculation contends, is undoubtedly a substance in cognition (whatever it may be in existence); because, although it may be an aggregate of mere phenomena, it can and does, nevertheless subsist in thought without any else subsisting there along with it; and thus it corresponds to the definition of known substance, which is all that is required to bear out the truth of the statement advanced in Proposition XVII. Anyone may convince himself, without much difficulty, that he can think of things *plus* himself without thinking of anything more (and can therefore conceive the substantial); and also that he cannot think of anything less than this without thinking of something more; and consequently, that whatever he thinks of as less than this completed synthesis, is

thought of as the phenomenal, in conformity with the definition of phenomenon. (The Institutional conception of known substance)

PROPOSITION XVIII
THE RELATIVE IN COGNITION

There is no *mere* relative in cognition: in other words, the relative *per se*, or by itself, is, of necessity, unknowable and unknown.

DEMONSTRATION

The demonstration commences with *the definition of the relative*, which is nearly identical with that of the phenomenal. "The relative is whatever can be known or conceived only when a correlative is known or conceived along with it." But that which can be known or conceived only when a correlative is known or conceived along with it cannot be known or conceived by itself. Therefore there is no *mere* relative in cognition; in other words, the relative *per se*, or by itself, is of necessity, unknowable and unknown.

PROPOSITION XIX
WHAT THE RELATIVE IN COGNITION IS

Objects, whatever they may be, are the relative in cognition; matter, in all its varieties, is the relative in cognition; thoughts or mental states whatsoever are the relative in cognition; the universal is the relative in cognition; the particular is the relative in cognition; the ego, or mind, or subject, is the relative in cognition.

DEMONSTRATION

The demonstration is a mere reiteration of demonstration XV; the word "relative" being substituted for the word "phenomenal." Each of the items specified in Prop. XIX is the relative in cognition, because each of them can be known only along with its correlative. Thus, objects can be known only in relation to some correlative subject—matter can be known only in relation to some correlative "me." The ego can be known only in relation to some correlative—*i.e.*, in relation to the non-ego (some thing or thought). Each of these, therefore, taken *singulatim*, is the relative in cognition.

PROPOSITION XX

THE ABSOLUTE IN COGNITION

There is an Absolute in cognition; in other words, something Absolute is knowable, and is known by us.

DEMONSTRATION

The demonstration commences with *the definition of the known absolute*, which is almost coincident with that of known substance. "Whatever can be known (or conceived) *out of relation*, that is to say, without any correlative being necessarily known (or conceived) along with it, is the known Absolute." But some such thing must be known, otherwise all knowledge would be impossible. Because, if everything had a correlative thing which required to be known before *it* could be known; and again, if the thing and its correlative had *another* correlative thing which required to be known before knowledge could arise, and so on perpetually, — it is obvious that no cognition could every take place; but cognition does take place. Therefore, something can, and *must* be known, out of relation, or without any correlative being known along with it; and this, whatever it may be, is the known Absolute conformably to the definition. Consequently there is an Absolute in cognition; in other words, the Absolute is knowable and is known by us.

OBSERVATIONS AND EXPLANATIONS

1. Here, as elsewhere in this section of the science, we are occupied only with the definition and consideration of the *known* Absolute, and not at all with the definition and consideration of the existing Absolute. Whatever the existing Absolute may be, it is certain, with all the certainty of necessary truth, as this demonstration proves that there is a known Absolute, or something which can be embraced in cognition, without any correlative being necessarily embraced in cognition along with it. (Nothing is affirmed as to the existing Absolute)

PROPOSITION XXI

WHAT THE ABSOLUTE IN COGNITION IS

Object *plus* subject is the absolute in cognition; matter *mecum* is the absolute in cognition; thoughts or mental states whatsoever, *together* with the self or subject, are the absolute in cognition; the universal in union with the particular is the absolute in cognition; the ego or mind in any determinate condition, or with any thought or thing present to it, is the absolute in cognition. This synthesis, thus variously expressed, is the Absolute, and the only absolute, in cognition.

DEMONSTRATION

This synthesis, thus variously expressed, is the known absolute, because it and it alone, can be known out of relation, or without any correlative being necessarily known along with it.

5. The truth is, that all men are equally cognizant of the absolute. Those who disavow this knowledge do, and must, entertain it, just as much as those who lay claim to it. No effort is required to get hold of it. Every man who is cognizant of himself, together with the things which come before him, has a knowledge of the absolute; because he apprehends this synthesis as detached and rounded off, and not in necessary association with anything else. It is true that our cognitions are linked together by such inveterate ties of association that it may be difficult, in point of fact, to obtain an absolutely isolated apprehension of oneself and any particular thing. But this is a question which is to be determined by reason, and not by experience. The laws of association are arbitrary and contingent, and their operation must at present be discounted. The question is, What is *all* that is strictly necessary to constitute a case of absolute and isolated cognition? and the answer is, "Me *plus* a grain of sand or less," even although, in point of fact, I should not be able to apprehend a grain of sand without taking cognizance, at the same time, of a whole seashore. The accidental enlargement of the objective element has no effect in essentially augmenting the absolute in cognition—(See Prop. III—Obs. 8.) (All men are equally cognizant of the absolute)

10. Kant was of opinion that he had hit upon a notable refutation of the doctrine of the Absolute when he declared that, "whatever we know must be known in conformity to the constitution of our faculties of cognition." Of course it must. And must not everything which *any* intelligence knows be known on the same terms—be known in conformity to the constitution of *its* cognitive faculties? And must not every intelligence, know *itself* along with all that it knows? And hence must not every intelligence, when it apprehends this synthesis (whatever the character of the particular element may be), apprehend that which is absolute, inasmuch as it must apprehend that which has no necessary correlative? Kant seems to have thought that although *we* could not know material things absolutely or out of rela-

tion to our faculties, other intelligences might possess this capacity, and might be competent to know them absolutely, or as they existed out of relation to *their* cognitive endowments—a supposition which carries a contradiction on the very face of it. If "the Absolute" can be known only when it is known out of relation to the faculties of *all* intelligence, it is obvious that there can be no cognizance of it in any quarter—not even on the part of Omniscience. Kant's refusal to generalize, or lay down as applicable to *all* intelligence, the law that *our* intellect can know things only as it is competent to know them, is one of the strangest cases of obstinacy to be found in the history of speculative opinion. Can any intellect, actual or possible, know things except as it is able to know them? (Kant on the Absolute)

11. The relations of which we usually speak, and which come before us in physical science, and in ordinary life, are relations between non-contradictories. Thus, for example, the relation that subsists between an acid and an alkali, between a father and a son, between the earth and the moon, are relations of non-contradictories, because each of these things is conceivable *out of* as well as *in* relation to the other. But the relationship of subject and object—of *me* and things, or thoughts, is a relationship of contradictories, because each term can be conceived only *in* relation to the other. A thing or thought with no "me" known or thought of in connection with it, is an expression of nonsense; and "me," with no thing or thought present to me, is equally an expression of nonsense. The known Absolute is thus a synthesis of two contradictories, and not of two non-contradictories. This should be particularly borne in mind. Psychology never gets beyond the position that the synthesis of subject *plus* object is the union of two non-contradictories, and thus sticks at the *pons asinorum* of speculation, which demands, as the condition of all further progress and enlightenment, an insight into the truth that the fusion of two contradictories—that is, of two elements which are necessarily unknowable *singulatim*—is the genesis of absolute cognition. (The relation of non-contradictories and the relation of contradictories)

PROPOSITION XXII

THE CONTINGENT CONDITIONS OF KNOWLEDGE

The senses are the contingent conditions of knowledge; in other words, it is possible that intelligences different from the human (supposing that there are such) should apprehend things under other laws, or in other ways, than those of seeing, hearing, touching, tasting, and smelling; or, more shortly, *our* senses are not laws of cognition, or modes of apprehension, which are binding on intelligence necessarily and universally.

12. Much of the perplexity and inconclusiveness of speculative thinking is to be attributed to the want of this analysis. To this cause the errors of representationism*[2] and the insufficiency of Berkleianism are mainly to be ascribed. It was formerly remarked (Prop. XI. – Obs. 10) that the doctrine of a representative perception is an obscure anticipation of the great law of all reason, which declares that nothing objective can be apprehended unless something subjective be apprehended as well. So far this system is true, and moves in a right direction. But the question is, *What* is the subjective part which *must* be apprehended whenever any objective counterpart is apprehended? Here it is that representationism goes astray. One part of the subjective contribution (the ego) enters *necessarily* into the constitution of cognition (a man must know himself along with all that he knows); another part of the subjective contribution (the senses) enters only *contingently* into the constitution of cognition (a man *might possibly* know things in other ways than those of seeing, touching, etc.) But the advocates of representationism, from being blind to this distinction, got entangled in a web of perplexity from which there was no extrication. They omitted to make out the analysis, and consequently they must be held either to have elevated the senses, considered as elements of cognition, to the same footing of necessity with the ego, or else to have reduced the ego, considered as an element of cognition, to the same footing of contingency with the senses. Whichever of these alternatives they may have adopted, the consequences were equally erroneous. If we suppose representationism to adopt the first alternative, and to hold that the senses are *necessary* to cognition – in other words, that no knowledge is possible except to an intelligence who is cognizant of such senses as we possess – in that case the material universe would be reduced to the predicament of a contradiction, if our senses were

---

[2] * In case any of our readers should be in doubt as to what is exactly meant by "representationism," it may be remarked, that this is the doctrine which holds that we are cognizant of, external objects only in or through some subjective medium, called indifferently by the name of *ideas, images,* or *species,* – in other words, that we are cognizant of things only in, or along with, our own *perceptions* of them; an undeniable truth, in spite of the exertions which Dr. Reid made to overthrow it. (See Prop. XI – Obs. 9)

withdrawn. It would become absolutely unknowable; because, upon this supposition, such senses as ours must necessarily be known along with it. And the only mode in which we could conceive it to subsist as a non-contradictory thing in our absence, would be by thinking it in synthesis with some mind which apprehended it exactly as we apprehend it — namely, by the way of seeing, hearing, touching, etc. But this is a species of anthropomorphical ontology which revolts us, and which we are by no means prepared to accept; and we refuse to accept it, because the conclusion is not logically reached. Reason does not assure us that all knowledge is impossible except under such sensational conditions as we are subject to. (The cause of the errors of representationism pointed out.)

13. Again, if we suppose representationism to adopt the second of these alternatives, and to hold that the ego is not a necessary, but is, like the senses, a mere contingent element of cognition — in other words, that knowledge is possible to an intelligence who is not cognizant of himself; in that case, the material universe would not be reduced to the predicament of a contradiction by the removal therefrom of every intelligent subject. It would still remain a knowable and intelligible thing, because upon this supposition no ego must necessarily be known or thought of along with it. But this is a species of materialistic ontology which revolts us as much as the other, and is fully more illogical. It assigns to matter an absolute and independent existence; and that step once taken, the descent into atheism is an inevitable (let people struggle against it as they please) as the gravitation of the stone towards the valley, when it has once been loosened from the overhanging mountain-top. But the ontology which assigns to matter *per se* an intelligible or non-contradictory existence, is founded on an abnegation of all the necessary principles of reason; and therefore the doctrine of a representative perception, if we suppose it to embrace the alternative now under consideration, or to hold that the subject is only contingently known along with the objects which it apprehends, is obnoxious to the most just censure. (The same subject continued.)

14. The system of Bishop Berkeley, also, was vitiated by the absence of this analysis, or by the neglect to distinguish the necessary from the contingent conditions of cognition. He falls into the error consequent on the adoption of the first of the alternatives just referred to. He saw that something subjective was a necessary and inseparable part of every object of cognition. But instead of main-

taining that it was the ego or oneself which clove inseparably to all that could be known, and that this element must be thought of along with all that is thought of, he rather held that it was the senses, or our perceptive modes of cognition, which clove inseparably to all that could be known, and that these required to be thought of along with all that could be thought of. These, just as much as the ego, were held by him to be the subjective part of the total synthesis of cognition which could not by any possibility be discounted. Hence the unsatisfactory character of his ontology, which, when tried by the test of a rigorous logic, will be found to invest the Deity—the supreme mind, the infinite ego, which the terms of his system necessarily compel him to place in synthesis with all things—with human modes of apprehension, with such senses as belong to man—and to invest Him with these, not as a matter of contingency, but as a matter of necessity. Our only safety lies in the consideration—a consideration which is a sound, indeed inevitable, logical inference—that our sensitive modes of apprehension are mere contingent elements and conditions of cognition; and that the ego or subject alone enters, of necessity, into the composition of everything which any intelligence can know. By occupying this ground, we neither require, on the one hand, to invest the Deity with such senses as ours; nor, on the other hand, to assign to matter an existence irrespective of all intelligence. The weak points in Berkeley's system are these three: first, he missed, though only by a hair's-breadth, the reduction of matter *per se* to a contradiction—an achievement which, until it be effected, speculation can accomplish nothing; secondly, in consequence of his neglect to distinguish the necessary from the contingent laws of knowledge, he failed to show that the supreme mind which the compulsory reason forced him to place in union with the universe, was not necessarily subject to our sensible modes of apprehension; and thirdly, he was hampered at every turn, as all philosophers have hitherto been, by the want of an agnoiology, or systematic doctrine of ignorance. In other respects, and viewed as approximations to the truth, the speculations of this philosopher, whether we consider the beauty and clearness of his style, or the depth of his insight, have done better service to the cause of metaphysical science than the lucubrations of all other modern thinkers put together. (The cause of Berkeley's errors pointed out.)

SELECTION 8
SECTION II
THE AGNOIOLOGY, OR THEORY OF IGNORANCE

PROPOSITION I

WHAT IGNORANCE IS

Ignorance is an intellectual defect, imperfection, privation, or shortcoming.

DEMONSTRATION

The deprivation of anything whose possession is consistent with the nature of the Being which wants it, is a defect. But ignorance is a deprivation of something which is consistent with the nature of intelligence: it is a deprivation of knowledge. Therefore ignorance is an intellectual defect, imperfection, privation, or shortcoming.

OBSERVATIONS AND EXPLANATIONS

1. The demonstration, and even the enunciation, of so obvious a truism may appear superfluous. It is introduced, however, in order that the doctrine of ignorance may be cleared from the very beginning, and to obviate any complaint to which the subsequent propositions might be exposed on the ground that their data of proof had been left doubtful or unexpressed. (Why this proposition is introduced.)

2. There have been many inquiries into the nature of knowledge: there has been no inquiry into the nature of ignorance. This section of the science has positively no forerunner; it is an entire novelty in philosophy—a circumstance which is mentioned merely to account for the fewness and brevity of the accompanying annotations. The agnoiology makes its way through a comparatively unencumbered field. There is something to pull down and something to build up; but the work both of demolition and of construction is much simpler than it was in the epistemology. (Novelty of the agnoiology)

3. This research, however, is indispensable. It is impossible to pass to the third section of the science except through the portals of this inquiry. For, suppose we were at once to carry forward the result of the epistemology into the ontology, and in answer to the question, What truly and absolutely is? were to reply, Objects *plus* a subject, the ego with something or thought present to it—this, and this alone, is what truly and absolutely is,—we should be instantly stopped by the rejoinder that this synthesis is, at best, merely the *known* abso-

lute, merely the substantial *in cognition*. It does not follow, the objector would say, that this synthesis alone is true and absolute Being—that it is the only true substantial *in existence*. He would argue that what truly and absolutely exists may be something very different from this—may be matter *per se* or mind *per se*, or something else of which we can form no sort of conception, and to which we can attach no predicate;—in short, that it may be, and is, that of which we are profoundly ignorant. (The agnoiology is indispensable.)

4. This plea has hitherto operated as an insurmountable barrier to the advance of metaphysics into the region of ontology. The fact of our extreme ignorance being undeniable, and the science of absolute existence being apparently inaccessible except on the postulation of a universal and unlimited knowledge, the difficulty of reconciling these two apparent incompatibilities seems to have disconcerted every system hitherto propounded. Any reasoned ontological conclusion establishing what alone absolutely exists, is obviously impossible in a system which admits our ignorance without entering into any critical inquiry as to its nature; while, on the other hand, the ontology of a system which denies our ignorance, or passes it over *sub silentio*, must either rest upon a false ground, or upon no ground at all,—on a false ground if our ignorance is denied—on no ground at all if it is not taken into account. In one or other of these predicaments all previous systems appear to be placed in reference to the problem of absolute existence: and hence a reasoned and systematic ontology has remained until this day a desideratum in speculative science, because a reasoned and systematic agnoiology has never yet been projected. (The plea of our ignorance a bar to ontology.)

5. The only way in which a deliverance from this dilemma can be effected is, by admitting our ignorance to the full, and then by instituting a searching inquiry into its nature and character. Conceding, then, that the conclusion of the epistemology cannot at present, with any logical propriety, be given out as valid for the ontology, the system proceeds to this investigation, and dealing not with the abstract, but only, or chiefly, with the concrete, it goes on to consider and to point out *what* we are, and can be, and *what* we are not, and cannot be, ignorant of. It is conceived that the research, thus conducted, will result in an effectual clearance of the ground for the establishment of a demonstrated ontology. (This obstacle can be removed only by an inquiry into the nature of ignorance.)

PROPOSITION II

IGNORANCE REMEDIABLE

All ignorance is *possibly* remediable.

DEMONSTRATION

No kind of knowledge is absolutely inconsistent with the nature of all intelligence. But unless all ignorance was *possibly* remediable, some kind of knowledge would be inconsistent with the nature of all intelligence, to wit, the knowledge by which the ignorance in question might be remedied. Therefore all ignorance is *possibly* remediable.

Or again, All defects are possibly remediable, otherwise they would not be defects. But ignorance is a defect (Prop. I.) Therefore all ignorance is possibly remediable.

OBSERVATIONS AND EXPLANATIONS

1. This proposition does not prove that all ignorance is *actually* remedied: in other words, that omniscience pervades the universe; but only that every form of ignorance is of such a character that it may *possibly* be removed; and that if certain kinds of ignorance are incident to certain orders of intelligence, they are not, of necessity, incident to other orders of intelligence. The subsequent movements of the system do not require that more than this should be proved. Neither does this proposition prove that all *human* ignorance is possibly remediable. It only proves that what man or any other intelligence may happen to be ignorant of, need not, of necessity, be unknown to all other intelligences (supposing that other intelligences exist). In other words, it merely proves that whatever any intelligence is ignorant of, may nevertheless be known, — known *actually* if an intelligence exists competent to know it — and known *potentially* even although no such intelligence should exist. Unless this were true, all ignorance would not be possibly remediable; and if all ignorance were not possibly remediable, some kind of knowledge would be inconsistent with the nature of all intelligence — in which case, ignorance would be no defect, because a defect is always the privation of some quality or attribute which is consistent with the nature of the being who is deprived of it. (All that this proposition proves.)

PROPOSITION III

THE LAW OF ALL IGNORANCE

We can be ignorant only of what can possibly be known; in other words, there can be an ignorance only of that of which there can be knowledge.

DEMONSTRATION

If we could be ignorant of what could not possibly be known by any intelligence, all ignorance would not be possibly remediable. The knowledge in which we were deficient could not be possessed by any intelligence. But all ignorance is possibly remediable (by Prop. II.) Therefore, we can be ignorant only of what can possibly be known; in other words, there can be an ignorance only of that of which there can be knowledge.

OBSERVATIONS AND EXPLANATIONS

1. This is the most important proposition in the agnoiology: indeed, with the exception of the first of the epistemology, it is the most fruitful and penetrating proposition in the whole system. It announces—for the first time, it is believed—the primary law of all ignorance, just as the first of the epistemology expresses the primary law of all knowledge. It is mainly by the aid of these two propositions that this system of Institutes is worked out. All the other propositions have an essential part to play in contributing to the final result; but these two are the most efficient performers in the work. If the reader has got well in hand these two truths—*first*, that there can be a knowledge of things only with the addition of a self or subject; and, *secondly*, that there can be an ignorance only of that of which there can be a knowledge—he will find himself in possession of a lever powerful enough to break open the innermost secrecies of nature. These two instruments cut deep and far—they lay open the universe from stem to stern. (Importance of this proposition.)

3. Ignorance, properly so called—that is, the ignorance which is a defect—must not be confounded with a nescience of the opposites of the necessary truths of reason; in other words, with a nescience of that which it would contradict the nature of all intelligence to know. Such nescience is no defect or imperfection—it is, on the contrary, the very strength or perfection of reason; and therefore such nescience is not to be regarded as ignorance. This simple but very important distinction must be explained and illustrated, for it is one

which is very apt to be lost sight of, or confounded; indeed, it has been altogether overlooked until now. (Distinction between ignorance and a nescience of the opposites of necessary truth)

4. When boys at school are taught Euclid, they learn that "the enclosure of space by two straight lines" is what cannot be known, — that "if equals be added to equals the wholes are *un*equal" is what cannot be known, — that "a part is greater than the whole" is what cannot be known, and so forth; but they do not learn that they are equally incapable of being ignorant of such matters. It is not necessary to apprise them of this in order to carry them forward in the study of mathematics. Nothing in geometry depends on the circumstance that we cannot be ignorant of what is deponed to in the opposites of the axioms. Hence this study merely shows us that there can be no knowledge of these opposites; it does not open our eyes to the fact that there can be no ignorance of them. It is obvious, however, that it is just as impossible for us to be ignorant of them as it is impossible for us to know them. No man can know that two and two make five, — but just as little can any man be ignorant of this; for suppose him ignorant of it, — in that case his ignorance could be removed only by teaching him that two and two *do* make five; but such instruction, instead of removing his ignorance, would remove his knowledge, and instead of giving him knowledge, would give him ignorance, or rather absurdity. The cure in this case would be itself the disease. (There can be no ignorance of the opposites of the geometrical axioms.)

5. An attention to the fact, that it is impossible for us (or for any intelligence) to be ignorant of the contradictory, that is, of the opposites of the necessary truths of reason, or, in other words, of that which cannot be known on any terms by any intelligence, though of no importance in mathematics, is of the utmost importance in metaphysics. Speculation can obtain a footing in ontology only by attending carefully to this circumstance, and by working it out through all its consequences. This truth is the key to the whole philosophy of ignorance. When we consider it well, we discover that the supposition that we can be ignorant of that which is absolutely and necessarily unknowable to all intelligence, is as extreme a violation of the law of contradiction as it is possible to conceive. We perceive that a nescience of the contradictory is not ignorance, but is the very essence of intelligence; and that there can be an ignorance only of that which can be known, or, otherwise expressed, of that which is

non-contradictory. With this discovery, light breaks into every cranny and recess of our science: the "holy jungle" of metaphysic is laid open to the searching day, and now no obstacle can stop the onward course of speculation. (There can be no ignorance of the contradictory.)

PROPOSITION IV

IGNORANCE OF OBJECTS PER SE

We cannot be ignorant of any kind of objects without a subject: in other words, there can be no ignorance of objects *per se*, or out of relation to a mind.

DEMONSTRATION

We can be ignorant only of what can possibly be known (Prop. III — Agnoiology). But objects without a subject cannot possibly be known (Props. I and II — Epistemology). Therefore we cannot be ignorant of objects without a subject; and thus there can be no ignorance of objects *per se*.

OBSERVATIONS AND EXPLANATIONS

1. The truths of the agnoiology now come down in a torrent. The epistemology has unlocked all the sluices. The opening propositions of the agnoiology have cleared away all obstructions which might remain; and we have now little more to do than to look on while the waters take their own unimpeded course. The counter-propositions will be rapidly swept away before the irresistible flood. (The truths now pour down fast.)

PROPOSITION V

IGNORANCE OF MATTER PER SE

We cannot be ignorant of material things out of all relation to a mind, subject, or self: in other words, there can be no ignorance of matter *per se*.

DEMONSTRATION

Material things out of all relation to a mind, subject, or self, cannot possibly be known (Prop. IV — Epistemology). But there can be no ignorance of what cannot possibly be known (Prop. III — Agnoiology). Therefore we cannot be ignorant of material things out of all relation to a mind, subject, or self; in other words, there can be no ignorance of matter *per se*.

OBSERVATIONS AND EXPLANATIONS

7. Many philosophers have seen that the human mind cannot know things *by and in themselves*, because it can show them only as modified and supplemented by its own faculties of cognition; in other words, that it can know them only as *seen* things, as *touched* things, and so forth—some subjective contribution being always added to the thing, and the total object apprehended being thus a composite product made up of a part which was objective and a part which was subjective. Hence they concluded, very rashly and inconsiderately, that we were ignorant of the objective part *per se*, or separated from the subjective part. They adopted this counter-proposition. They gave out that we were ignorant of matter *per se*, of things by and in themselves. This conclusion is more particularly embraced and insisted upon by Kant. (Psychological conclusions as to our ignorance of matter *per se*.)

8. This conclusion, however, rests on an assumption which contradicts the strongest and most essential principles of reason. It is founded on the assumption that these things may *possibly* be known as they are, by and in themselves, and out of relation to all intelligence. This premise must be postulated by those who maintain that we are ignorant of material things *per se*; because it would be manifestly absurd to assert that we could be ignorant of what could not possibly be known. This, then, is their postulation; and if it were true, or if it could be conceded, their conclusion would be perfectly legitimate. (It rests on a contradictory assumption.)

9. But the whole tenor of this work has proved that the postulation in question is contradictory. It stands opposed to the primary law of all knowledge, as expressed in the first proposition of the epistemology, which declares that all cognition of material or other things *per se* is impossible, inasmuch as every intelligence (actual or possible) which apprehends material things, must apprehend itself along with them; in other words, must apprehend them, not *per se*, but *cum alio*. Hence the conclusion now under discussion is contradictory, because it is founded on an assumption which is contradictory: and thus the counter-proposition which contends for our ignorance of matter *per se*, or of the universe as it exists by and in itself, is annihilated, by the artillery of necessary truth. (The psychological conclusion therefore, is contradictory.)

10. From these remarks it is obvious that Kant and other philosophers have fallen into the mistake of supposing that we would be

ignorant of material things *per se* through an inattention to the causes which render them absolutely unknowable. They supposed that they were simply unknowable by us on account of the limitation or imperfection of our faculties of cognition, but that they were still possibly knowable by intelligences competent to know them. In the course of this work, however, it has been repeatedly shown that our incompetency to know matter *per se* is due to no such cause, but is attributable to the essential structure of all intelligence, and to the necessary laws of all cognition. Hence matter *per se* is not the simply unknowable and inconceivable to us — it is the absolutely unknowable and inconceivable in itself; in other words, it is the contradictory, — a consideration which dislodges it from our ignorance just as effectually as it dislodges it from our knowledge, as must be apparent to all who have mastered the very simple argument by which this conclusion is established. (The origin of the psychological mistake pointed out.)

PROPOSITION VI

IGNORANCE OF THE UNIVERSAL AND PARTICULAR

We cannot be ignorant either of the universal element of cognition *per se*, or of the particular element of cognition *per se*.

DEMONSTRATION

We cannot be ignorant of the universal element apart from the particular element, or of the particular element apart from the universal element of cognition, because (by Prop. VI — Epistemology) there can be no knowledge of the universal apart from the particular, or of the particular apart from the universal. But what there can be no knowledge of there can be no ignorance of (Prop. III. — Agnoiology.) Therefore we cannot be ignorant of the universal element of cognition *per se*, or of the particular element of cognition *per se*.

PROPOSITION VII

IGNORANCE OF THE EGO PER SE

We cannot be ignorant of the ego *per se*, in other words, there can be no ignorance of the mind in a state of pure indetermination, or with no thing or thought present to it.

DEMONSTRATION

There can be no ignorance of the ego or mind *per se*, because (by Prop. IX – Epistemology) there can be no knowledge of it; and because (by Prop. III – Agnoiology) there can be no ignorance of that of which there can be no knowledge.

PROPOSITION VIII

THE OBJECT OF ALL IGNORANCE

The object of all ignorance, whatever it may be, is always something more than is usually regarded as the object. It always is, and must be, not any particular thing merely, but the synthesis of the particular and the universal: it must always consist of a subjective as well as of an objective element; in other words, the object of all ignorance is, of necessity, some-object-*plus*-some-subject.

DEMONSTRATION

There can be ignorance only of the knowable (Prop. III – Agnoiology.) But the only knowable is the union of the objective and subjective – the synthesis of the universal and particular – the concretion of the ego and the non-ego. (Props. I.; II.; III.; VI.; and IX – Epistemology.) Therefore there can be an ignorance only of the objective and subjective in union, only of the synthesis of the universal and particular, only of the concretion of the ego and the non-ego; in other words, the object of all ignorance is, of necessity, some-object-*plus*-some-subject.

2. Novel, and somewhat startling, as this doctrine may seem, it will be found, on reflection, to be the only one which is consistent with the dictates of an enlightened common sense; and the more it is scrutinized, the truer and the more impregnable will it appear. If we are ignorant at all (and who will question our ignorance?) we must be ignorant of something; and this something is not nothing, nor is it the contradictory. That is admitted on all hands. But every attempt to fix the object of our ignorance as anything but object + subject *must* have the effect of fixing it either as nothing, or as the contradictory. Let it be fixed as things *per se*, or as thoughts *per se* – that is, without any subject; but things or thoughts, without any subject, are the contradictory, inasmuch as they are the absolutely unknowable and inconceivable. Therefore, unless we can be ignorant of the contradictory (a supposition which is itself contradictory, and in the highest degree absurd), we cannot be ignorant of things *per se*, or of thoughts

per se. Again, let it be fixed as subject *per se*, as the ego with no thing or thought present to it. But the subject *per se* is equally contradictory with object *per se*. It cannot be known on any terms by any intelligence; and therefore, unless we entertain the absurd supposition that we can be ignorant of the contradictory, we cannot be ignorant of the subject, or ego, or mind, *per se*. Again, let the object of our ignorance be fixed as nothing. But who was ever so foolish as to maintain that we were ignorant of nothing? By the very terms of the research, in which our ignorance is admitted, we confess ourselves to be ignorant or something. And therefore, since this something cannot be things by themselves, or the non-ego *per se*, and cannot be the mind by itself, or the ego *per se*, and moreover cannot be nothing, it must be the synthesis of things and some mind—the non-ego *plus* some ego—in short, some-object-plus-some-subject. If any other alternative is left which the object of our ignorance may be, this system will be glad to learn what that alternative is. (The object of ignorance is neither nothing nor the contradictory.)

4. If this doctrine of ignorance has been missed by previous inquirers, the cause of the oversight is to be found in the inaccuracy of their observations in regard to the object of all knowledge. Until this had been fixed as consisting necessarily of an objective and a subjective element, no theory determining demonstrably the object of all ignorance was possible. But we have seen throughout the epistemology, how loose, wavering, inexact, erroneous, and indeed contradictory, the opinions of philosophers in general, and of psychologists in particular, have been in regard to the object of knowledge; and hence it is not surprising that their opinions should have been equally confused, or rather more confused and unsettled, in regard to the object of ignorance. Many previous approximations, indeed, have been made to the true theory of knowledge. It has been seen, more than once, that the unity of object and subject is the only possible object of cognition. But this doctrine, not having been worked through all its phases, or followed out into all its consequences, remained, as has been said, a mere approximation to the truth. It was left very far in arrear; and hence the true doctrine of ignorance, which depends entirely on the perfecting of that antecedent speculation, has never shown itself until now. (What has caused this doctrine to be missed?)

5. Another cause of the omission is to be found in the circumstance that philosophers hitherto have been satisfied with making our ignorance a theme for moral declamation, instead of making it a sub-

ject for metaphysical inquiry. Its quantity has distracted their attention from its quality. "Heu, quantum est quod nescimus!" they exclaim pathetically. "What an immensity of ignorance is ours!" True; but these whinings will never teach us what ignorance is, what its law is, and what its object is: and this alone is what we, as searchers after truth, are interested in finding out. To tell us *how much* a thing is, will never teach us *what* it is, as our psychologists, moralizing on the boundlessness of human ignorance, seem to suppose. "What does this cheese *consist of*?" says a customer to his grocer. "Consist of!" answers the man, "consist of; why, it *weighs* twenty pounds to a hair, and *that* is what it consists of." Our psychologists are that grocer. We ask them *what* ignorance is, and *what* we are ignorant of? and they reply that, while our knowledge is as mere dust in the balance, our ignorance is *so great* that it might ballast the whole British navy. This, as has been said, is to mistake a question as to quality, for a question as to quantity—rather a serious error for a philosopher to fall into. (Another circumstance which has caused it to be missed.)

8. The advantage of discriminating the necessary from the contingent conditions of knowledge effected in the twenty-second proposition of the epistemology now becomes apparent. The object of our ignorance must be a subject *plus* some object. But the subject comprised in this synthesis need not know things in the ways in which we know them, but may be cognizant of them in ways totally different, and the objects comprised in this synthesis may be altogether different from the objects of which we are cognizant. All that is fixed by reason as necessary is, that the object of which we are ignorant should be objects *plus* a subject; because any other object than this is contradictory, as has been shown, again and again, on necessary grounds of reason. But had this analysis not been effected, the important conclusion referred to could not have been reached. If the discrimination had not been made—in other words, if the necessary laws had been reduced to a level with the contingent laws—objects *per se*, or without any subject, would have been fixed as the object of our ignorance; in which case materialism would have triumphed, and all the higher interests of man, in behalf of which speculation so zealously contends, would have been placed in jeopardy: reasoning at least could have done nothing towards their extrication and security. Again, if the contingent laws had been elevated to a level with the necessary laws, the only possible object of our ignorance would

have been a subject apprehending things *exactly as we apprehend them*. This would have been the only possible object of ignorance, because, in the circumstances supposed it would have been the only possible object of knowledge; in which case the sophism of Protagoras would have been verified, that man is the measure of the universe. Our ontology would have been anthropomorphical and revolting. But the accomplishment of the analysis referred to, extricates the system from this dilemma. By distinguishing the necessary from the contingent laws of cognition, we were able to obtain demonstrably in the epistemology a mind, or self, or subject plus *some* objects (though *what* objects it is impossible to say—this being the particular, variable, and inexhaustible element of cognition) as the only possible object of all knowledge; and in like manner, this distinction enables us to obtain demonstrably in the agnoiology a mind, or self, or subject plus *some* objects (though *what* objects it is impossible to say—this being the particular, variable, and inexhaustible element of ignorance) as the only possible object of all ignorance. The system is thus advancing in strength towards the position where ontology lies in-trenched; it is drawing closer and closer its lines of circumvallation around the encampment of Absolute Existence, and has already driven in its outposts. (The advantage of discriminating the necessary from the contingent laws of knowledge.)

9. From these remarks it will be seen, that this doctrine, so far from denying our ignorance, rather represents it as double. In fixing the object of ignorance as non-contradictory—in other words, in insisting (and in proving) that whenever we are ignorant of an object we must also be ignorant of a subject—this system teaches that we are ignorant of an intelligible, that is, not-nonsensical, *whole*; whereas ordinary thinking and psychology teach that we are ignorant of an unintelligible and nonsensical *half* (objects *per se*). It is true that the system, in concluding that there can be no ignorance of the contradictory, limits or abridges our ignorance in that particular direction. But, as has been said, it extends it in another direction, by showing that, in so far as we are ignorant, our ignorance must have for its object not merely one of the factors or elements of cognition, but must have for its object both of them,—the universal no less than the particular element, the subjective no less than the objective factor. Whenever we suppose that we can be ignorant of either of these without being ignorant of the other, we suppose that we can be ignorant of the contradictory,—an option which everyone who reflects

upon its absurdity will be inclined forthwith to abandon. Hence it is submitted that these Institutes are more humble in their pretensions, and acknowledge more fully the extent of man's ignorance, than any of those systems which lay claim ostentatiously to the virtue of humility, and talk about the infinite particulars which lie beyond our cognizance, without considering very critically what they are saying. (This system is more humble in its pretensions than other systems.)

13. As a corollary of this proposition, it follows that object + subject is the only substantial, and absolute in ignorance, just as this synthesis is the only substantial and absolute in cognition. It is, however, unnecessary to enunciate this truth in a distinct and separate proposition; suffice it to say, that the mere factors of this synthesis cannot either of them be the substantial and absolute in ignorance, because there can be no knowledge of them apart from each other; and there can be no ignorance of what there can be no knowledge of. Hence the only absolute and substantial reality of which we can be ignorant is a subject in union with objects of some kind or other. (The substantial and absolute in ignorance.)

SELECTION 9

SECTION III
THE ONTOLOGY, OR THEORY OF BEING

PROPOSITION I

THE THREE ALTERNATIVES AS TO ABSOLUTE EXISTENCE

That which truly is, or, as it shall be usually termed, Absolute Existence, is either, *first*, that which we know; or it is, *secondly*, that which we are ignorant of; or it is *thirdly*, that which we neither know nor are ignorant of; and no other alternative is possible.

DEMONSTRATION

If a thing is not *this*, it may be *that*; but if it is not this, and not that, it *must* be neither this nor that. (This is one of the strongest forms in which the law of contradiction, the criterion of all necessary truth, can be expressed.) Hence if Absolute Existence is not that which we know, it may be that which we are ignorant of; but if it is not that which we know, and not that which we are ignorant of, it must be that which we neither know nor are ignorant of. Therefore Absolute Existence is either, *first*, that which we know; or, *secondly*, that which we are ignorant of; or, *thirdly*, that which we neither know nor are ignorant of; and no other alternative is possible.

OBSERVATIONS AND EXPLANATIONS

1. The problem of ontology, as announced in the Introduction, § 54, is, What is? in the proper and emphatic sense of the word IS. What absolutely and independently exists? What, and what alone, possesses a clear, detached, emancipated, substantial, genuine, or *un-parasitical* Being? What can that which possesses this be declared to be? What is its character? What predicate can be attached to it? This is the problem which ontology is called upon to resolve; and it will be seen as we advance, that without the whole of the preceding demonstrations, this question is insoluble, but with them its reasoned settlement may be reached. (The problem of ontology stated.)

PROPOSITION II

A PREMISE BY WHICH THE THIRD ALTERNATIVE IS ELIMINATED

Whatever we neither know nor are ignorant of is the contradictory.

DEMONSTRATION

If that which we neither know nor are ignorant of were not the contradictory, it would be knowable; because whatever is not contradictory is knowable. But if it (that, viz., which we neither know nor are ignorant of) were knowable, we must either know it or be ignorant of it. If we know it, we cannot neither know it nor be ignorant of it; and if we are ignorant of it, we cannot neither know it nor be ignorant of it. Therefore whatever we neither know nor are ignorant of cannot be knowable; and not being knowable, it must be the contradictory; because everything except the contradictory is knowable. Consequently, whatever we neither know nor are ignorant of, is, and must be, the contradictory.

PROPOSITION III

A PREMISE BY WHICH THE THIRD ALTERNATIVE IS ELIMINATED

Absolute Existence, or Being in itself, is not the contradictory.

DEMONSTRATION

There is no absurdity or contradiction involved in the supposition that something (whatever it may be), really and truly, and absolutely exists. And therefore, inasmuch as no absurdity or contradiction attaches to this supposition, no absurdity or contradiction attaches to that to which this supposition refers—namely, to Being in itself. Consequently Absolute Existence, or Being in itself, is not the contradictory.

OBSERVATIONS AND EXPLANATIONS

1. Although a demonstration of this proposition is given, none, strictly speaking, is required. The proposition is postulated or presupposed by the very terms of the inquiry, and must be conceded by all who enter on the study of metaphysics. The ultimate problem of the science is, *what is truth?* – (See Introduction § 54.) This problem necessarily takes for granted two points: first, that truth is; and secondly that truth is not nonsense or the contradictory. The science is not called upon to prove *that* truth is, and that it is not the contradictory. This must be conceded. The science is merely called upon to find out and prove *what* truth is; it merely undertakes to affix to truth some predicate descriptive and explanatory of its character. In the same way the science is not called upon to prove either *that* Absolute Existence is, or that it is not the contradictory. It takes, and must be allowed to take, this for granted: it is merely called upon to find out and demonstrate *what* Absolute Existence is; in other words, to affix to it some predicate declaratory of its nature and character. In this respect the metaphysician resembles the mathematician, who is not called upon to prove either that his diagrams *are*, or that they involve no contradiction, but simply to demonstrate *what* relations they and their various parts bear to one another. So that if the foregoing demonstration should appear not altogether satisfactory, the reader is requested to remember that the proposition is one which the science is entitled to postulate, and one which even the most extravagant skepticism cannot call in question. No form of skepticism has ever questioned the fact *that* something absolutely exists, or has ever maintained that this something was the nonsensical. The skeptic, even when he carries his opinions to an extreme, merely doubts or denies our competency to find out and declare *what* absolutely exists. (The truth of this proposition is presupposed by the very nature of this inquiry.)

PROPOSITION IV

ELIMINATES THE THIRD ALTERNATIVE

Absolute Existence is not what we neither know nor are ignorant of.

DEMONSTRATION

Whatever we neither know nor are ignorant of is the contradictory (Prop. II.) Absolute Existence is not the contradictory (Prop. III.) Therefore Absolute Existence is not what we neither know nor are ignorant of.

PROPOSITION V

THE REMAINING ALTERNATIVES

Absolute Existence is either that which we know or that which we are ignorant of.

DEMONSTRATION

It was proved by Proposition I, that Absolute Existence has only three alternative characters: it is either, first, that which we know; or secondly, that which we are ignorant of; or, thirdly, that which we neither know nor we are ignorant of. The third alternative has been excluded by Proposition IV. Absolute Existence, therefore, must be the one or other of the two remaining alternatives: in other words, it is either that which we know or that which we are ignorant of.

OBSERVATIONS AND EXPLANATIONS

1. The elimination of the third alternative, and the proof that Absolute Existence is either that which we know or that which we are ignorant of, secures the key of the ontology, and renders her position impregnable. Her victory is now assured against whatever force may be brought against her. She has now but to put forth her hand to pluck the fruit of all her previous labors. Because the alternative characters of Absolute Existence having been reduced to two — in other words, Absolute Existence having been proved to be either that which we know or that which we are ignorant of, the system is able to deal with it and to declare what it is, whichever of the two alternatives be embraced. Should "Being in itself" be held to be that which we know, the result of the epistemology enables us to affix to it a predicate declaratory of its nature — for the epistemology has settled what alone it is possible for us to know. Should "Being in itself" be held to be that which we are ignorant of, the result of the agnoiology (which has been proved to be coincident with the result

of the epistemology) enables us to affix to it *the very same* predicate declaratory of its nature. Thus the system makes good its point, and redeems its pledge (see Introduction § 60), whichever horn of the dilemma be presented to it, as shall be shown articulately in Proposition X. Meanwhile a few articles must be introduced for the purpose of clearing away the wrecks of antecedent systems, and of giving the finishing stroke to the cardinal doctrines of psychology, which are still dragging out, in book and in lecture room, a debilitated and semi-animate existence. (This proposition secures the key of the ontology.)

PROPOSITION VI

WHAT ABSOLUTE EXISTENCE IS NOT

Absolute Existence is not matter *per se*: in other words, *mere* material things have no true and independent Being.

DEMONSTRATION

Matter *per se* is neither that which we know (Prop. IV — Epistemology) nor that which we are ignorant of (Prop. V. Agnoiology). But Absolute Existence is either that which we know or that which we are ignorant of (Prop. V — Ontology). Therefore Absolute Existence is not matter *per se*; in other words *mere* material things have no true and independent Being.

Or again — Matter *per se* is the contradictory, inasmuch as it is necessarily unknowable by all intelligence (Prop. IV — Epistemology). But Absolute Existence is not the contradictory (Prop. III — Ontology). It may possibly be known. Therefore Absolute Existence is not matter *per se*, etc.

OBSERVATIONS AND EXPLANATIONS

1. *Sixth Counter-proposition* — "Absolute Existence is, or at least may be, matter *per se*; in other words, *mere* material things have, or may have, a true and independent Being." (Sixth counter-proposition)

2. There can be no doubt that ordinary thinking embraces this counter-proposition in its most dogmatical expression, and asserts positively that mere material things not only may have, but have a true and absolute and independent existence. Psychology, too, has a decided leaning towards this positive asseveration, which is advocated more particularly by our whole Scottish philosophy of commonsense. After all that has been said, it is unnecessary to do more than refer to this opinion as part of the *debris* of a defunct and

exploded psychology, which is now swept away and effaced forever from science by these ontological institutes. (Is approved of by ordinary thinking, and by psychology)

3. When it is asserted that material things have no *Absolute* Existence, this must not be confounded with the affirmation that they have no existence *at all*. They have a spurious, or inchoate, or dependent existence. This has always been conceded by genuine speculation, although even this kind of existence may have been denied to them by some spurious systems of idealism. But absolute or independent existence only arises when the incipience of material things is supplemented by the element necessary to complete it. In short, they are what the Greek speculators called the μή ὄντα (that is, the contradictory), but they are not the οὐκ ὄντα (that is, the intelligibly non-existent). By themselves, material things are not *nothing*, but they are *nonsense*. (In what sense material things exist.)

PROPOSITION VII

WHAT ABSOLUTE EXISTENCE IS NOT

Absolute Existence is not the particular by itself, nor is it the universal by itself; in other words, particular things prescinded from the universal have no absolute existence, nor have universal things prescinded from the particular any absolute existence.

DEMONSTRATION

There can be no knowledge of the particular by itself (Prop. VI – Epistemology). There can be no ignorance of the particular by itself (Prop. VI – Agnoiology). But Absolute Existence is that of which there is either a knowledge or an ignorance (Prop. V – Ontology). Therefore Absolute Existence is not the particular by itself. Again, there can be no knowledge of the universal by itself (Prop. VI – Epistemology). There can be no ignorance of the universal by itself (Prop. VI – Agnoiology). But Absolute Existence is that of which there is either a knowledge or an ignorance (Prop. V – Ontology). Therefore Absolute Existence is not the universal by itself. And thus particular things prescinded from the universal have no absolute existence, nor have universal things prescinded from the particular any absolute existence.

PROPOSITION VIII
WHAT ABSOLUTE EXISTENCE IS NOT

Absolute Existence is not the ego *per se*, or the mind in a state of pure indetermination — that is, with no such thing or thought present to it: in other words, the ego *per se* is not that which truly and absolutely exists.

DEMONSTRATION

The ego *per se*, or the mind in a state of pure indetermination, is what we cannot know (Prop. IX — Epistemology): it is what we cannot be ignorant of (Prop. VII — Agnoiology). But absolute Existence is what we either know or are ignorant of (Prop. V — Ontology). Therefore Absolute Existence is not the ego *per se*, or the mind in a state of pure indetermination; in other words, the ego *per se* is not that which truly and absolutely exists.

PROPOSITION IX
THE ORIGIN OF KNOWLEDGE

Matter is not the cause of our perceptive cognitions; in other words, our knowledge of material things is not an effect proceeding from, and brought about by, material things.

DEMONSTRATION

Matter is the particular part, or peculiar element, of some of our cognitions — of those, viz., which we term perceptions (Prop. VII — Epistemology). But the *part* of a cognition, cannot be the *cause* of a cognition. Therefore matter is not the cause of our perceptive cognitions; in other words, our knowledge of material things is not an effect proceeding from, and brought about by, material things.

OBSERVATIONS AND EXPLANATIONS

1. It is at this place that the question as to the origin of our knowledge falls to be discussed, and that the opinions of philosophers respecting it come under review: for this question is ontological, just as the inquiry into the actual character and composition of our cognitions is epistemological. It is of the utmost importance that these inquiries should be kept distinct, and that the *nature* of our knowledge should be accurately ascertained, before any attempt is made to explain its *origin*. This order, however, has been reversed: philosophers have treated of the origin of knowledge before they had attained to any definite conception of its nature; they explored the causes of the fact,

but the fact itself they left undetermined: and to this reversal of the right method of research are to be attributed all the perplexities and errors in which they got involved in the course of the controversy. (Question as to the origin of knowledge—has been erroneously treated.)

2. The fundamental assumption which has hitherto rendered abortive every attempt to settle this question is the hypothesis that matter exists, not as an element of cognition, but in an absolute capacity, or irrespective of all intelligence. Whether this assumption be true or not, it was not a position to start from. It is an ontological offshoot from an uncritical and erroneous epistemology. To comprehend the salient points of the controversy respecting the origin of knowledge, and the perplexities by which it has been beset at every stage, we have but to trace this assumption into its consequences. (The assumption which vitiates the discussion)

3. The attribution of absolute existence to material things leads at once to the inference that matter operates as a cause in the production of our cognitions. And accordingly, when the question as to the origin of knowledge arose, this was the solution proposed—an explanation which finds expression in the following counter-proposition. *Ninth Counter-proposition*: "Matter is the *cause* of our perceptive cognitions; in other words, our knowledge of material things is an *effect* proceeding from, and brought about by, material things." This opinion is the first consequence which flows from the assumption referred to. (First consequences of the assumption Ninth counter-proposition,)

4. This consequence may seem harmless enough; the next is more serious. If our knowledge, or perception, of material things be an effect produced by material things, this knowledge (the effect) must be all that we truly apprehend: the material things themselves (the cause) must elude or transcend our observation. The position is that matter is not itself our knowledge, or any part of our knowledge, but is merely the cause of our knowledge, the originator of our perceptions: hence the perceptions alone are the objects of the mind; their cause comes not within the pale of our cognition. And thus the second consequence of the assumption that material things have an absolute existence is the inevitable conclusion that we have no knowledge of *them*, but only a knowledge of their *effects*. Thus arises, and thus arose, the doctrine of a representative perception—a doctrine which, substituting for the real material universe what Berke-

ley calls "a false imaginary glare," is alike unsatisfactory to the philosophical and to the un-philosophical mind. (Second consequence — the doctrine of representationism)

5. The earliest form of the representative hypothesis is that which is known in the history of philosophy under the name of Physical Influx (*influxus physicus*). The advocates of this scheme maintained that real things are the efficient causes of our perceptions, the word "efficient" being employed to signify that the things, by means of some positive power or inherent virtue which they possessed, were competent to transmit to the mind, knowledge of themselves. This theory held that man was cognizant, not of things themselves, but only of certain ideal copies, or intelligible transcripts of them; and that these were caused, first, or remotely, by the operation of material things on the senses, and secondly, or proximately, by the operation of the senses on the mind; so that the doctrine of physical influx was rather an hypothesis explanatory of the way in which the senses or nervous system affected the mind, than of the way in which external objects affected the nervous system. If attempted, by invoking the casual relation, to explain the intercourse which subsists between the body and the mind. External objects were supposed to operate on the nervous system by the transmission of some kind of influence — the nervous system was supposed to carry on the process by the transmission of certain images or representations — and thus our knowledge of external things was supposed to be brought about. The representations alone came before the mind; the things by which they were caused remained occult and unknown. (The earliest form of representationism, Physical Influx.)

6. The first important correction which this crude hypothesis sustained was at the hands of the French philosopher Des Cartes. The doctrine was, that things remotely, and the senses proximately, transmitted to the mind a knowledge of external objects. Des Cartes had an eye for the fallacy of that position. He saw that things and the senses could not more transmit cognitions to the mind than a man can transmit to a beggar a guinea which he has not got. Material things, including of course the organs of sense, have no knowledge to give to man; and therefore man cannot receive his knowledge from material things; in other words, matter cannot be the *efficient* cause of our perceptions. The explaining cause is not adequate to the production of the effect to be explained. To derive our perceptions of materials things from material things, is to derive them from a

source in which they are not contained, and which is therefore not competent to impart them. Such is the substance of the revolution effected by Des Cartes on this the standard opinion in the common schools of philosophy; and the downfall of the hypothesis of Physical Influx was the result. (Correction of this doctrine by Des Cartes)

7. The Cartesian reform was followed by important consequences. The question now arose — What, then, is the cause of our knowledge; from whence do we derive our cognitions of external objects? If material things and the organs of sense do not originate them, — *what* originates them? Their efficient cause, answers Des Cartes, their true source, is the power and will of the Deity, who, containing within Himself every perfection, is competent to produce and to impart to us perceptions, or whatever else he may be pleased to produce and to impart. (Consequences of the Cartesian correction)

8. This solution gave a new turn to the discussion. *Now* skepticism in regard to the existence of material things broke loose. *Now* the question emerged — What proof is there that matter exists at all? So long as material things were held to be the causes of our perceptions, a sufficient guarantee for their existence was obtained; for we can scarcely maintain that one thing is the cause of another, without conceding that the former thing exists. But now, when this doctrine is set aside as untenable — now, when it is held that material things are not, and cannot be, the causes of our perceptions, and when it is further maintained that these are to be attributed to an entirely different origin, the question may reasonably be put — What evidence is there in support of the existence of matter? The material universe is now superfluous and otiose. It has no part to play — no purpose to fulfill. Our perceptive cognitions are brought about without its aid. All goes on as well, or better, without it. It is a mere cumberer of the ground,

' Αχρεῖον καί παράορον δέμας.

Why not say at once that it is a nonentity? Thus skepticism and idealism are the consequences, not very far removed, of the assumption that matter has an absolute existence. Commencing with the hypothesis that matter exists *absolutely*, philosophers have been led on, by the inevitable windings of the discussion, to doubt or to deny that it exists *at all*. (Skepticism and idealism arise)

9. It might have been expected that these perplexities would have thrown philosophers back upon a severer examination of the data on

which they were proceeding, and would have suspended their inquiry into the origin of our knowledge until the state of the fact as to its actual nature had been determined. But no such result ensued. Philosophers still busied themselves about its causes; and in order to salve the skepticism which his own reform had provoked, Des Cartes came to the rescue of the material universe armed with these two arguments: first, that matter, although not the *cause*, is nevertheless the *occasion*, of our perceptions. It affords the occasions on which the Deity (the efficient cause and true source of all our knowledge) calls up in our minds the appropriate presentations. This is the Cartesian doctrine of occasional, as distinguished from efficient, causes. And secondly, he argues that the Deity, from whom can proceed no fallacious beliefs, has implanted within us a conviction of the independent existence of material things. To which arguments the answer is, that if our perceptions are originated by the Divine Power, it is more probable that they are called into being *directly*, and not through the circuitous process alleged by the Cartesians, in which certain material existences, of which we know nothing, are supposed to serve as the occasions on which the Deity is pleased to bring about in our minds certain corresponding representations; and secondly, that it is not true that any man really believes in the existence of material things out of all relation to an intelligent mind — for, however much we may deceive ourselves on this point, it is certain that we cannot believe in that which we cannot, by any possibility, think of — and it is certain that we can think of material things only in association with our own, or some other, intelligence. (The Cartesian salvo-hypothesis of "Occasional Causes: its insufficiency.)

10. Mallebranche, following in the wake of Des Cartes, advocated similar opinions. He perceived and avoided, the contradiction involved in the supposition that material things *cause* our cognitions. Our perceptions of extension, figure, and solidity (the primary qualities, as they are called), he attributed to the direct operation of the Deity. This is what he means by our "vision of all things in God," who, according to Mallebranche, is the "light of all our seeing." Our sensations of heat, color, and so forth, he referred to certain laws of our own nature. Although material things are superfluous and otiose by the terms of this, no less than by the terms of the Cartesian hypothesis, still Mallebranche asserts their independent existence on the authority of revelation, as Des Cartes had attempted to vindicate it on the ground of natural belief — "In the beginning God cre-

ated the heavens and earth" — as if that statement was equivalent to the declaration that material things were invested with an absolute existence, and had a subsistency out of relation to all intelligence! (Mallebranche: His "Vision of all things in God.")

11. Leibnitz, also, studiously avoided all acknowledgment of matter as the transmitting cause of our cognitions. He supposed a double series of phenomena running on simultaneously in the mind and in the body, and coincident, although absolutely independent of each other. No influence of any kind passed from mind to body, or from body to mind; but the pre-concerted arrangements of each brought about an entire concordance between the two series of changes — a concordance in which the mental representations were never at variance with the bodily impressions, although in no respect induced by them; nor the bodily movements ever at cross-purposes with the mental volitions, although in no degree dependent upon them — just as two clocks may keep time together, although no sort of influence is transmitted from the one to the other. This is the doctrine of Pre-established Harmony — a scheme which differs from that of "occasional causes" only in this respect, that by the former hypothesis the accordance of the mental and the bodily phenomena was supposed to be prearranged, once for all, by the Divine Power, while by the latter their harmony was supposed to be effected by His constant and ever-renewed interposition. (Leibnitz: His "Pre-established Harmony.")

12. Extravagant as these hypotheses may seem, they are less so than the position which they controverted; the doctrine, namely, of physical influx, which asserted that our cognitions were caused or produced by material things operating upon our minds. They are commendable, as evidences of a reaction or struggle against that contradictory position. But they did not go to the root of the mischief: they involved no critical inquiry into the essential structure of all cognition; and hence they failed to reduce matter *per se* to the condition of a contradiction. (Character of these hypotheses)

13. Locke's explanation of the origin of our knowledge differs from the opinions of his predecessors only by being more ambiguous and perfunctory. Material things exist, and give rise to our sensible ideas or perceptions, because they are fitted to do so by the Divine law and appointment. That sentence contains the substance of all that has been advanced by Locke on the subject now under consideration, and the doctrine which it expresses is obviously a mere

jumble of the four hypotheses which have just been commented on. Like his predecessors, Locke was a stanch representationist. The philosopher next to be named was the first who distinctly promulgated a doctrine of intuitive perception, although he seldom gets credit for having done so. (Locke's explanation)

14. Berkeley's merits and defects have been already touched upon (see Epistemology, Prop. XXII. Obs. 14). His system, with all its imperfections, was an immense improvement upon those which had preceded it. It was an inquiry, not so much into the origin as into the nature of our knowledge. It was mainly a polemic against the doctrine of representationism in all its forms. Other systems had declared that our perceptions were representative of material realities—that the perceptions alone were known—that the realities themselves were occult. Looking merely to the actual structure, and not to the supposed origin, of our cognitions, Berkeley brought the material reality itself into the immediate presence of the mind, by showing, not indeed that it was the object, but that it was *part* of the object of our cognition. The total and immediate object of the mind is, with Berkeley, the material thing itself (and no mere representation of it), with the addition, however, of some subjective and heterogeneous element. It is a synthesis of the objective and the subjective; the thing *plus* the sense (sight or touch, etc.), a unit indivisible *by us* at least. Berkeley thus accomplished the very task which, fifty or sixty years afterwards, Reid labored at in vain. He taught a doctrine of intuitive, as distinguished from a doctrine of representative, perception; and he taught it on the only grounds on which such a doctrine can be maintained. (Berkeley: His doctrine of intuitive perception.)

15. Berkeley's system, however, was invalidated by a fundamental weakness, which was this, that it was rather an exposition of the contingent structure of *our* knowledge, than an exposition of the necessary structure of *all* knowledge. As has been stated elsewhere, he does not sufficiently distinguish the necessary from the contingent laws of cognition, or distinctly lay down the former as binding on intelligence universally. He saw that every object of *our* cognition must contain and present a subjective element. But he neither declared what that element was, nor did he clearly show that all intelligence was necessarily subject to the same law, and that every object of *all* cognition must involve a subjective or non-material ingredient. Hence he failed to reduce matter *per se* to the condition of a contradiction; because if matter can be known *per se* by any possible

intelligence—if it can, in any circumstances, be apprehended without some subjective ingredient being apprehended along with it—we are not entitled to set it down as the contradictory in itself. To fix it as this, it must be fixed as the absolutely and necessarily and universally unknowable. Berkeley's system scarcely rises to this position. He has nowhere made out clearly that matter *per se* is the contradictory to *all* intelligence, although he may have shown with sufficient distinctness that it is the contradictory to *our* intelligence. But if matter *per se* is not the contradictory to all intelligence, it may possible exist—exist with a true and absolute existence. But if matter *per se* can exist exclusively, Berkeley's ontology breaks down—for his conclusion is that the subject and the object *together*, the synthesis of mind and the universe, is what alone truly and absolutely exists, or can exist. (His fundamental defect)

16. Reid mistook entirely the scope of the Berkeleian speculations. He actually supposed Berkeley to have been a representationist, and that the only difference between him and the ordinary disciples of this school was, that while *they* admitted the existence of matter, *he* denied it, and was what is vulgarly termed an idealist. Berkeley is supposed by Reid to have agreed with the respresentationists in holding that mere ideas or perceptions were the immediate objects of the mind; but to have differed from them in throwing overboard the occult material realities which these ideas were supposed to represent. This interpretation of Berkeleianism is altogether erroneous. Instead of exploding the material reality, Berkeley, as has been said, brought it face to face with the mind, by showing that it was a *part*, although never the *whole*, of the object of our cognition; and this, it is submitted, is the only tenable or intelligible ground on which the doctrine of intuitive perception can be placed. This position, however, was totally misconceived by Dr. Reid; and hence he has done very gross, although unintentional, injustice to the philosophical opinions of his predecessor. (Reid: His misunderstanding of Berkeley.)

17. In regard to Dr. Reid's own doctrine of intuitive perception and his supposed refutation of representationism, it must not be disguised that both of them are complete failures. His ultimate object was to vindicate the absolute existence of the material universe, which, having been rendered problematical by the Cartesian speculations, had been denied on much better grounds by the dialectic of Berkeley—these grounds being, that we could only know it *cum alio*,

and therefore could neither conceive nor believe in it *per se*. To accomplish this end, Reid set on foot a doctrine of intuitive perception, in which he endeavored to show that material realities stand face to face with the mind, *without anything more* standing there along with them. This at least must be understood to have been his implied, if not his express, position; for what kind of logic would there be in the argument—material things are known to exist, *not* by themselves, but only in connection with something else, *therefore* they exist by themselves, or out of connection with everything else? Unless, then, we are to charge Dr. Reid with this monstrous paralogism, we must suppose him to have held that we apprehend material things without apprehending anything else at the same time. If that position could be made good, it would at once establish both the independent existence of matter, and a doctrine of intuitive perception. But the position is one which runs counter to every law of human knowledge, both contingent and necessary. Whenever we know material things, we are cognizant of our own senses (sight or touch, etc.) as well: it thus runs counter to the contingent laws. Again, whenever we know material things, we know ourselves as well: it thus runs counter to the necessary laws. This doctrine of intuitive perception, therefore, is a theory which sets at defiance every law of intelligence, and which consequently fails to overtake either of the aims which its author had in view. (Reid failed to establish a doctrine of intuitive perception.)

18. But Dr. Reid, honest man, must not be dealt with too severely. With vastly good intentions, and very excellent abilities for everything except philosophy, he had no speculative genius whatever—positively an anti-speculative turn of mind, which, with a mixture of shrewdness and *naïveté* altogether incomparable, he was pleased to term "common sense;" thereby proposing as arbiter in the controversies in which he was engaged, an authority which the learned could not well decline, and which the vulgar would very readily defer to. There was good policy in this appeal. The standard of the exact reason did not quite suit him, neither was he willing to be immortalized as the advocate of mere vulgar prejudices; so that he caught adroitly at this middle term, whereby he was enabled, when reason failed him, to take shelter under popular opinion; and when popular opinion went against him, to appeal to the higher evidence of reason. Without renouncing scientific precision when it could be attained, he made friends of the mammon of un-philosophy. What

chance had a writer like David Hume, with only one string to *his* bow, against a man who thus avowed his determination to avail himself, as occasion might require, of the plausibility of uncritical thinking, and of the refinements of logical reflection? This amphibious method, however, had its disadvantages. At home in the submarine abysses of popular opinion, Dr. Reid, in the higher regions of philosophy, was as helpless as a whale in a field of clover. He was out of his proper element. He blamed the atmosphere: the fault lay in his own lungs. Through the gills of ordinary thinking he expected to transpire the pure ether of speculation, and it nearly choked him. His fate ought to be a warning to all men, that in philosophy we cannot serve two mistresses. Our ordinary moods, our habitual opinions, our natural prejudices, are not compatible with the verdicts of our speculative reason. (His character as a philosopher)

19. The truth is, that Dr. Reid mistook, or rather reversed, the vocation of philosophy. He supposed that the business of this discipline was, not to correct, but to confirm the contradictory inadvertencies of natural thinking. Accordingly, the main tendency of his labors was to organize the irrational, and to make error systematic. But even in this attempt he has only partially succeeded. His opinions are even more confused than they are fallacious, more incoherent than they are erroneous; and no amount of expositorial ingenuity has ever succeeded in conferring on his doctrines even the lowest degree of scientific intelligibility. His claim to take rank *par excellence*, as *the* champion of common sense, is preposterous, if by common sense anything more be meant than vulgar opinion. When the cause of philosophy is fairly, and fully, pled at the bar of *genuine* common sense, it is conceived that a decision will be given by that tribunal in favor of the necessary truths of reason, and not in favor of the antagonist verdicts of the popular and unreflective understanding which Dr. Reid took under his protection. Oh, Catholic Reason of mankind, surely thou art not the real, but only the reputed, mother of this anti-philosophical philosophy! *Thy* children, I take it, are rather Plato's Demigods and Spinoza's Titans. (He mistook this vocation of philosophy.)

20. At this place, and in special reference to the philosopher (Kant) whose opinions have next to be considered, it will be necessary to introduce a short account of the doctrine of "innate ideas," viewed both in itself and in its history. This theory has been generally, if not universally, misunderstood: and, as has usually happened in philo-

sophical controversies, its supporters and its impugners have been both equally at fault. Before commenting on the false, it will be proper to give the true, version of this celebrated opinion—and before showing in what sense it is wrong and untenable, to show in what sense it is tenable and right. (Kant, "Innate ideas")

21. Rightly understood, the doctrine of innate ideas is merely another form of expression for the initial principle (Prop. I.) of these Institutes. From an accurate observation of *the fact* in regard to knowledge, we learn that every cognition, or perception, or idea, consists, and must consist, of two heterogeneous parts, elements, or factors,—one of which is contributed from within—belongs to the mind itself, and hence is said to be *innate*; the other of which is contributed from without, and hence may be said to be *extranate* (if such a word may be used), or of foreign extraction. To render this somewhat abstract statement perfectly intelligible and convincing, all that we have to do is to translate it into the concrete; and to affirm that whenever a man apprehends an external thing (this is the foreign, the extranate ingredient in the total cognition), he must apprehend *himself* also (this is the innate, or home ingredient in the total cognition); and conversely, that whenever a man apprehends *himself* (the innate element), he must always apprehend something else, be it a thing, or a thought, or a feeling (the foreign element), as well. So that every cognition, or idea, or perception, necessarily consists of two parts, the one of which is native to the mind, and is often denominated *a priori*—to indicate that it is the essential or grounding element; and the other of which is extraneous to the mind, and is frequently termed *a posteriori*, to signify that it is the changeable, or accidental, or accruing element. It is thus obvious that the doctrine of innate ideas, when properly understood, is merely another form of the doctrine advanced in the first proposition of the epistemology; and further, that it is merely another phasis of the doctrine of "the universal and the particular" propounded in the sixth proposition of that same section. The *me* is the innate, or *a priori*, or universal, part of every congnition, perception, or idea: things, or thoughts, or states of mind whatsoever (the not-me), are the extranate, *a posteriori*, or particular part of every cognition, perception, or idea. (Right interpretation of this doctrine)

22. The circumstance, then, above all others, to be attended to in coming to a right comprehension of this theory is, that the word "innate" is never to be understood in reference to ideas, but only in

reference to a part of every idea; and that neither is the word "foreign, or acquired, or extraneous," ever to be understood in reference to ideas, but only in reference to a part of every idea. There are thus no innate ideas, and no extranate ideas; but every idea or cognition has an element which is innate, and an element which is not so—every cognition, in short, is both innate and extranate—is a synthesis constituted by an *a priori* part and an *a posteriori* part. This consideration, of course, fixes these elements (when considered apart from each other), as necessarily unknowable and contradictory. (The circumstance to be particularly attended to in considering this doctrine)

23. Hence the misconception, above all others to be avoided, if we would form a correct notion—indeed, any notion at all of this theory—is the supposition that some (one class) of our cognitions or ideas are innate; and that others (another class) are originated from without; in other words, the blunder most particularly to be guarded against, is the opinion that the two factors (original and derivative) of our cognitions are themselves cognitions, or can be themselves *whole* ideas. If *this* were the theory, it would indeed be a portentous, purposeless, and unintelligible chimera. (The misconception to be particularly guarded against)

24. Strange to say, no philosopher that can be named has avoided this error. They have agreed, to a man, in thinking that the word "innate" referred to a particular *class* of our ideas—and not to a *part* of each of our ideas; and that the word "foreign" or "derived" or "extraneous," referred to another *class* of our ideas and not to a *part* of each of them. In short, they have fallen into the mistake already explained at considerable length under the Sixth Proposition of the Epistemology, Obs. 13-17. The advocates, equally with the opponents of the theory, have misapprehended the nature of the analysis on which it proceeded. They have mistaken elements for kinds. Those who maintained the doctrine, supposed that one kind or class of our ideas had its origin from within the mind, and that another kind or class of our ideas had its origin from without; while their opponents, never doubting that this was the point properly at issue, denied that any of our ideas were innate, and attributed the whole of them to an extraneous origin. Accordingly, the controversy concerning innate ideas has been one in which neither of the parties engaged had any conception of the question properly under litigation. (This misconception has never been guarded against by any philosopher)

25. This fundamental mistake has beset the controversy during every period of its history. Des Cartes, Mallebranche, and Leibnitz were of opinion that some of our ideas came to us from without, and that others were generated from within; that one class of our cognitions was innate, or original; that another class was factitious, or acquired. Over the theory thus irrationally propounded, Locke obtained an easy victory. Had the controversy been put upon the right footing—had the true question been raised, is there an innate *part* and an extraneous *part* in every one of our cognitions—and had Locke answered in the negative, and maintained that each of our cognitions embraced *only one* element—namely, the extraneous or sensible part,—in that case his position would have been untenable, because it would have been equivalent to the assertion that both factors (inner and outer) were not essential to the formation of all knowledge, and that an idea could subsist with one of its necessary constituents withdrawn. But, as against Des Cartes, Mallebranche, and Leibnitz, who held that some of our ideas are from without, and others from within, his refutation was triumphant. If any one cognition has its origin *wholly* from without, we may safely generalize that fact, and assert that the whole of our knowledge is due to an external source. The postulation of an internal element is permissible only because the external element by itself (the mere objective) is no cognition at all, but is pure nonsense, just as the postulation of an external element is permissible only because the internal element by itself (the mere subjective, the indeterminate *me*) is no cognition at all, but is pure nonsense. This, however, was not the acceptation in which the doctrine of innate ideas was understood at the time when Locke wrote, and therefore he is less to be blamed for having impugned, than his opponents are for having advanced, so inept and irrelevant an hypothesis. (Hence the ineptitude of the controversy)

26. Locke's refutation of the doctrine, as it was at that time understood, was so complete, that little or nothing was heard of "innate ideas" for many years afterwards. This speculation lay dormant during the ascendancy of sensualism, or the scheme which derives all our knowledge from without, until towards the close of the eighteenth century, when it was again revived under the auspices of the German philosopher Kant. And on what footing does Kant place the resuscitated opinion? Precisely on the same footing as before. He understands, or rather misunderstands, the doctrine, just as its former upholders had misunderstood it. He mistakes elements for

kinds. In explaining the origin of our knowledge, he does not refer one part of each of our cognitions to the mind itself, and another part of each of our cognitions to some foreign source; but, he refers some of our cognitions entirely to the one source, and some of them entirely to the other. It is true that Kant is ambiguous, and appears at times as if he had got hold of the right doctrine—namely, that the words *a priori*, or *native*, on the one hand, and *a posteriori*, or *empirical*, on the other, apply only to the elements of our ideas, and not to our ideas themselves. But he more frequently repeats the old error, characterizing some of our cognitions as *a priori*, or original, and others as empirical or acquired. At any rate, his misconception of the true doctrine is proved by the consideration that he nowhere proclaims that the empirical element of cognition (that supplied by the senses) is nonsensical and contradictory, when divorced from the element which is supplied by the mind; and conversely, that the latter element is nonsensical and contradictory, unless when associated with some empirical or extraneous ingredient. Not having made this announcement, Kant must be held to have missed the true theory, and to have taught a doctrine of innate ideas fully as untenable and inept as any propounded by his predecessors. He regards matter *per se* as the cause of our sensible cognitions; and altogether he cannot be complimented on having thrown any new light on the origin of knowledge, or on having extricated the controversy from the confusion into which it had run. (In this controversy Kant is as much at fault as his predecessors)

27. The errors and perplexities which have been passed under review might have been avoided, had philosophers addressed themselves assiduously to the consideration of knowledge as it actually is, and eschewed at the outset all inquiry into its origin. This is the method which these Institutes have endeavored uniformly to pursue throughout the first section of the science: and to its observance is to be attributed any credit which they may obtain for having steered clear of the shoals and whirlpools which have shipwrecked all previous systems. The following recapitulation may serve as a memorandum of some of the leading points of the system. (How this system of Institutes avoids these errors.)

28. *First*, and generally, this system obtains a great advantage in starting from no hypothesis, either affirmative or negative, in regard to the absolute existence of the material universe. The affirmative assumption has disconcerted every attempt which has hitherto been

made to propound a reasoned theory of knowing; and the negative assumption is, of course, equally unwarrantable. The system, therefore, indulges, at the outset, in no opinion in regard to independent material existence either *pro* or *con*; it leaves that point to be determined by the result of the inquiry into the actual character and constitution of knowledge. To this inquiry it adheres closely until it has exhausted all its details, and, tracking the knowable through all the disguises and transformations which it can assume, has found that, under all its metamorphoses, it is, at bottom and in the last resort, essentially *the same*—the same knowable in all essential respects, susceptible though it be of infinite varieties in all its accidental features. (*First*: It starts from no hypothesis.)

29. *Secondly*. A rigorous inquisition into the structure of the known and knowable, shows us that *oneself* must always be a part of everything that is known or knowable. The two constituents, therefore, of every cognition which any intelligence can entertain, are itself and - whatever else the other element may be; for this element, being indefinite and inexhaustible, cannot be more specially condescended upon. (Secondly: it finds that all cognition consists of two elements.)

30. *Thirdly*. This analysis necessarily reduces to a mere part of cognition everything which is known along with that definite part called self; because, if this definite element must be known (as it must) along with whatever is known, that which is known along with it cannot be a known or knowable whole; but only a known and knowable part. Thus many things—indeed, everything—which we heretofore regarded as the objects of cognition, turn out, on examination, to be only *part-objects* of cognition. (*Thirdly*: it finds that each element is no cognition, but only a half or part-cognition.)

31. *Fourthly*. This analysis further reduces the material universe, whether considered in the aggregate or in detail, to a mere part or element of cognition. It can be known only along with the other element. *The* cognition is always the material universe (or a portion of it), *plus* the mind or person contemplating it. This synthesis is not merely the only known, but the only knowable. (*Fourthly*: it finds that matter is only a *half* cognition.)

32. *Fifthly. Now*, a doctrine of intuitive perception can be established on reasonable grounds; *now*, the downfall of representationism is insured. A doctrine of intuitive perception arises, indeed, of its own accord, out of the data which have been laid down. Matter, or

the external thing, is just as much the immediate object of a man's mind as he himself is the immediate object of his mind, because it is part and parcel of the total presentation which is before him. Thus the material universe is neither representative of something else, nor is it represented by anything else. It is representative of nothing except itself; and we apprehend it intuitively — the consideration being borne in mind that we always do and must apprehend ourselves along with it. (*Fifthly*: it establishes "intuitive," and overthrows "representative," perception.)

33. *Sixthly*. This system steers clear of materialism, of the doctrine which holds that matter has an absolute existence — is an independent and completed entity. The same stroke which reduces matter to a mere element of cognition, reduces matter *per se* (that is, matter dissociated from the other element of cognition) to the predicament of a contradiction. But the contradictory can have no true or absolute existence; and thus materialism is annihilated. Its whole strength is founded on the assumption that material objects are *completed* objects of cognition; in other words, that they can be known without anything else being known along with them. This assumption has been found to be false. The materialist is asked *where* is the matter *per se* of which you speak? *There* it is, said Dr. Johnson, kicking against a stone. But, good Doctor, that it is not matter *per se*, — that is matter *cum alio*; and this, we need scarcely say, is what no man ever doubted or denied the existence of. (*Sixthly*: it steers clear of materialism.)

34. *Seventhly*. This system steers clear of spurious idealism, or the doctrine which holds that matter, in the supposed withdrawal of all intelligence, is a nonentity. Matter is an element, or half-object of cognition. The withdrawal, therefore, of the other element or half-object (the ego), cannot have the effect of reducing matter to a nonentity; first, because the *whole* object of cognition is matter-*plus*-me, and only *half* of it has been supposed to be withdrawn; and secondly, because there are no nonentities anymore than there are entities out of relation to some *me* or mind. Knowable nonentity is always nonentity *plus* me, just as much as knowable entity is always entity *plus* me. So that to suppose matter to become a nonentity in the supposed withdrawal or annihilation of (every) me, would be to suppose it still in connection with the very factor which we profess to have withdrawn. Accordingly the conclusion is, first, *if* we can suppose all intelligence at an end, matter, although it would cease to be an entity, would not become a nonentity. It would

become the contradictory—it would be neither nothing nor anything.*[3] And secondly, we *cannot* conceive all intelligence at an end, because we *must* conceive, under any circumstances, either that something exists or that nothing exists. But neither the existence nor the non-existence of things is conceivable out of relation to an intelligence—and therefore the highest and most binding law of all reason is, that in no circumstances can a supreme mind be conceived to be abstracted from the universe. The system which inculcates these truths may be termed a philosophy of real-idealism. It loses hold of nothing which the unreflective mind considers to be real; but seizing on the material universe, and combining it inseparably with an additional element, it absorbs it in a new product, which it gives out as the only true and substantial universe—the only universe which any intellect can think of without running into a contradiction. (*Seventhly*: it steers clear of spurious idealism.)

35. *Eighthly*. By these considerations this system is absolved from all obligations to point out the causes or origin of cognition. The truths which it has reached render that question absurd. It is unanswerable, because it is unaskable. The question is, What are the conceivable causes in existence which generate knowledge? And the answer is, That no existence at all can be conceived by any intelligence anterior to, and aloof from, knowledge. Knowledge of existence—the apprehension of oneself and other things—is alone true existence. This is itself the First, the Bottom, the Origin—and this is what all intelligence is prevented by the laws of all reason from ever getting beyond or below. To inquire what this proceeds from, is as inept as to ask what is the Beginning of the Beginning. All the explanations which can be proposed can find their data only by presupposing the very knowledge whose genesis they are professing to explain. In thinking of things as antecedent to all knowledge, some *me* or mind must always be thought of along with them; and in thinking of some *me* or mind as antecedent to all knowledge, some things or determinations must always be thought of along with it. But the conception of this synthesis is itself the conception of knowledge; so that we are compelled to assume as the ground of our explanation, the very thing (knowledge) which that ground had been brought

---

[3] * It is a remarkable confirmation of this conclusion, that Plato found himself unable to affirm either the existence or the non-existence of the material universe *per se*. But not having distinctly reduced matter *per se* to a contradiction, he failed to fathom and to exhibit the grounds of this inability.

forward to explain. (*Eighthly*: it is under no obligation to explain the origin of knowledge, because knowledge itself is *the Beginning*.)

36. And finally, it must be borne in mind that although all cognition has been characterized by this system as a fusion or synthesis of two contradictories (the ego and non-ego) — that is, of two elements which, out of relation to each other, are necessarily unknowable — this does not mean that the synthesis is brought about by the union of two elements which *existed* in a state of separation *previous* to the formation of the synthesis. The synthesis is the primary or original; the analysis is the secondary or posterior. The contradictory elements are found by an analysis of the synthesis, but the synthesis is not generated by putting together the parts obtained by the analysis, because these parts can be conceived only in relation to each other, or as *already* put together. (The synthesis of ego and non-ego is original, and not factitious or secondary.)

PROPOSITION X

WHAT ABSOLUTE EXISTENCE IS

Absolute Existence is the synthesis of the subject and object — the union of the universal and the particular — the concretion of the ego and non-ego; in other words, the only true, and real, and independent. Existences are minds-together-with-that-which-they-apprehend.

DEMONSTRATION

Absolute Existence is either that which we know or that which we are ignorant of (Prop. V. — Ontology). If Absolute Existence is that which we know, it must be the synthesis of subject and object — the union of the universal and the particular, the concretion of the ego and the non-ego, because this, and this alone, is knowable (Props. I, II, VI, IX. — Epistemology). This synthesis alone is the conceivable (Prop. XIII. — Epistemology). This, and this alone, is the substantial and absolute in cognition (Props. XVII, XXI. — Epistemology). Again, if Absolute Existence is that which we are ignorant of, it must equally be the synthesis of subject and object, the union of the universal and the particular, the concretion of the ego and the non-ego, because this, and this alone, is what we can be ignorant of (Prop. VIII. — Agniology). Therefore, whichever alternative be adopted, the result is the same. Whether we claim a knowledge, or profess an ignorance, of the Absolutely Existent, the conclusion is inevitably forced upon us that the Absolutely Existent is the synthesis of the subject and object—the union of the universal and the particular—the concretion of the ego and non-ego; in other words, that the only existences to which true, and real, and independent Being can be ascribed, are minds-together-with-that-which-they-apprehend.

2. The solution of the ontological problem affords, moreover, an answer to the ultimate question of philosophy—What is truth?—(See Introduction, § 60.) Whatever absolutely is, is true. The question, therefore, is—But what absolutely is? And the answer, as now declared, is, that object *plus* subject is what absolutely is—that this, and this alone, truly and really exists. This synthesis, accordingly, is THE TRUTH: the Ground—below which there is neither anything nor nothing. (It answers the question: What is truth?)

PROPOSITION XI

WHAT ABSOLUTE EXISTENCE IS NECESSARY

All absolute existences are contingent *except one*; in other words, there is One, but only one, Absolute Existence which is strictly *necessary*; and that existence is a supreme, and infinite, and everlasting Mind in synthesis with all things.

DEMONSTRATION

To save the universe from presenting a contradiction to all reason, intelligence must be postulated in connection with it; because everything except the synthesis of subject and object is contradictory, is that of which there can be no knowledge (Props. I, II.—Epistemology) and no ignorance (Prop. VIII.—Agnoiology). But *more* than *one* intelligence does not require to be postulated; because the universe is rescued from contradiction as effectually by the supposition of one intelligence in connection with it, as by the supposition of ten million, and reason never postulates more than is necessary. Therefore all absolute existences are contingent except one; in other words, there is One, but only one, Absolute Existence which is strictly *necessary*; and that existence is a supreme, and infinite, and eternal Mind in synthesis with all things.

OBSERVATIONS AND EXPLANATIONS

1. In this proposition a distinction is taken between contingent absolute existences (for example, human beings *together with* what they apprehend) and the One Absolute Existence which is necessary. All absolute existences except one are contingent. This is proved by the

consideration that there was a time when the world was without man; and by the consideration that in other worlds there may be no intelligences at all. This is intelligible to reason. But in the judgment of reason there never can have been a time when the universe was without God. *That* is unintelligible to reason; because time is not time, but is nonsense, without a mind; space is not space, but is nonsense, without a mind; all objects are not objects, but are nonsense, without a mind; in short, the whole universe is neither anything nor nothing, but is the sheer contradictory, without a mind. And therefore, inasmuch as we cannot help thinking that there was a time before man existed, and that there was space before man existed, and that the universe was something or other before man existed; so neither can we help thinking that before man existed, a supreme and eternal intelligence existed, in synthesis with all things. In the estimation of natural thinking, the universe by itself is not the contradictory; in our ordinary moods we suppose it capable of subsisting by itself. Hence, in our ordinary moods, we see no *necessity* why a supreme intelligence should be postulated in connection with it. But speculation shows us that the universe, by itself, is the contradictory; that it is incapable of self-subsistency, that it can exist only, *cum alio*, inasmuch as it can be known only *cum alio*, and can be ignored only *cum alio*; that all true and cogitable and non-contradictory existence is a synthesis of the subjective and the objective; and *then* we are compelled, by the most stringent necessity of thinking, to conceive a supreme intelligence as the ground and essence of the Universal Whole. Thus the postulation of the Deity is not only permissible, it is unavoidable. Every mind thinks, and *must* think of God (however little conscious it may be of the operation which it is performing), whenever it thinks of anything as lying beyond all human observation, or as subsisting in the absence or annihilation of all finite intelligences.

VI

Scottish Philosophy: The Old and the New

Selection 10
A STATEMENT BY PROFESSOR FERRIER (ABRIDGED)

The Government of the country has relieved the University of Edinburgh of one test, and they, of their own authority, have imposed upon it another; and, as most people will think, a much more obnoxious one. Chiefly through their liberalism the religious test was abolished, and entirely through their illiberalism, a philosophical test of the most exclusive character, has been substituted in its room. It is well to know that a candidate for a philosophical chair in the University of Edinburgh need not now be a believer in Christ or a member of the established Church; but he must be a believer in Dr. Reid, and a pledged disciple of the Hamiltonian system of philosophy.

Philosophy is not traditional. As a mere inheritance it carries no benefit to man or boy. The more it is a received dogmatic, the less it is a quickening process

Truth, under the relation in which we have at present to consider it, is not truth *simply*, but truth *in philosophy*. An illustration will make this distinction plain. Suppose that we are discussing the subject of salt, and that we say, "salt is white and gritty, it is in some degree moist, it is sometimes put into a salt-cellar and placed on the dinner table, and sometimes it is kept in a box in the kitchen; it is eaten with most articles of food, and usually helped—although never to one's neighbor—with a small spoon." These statements about salt are all truths; they are truths, as we may say, *simply*, but they are not truths *in chemistry*. No man would be considered much of a chemist, who was merely acquainted with these and other such circumstances, concerning salt. So in philosophy, no man can be called a philosopher who merely knows and says, that he and other people exist, that there is an external world, that a man is the same person today that he was yesterday, and so forth. These are undoubtedly truths, but I maintain that they are not truths in philosophy any more than those others just mentioned, are truths in chemistry. Our old Scottish school, however, is of a different way of thinking. It represents these and similar facts as the first truths of philosophy, and to these it has recourse in handling the deeper questions of metaphysics. I have no objections to this, for those who like it—only my system deals with first truths of a very different order; and it denies, that the first truths of the old Scottish school are truths of philosophy at all. This is one very fundamental point of difference between the old and the new Scottish system of metaphysics; and I am not at all ashamed to confess it.

The first truths of the old Scottish school have not only no value in philosophy, they have no value in any intellectual market in the world. They possess no exchangeable worth: they are positively not vendible; yet, Dr. Reid and his successors have been in the habit of charging their students for them, at the rate of three guineas a head, and of doing this while all the rest of the world was obtaining them in unlimited abundance for nothing. That was scarcely fair. "I exist," says Dr. Reid: surely that is a truth worth knowing. "So do you:"—is not that one also worth knowing? Is not the fact, too, worth knowing, "that there is an external universe?" That there may be no mistake as to these interesting "first truths," of the old Scottish philosophy, a few of them shall be given in Dr. Reid's own words. "The thoughts of which I am conscious are the thoughts of a being which I call *myself*, my *mind*, my *person*." — (Reid's works, p. 443, Sir W. Hamilton's edition). "Those things did really happen which I distinctly remember!" — (P. 444.) "Those things do really exist which we perceive by our senses, and are what we perceive them to be." — (P. 445.) "There is life and intelligence in our fellow-men with whom we converse!" — (P. 448.) There are truths for you! — Dr. Reid may be supposed to exclaim: are they not well worth knowing? I answer, certainly, all these things are worth knowing, but they are not worth *paying* to know, and for this reason, that every person is already acquainted with them *gratis*. So that what I have to complain of is, that our Scottish students of philosophy appear to me generally to have been made to purchase, and to pay a high price, too, in hard cash, for bottled air, while the whole atmosphere around was floating with liquid balm, that could be had for nothing. The fundamental principles of the old Scottish philosophy have either no proper place in metaphysics, or else it is just such a place as the facts, that people usually take sugar with their tea, and generally take-off their clothes before getting into bed, occupy in the sciences of chemistry, botany, and physiology.

Hence it appeared to me necessary that philosophy should undergo a somewhat different development, if her instructions were to become profitable as an exercise and discipline of the mind. What the first principles of the science are, may be a somewhat disputed question; and, a still more debatable point may be, whether I have succeeded in reaching them. But one thing is certain, that the first principles of philosophy are *not* the elementary truths which have been enunciated as such by our old Scottish philosophy. These, I conceive, must be set aside, as good for nothing in science, however indispensable they may be in life. That our antecedent philosophy is valuable on other accounts, although not on account of its first principles, is what may be readily conceded.

Another point of difference—indeed the fundamental difference—between the two Scottish philosophies, the Old and the New, is this, that while I hold that philosophy exists for the sole purpose of correcting the natural inadvertencies of loose, ordinary thinking—that this is her true and proper vocation; the old school, on the contrary, are of opinion that philosophy exists for the very purpose of ratifying, and, if possible, systematizing these inadvertencies. This is held by Reid and his followers to be the proper business of metaphysical science. It may easily be seen what a vast difference in our respective modes of treatment and inquiry this fundamental discrepancy must give rise to. Yet, amid all the opposition which my system has provoked, no one has ventured to deny what I have proclaimed to be the true vocation of philosophy. A not unfavorable inference is suggested by this significant admission.

It has been asserted, that my philosophy is of Germanic origin and complexion. A broader fabrication than that never dropped from human lips, or dribbled from the point of pen. My philosophy is Scottish to the very core; it is national in every fiber and articulation of its frame. It is a natural growth of old Scotland's soil, and has drunk in no nourishment from any other land. Are we to judge of the productions of Scotland by looking merely to what Scotland has *hitherto* produced? May a philosopher not be, heart and soul, a Scotsman—may he not be a Scotsman in all his intellectual movements, even although he should have the misfortune to differ, in certain respects, from Dr. Reid and Sir William Hamilton? To expatriate a man and his works on such grounds, would be rather a severe sentence, and one which the country, I take it, would be very slow to confirm. If my system presents points of contact or coincidence with the speculations of foreign thinkers, I cannot help that. Is a man to reject the truth which he has discovered by his own efforts, because a person in another country has touched upon something like it? The new Scottish philosophy would have been exactly what it is, although Germany and the whole continent of Europe had been buried, centuries ago, in the sea. Whatever my dominion over truth may be, small or great, I have conquered every inch of it for myself. The "Institutes of Metaphysics" seem very plain-sailing, and so does railway traveling; but if some of my critics "had seen these roads before they were made," they would have a better idea of the difficulties of intellectual tunneling, and of bridging chasms in the land of thought, over which they may now be wafted in their sleep. But what I assert is, that my system of philosophy—whatever its merit or demerit may be—was born and bred in this country, and is essentially native to the soil. Scotland, and Scotland alone, shall get the credit, if it is good for anything, just as she must submit to the dishonor, if it is found fraught with principles of folly, danger, or disgrace.

Every expedient of malice was resorted to, in order to damage me in the late canvass; and of these, one of the most effectual was the artifice on which I have just commented. Some of my assailants endeavored (and, I fancy, with only too much success) to frighten the electors from their propriety, with the portentous name of HEGEL, and by dinning in their ears that my philosophy was nothing but an echo of his. Other critics, however, have doubted whether I knew anything at all about that philosopher. Thus, one gentleman, Monsieur A. Vera, the most recent expositor of Hegel, asks (simple soul!), "Is Professor Ferrier acquainted with Hegel's philosophy?" So that, while I am abused, on the one hand, for being Hegel all over, I am suspected, on the other, of being almost ignorant of his existence. It is difficult to escape from such a cross-fire as that. The exact truth of the matter is this: I have read most of Hegel's works again and again, but I cannot say that I am acquainted with his philosophy. I am able to understand only a few short passages here and there in his writings; and these I greatly admire for the depth of their insight, the breadth of their wisdom, and the loftiness of their tone. More than this I cannot say. If others understand him better, and to a larger extent, they have the advantage of me, and I confess that I envy them the privilege. But, for myself, I must declare that I have not found one word or one thought in Hegel which was available for my system, even if I had been disposed to use it. There is a joke current about Hegel, that, towards the close of his career, he remarked that there was only one man in Germany who understood him, and that he misunderstood him. If Hegel follows (as I do) the demonstrative method, I own I cannot see it, and would feel much obliged to anyone who would point this out, and make it clear. In other respects, my method is diametrically opposed to his: he begins with the consideration of Being; my whole design compels me to begin with the consideration of Knowing.

Another great name which has been conjured up against me is that of Spinoza. Is not that a horrible man to be in any way related to? Do not undefined terrors seem to encircle the very letters of his name? A poor Jew of Amsterdam, a needy grinder of glass lenses for his frugal livelihood, and the most peaceful, and, by all accounts, the most amiable and disinterested of men—this thinker, more terrible than Swedish Charles, in all his sweeping forays,

> "Has left a name at which the world grows pale."

The world, methinks, grows pale at very little. I owe no fealty to Spinoza. I preach none of his opinions. Indeed, I am not charged with adopting anything of his except a method, which he has in common with all rigorous reasoners. But this I will avouch, that all the outcry which has been raised against Spinoza has its origin in nothing but ignorance, hypocrisy, and cant. These traditional malignancies are perfectly sickening to listen to. Parrots in their ignorance, but worse than parrots in their spite, those pests who screech such hereditary malice ought to be nailed flat against the door of every philosophical classroom in the kingdom. If Spinoza errs, it is in attributing, not certainly too much to the great Creator, for that is impossible, but too little to the creature of His hands. He denies, as many great and pious divines have done, the free agency of man: he asserts the absolute sovereignty of God. He is the very Calvin of philosophy.

I repeat, then, that I disclaim for my philosophy the paternity either of Germany or Holland. I assert, that in every fiber it is of home growth and national texture.

Index

Berkeley, B., 2, 8, 11-12, 75-82, 85-88, 98, 121, 148, 155-156, 181-182
Blackwood's Magazine, 1, 6
Boucher, D., 2
Brown, T., 29

Caird, E., 2
Chalmers, T., 28-29, 72
Coleridge, S.T., 67
Common sense, 1-4, 8, 10, 12, 18, 21-26, 75-76, 80, 82, 85, 89, 93, 96, 100, 103, 106, 110, 118-119, 165, 173, 183-184
Consciousness, 2-3, 6-8, 10, 12, 17-22, 25-32, 34-37, 40-42, 44-56, 60-64, 66, 71-74, 96-97, 99, 104, 112, 127-129, 133, 139
  Self-consciousness, 2-3, 7, 127-129

Davie, G., 1
Descartes, R., 7, 44-45, 177-179, 187
De Quincey, T., 1

Ferrier, S., 1
Fichte, J.G., 2, 85, 133

Hamilton, W., 2, 9, 196, 198
Hegel, G.W.F., 2, 7, 114, 133-134, 198-199
Hume, D., 79-80, 102-103, 184

Idealism, 1-2, 7-9, 11, 76-77, 85-86, 89-91, 95, 98-103, 112, 115, 118, 120, 136, 174, 178, 190-191
  Absolute idealism, 1, 2, 8-9, 76
  Genuine idealism, 85, 136
  Spurious idealism, 85, 190-191

Subjective idealism, 11, 85, 90, 115, 118
Ignorance, 5-6, 10-12, 125, 156-169, 192-193
Immaterialism, 17
Immaterialist, 14-17

Johnson, S., 77-78, 190

Kant, I., 2, 8, 10, 133-134, 152-153, 163, 184-185, 187-188

Leibnitz, G., 180, 187
Locke, J., 180-181, 187

Mackintosh, J., 65
Malebranche, N., 121, 179-180, 187
Materialism, 16, 38, 167, 190
Materialist, 16-17, 140-141, 190
Materialistic ontology, 155
Metaphysic(s), 1-4, 6,9, 12, 25, 36, 38, 41-42, 94, 113-120, 123-124, 137, 148, 158, 161-162, 171, 196-197

North, C., 1

Perception, 4, 9, 38, 41, 48, 64, 66-67, 78-81, 84-85, 93-121, 128-130, 154-155, 175-183, 185, 189-190
  Perception of matter, 4, 9, 93-99, 102-103, 108, 110-113, 115-121
Plato, 114, 184, 191
Protagoras, 168
Psychology, 6, 13, 15-18, 21, 26, 35, 42, 49, 56, 67, 94, 97, 113-117, 131, 138, 148-149, 153, 168, 173-174
Pythagoras, 132

Realism, 4, 85, 89
Realist, 88
Reid, T., 2-4, 6, 8-9, 11-12, 81, 93-95, 97-103, 106, 108-110, 112, 118, 154, 181-184, 195-198
Representationism, 4, 9, 96-99, 112, 120, 154-155, 177, 181-182, 189
   Representationist, 96-98, 181, 182
   Representative theory of perception, 95, 98
Ritchie, D.G., 2

Schelling, F.W.J., 2, 114, 133
Science of man, 2-3, 6-7, 9, 13, 76
Science of mind, 137-138
Scottish philosophy, 1-2, 12, 173, 196, 198
Skepticism, 43-45, 78, 80, 95, 98-103, 112, 118, 120, 171, 178-179
Spinoza, B., 9, 184, 199
Stewart, D., 14-17, 108-110, 112

Wilson, J., 1